Articles of War

To Arlan Gilbert:

For many years a distinguished teacher at,
and destined to be forever the
greatest historian of, Hillsdale College.

In appreciation of his friendship.

ARTICLES OF WAR

Winners, Losers,
and Some Who Were Both
during the Civil War

ALBERT CASTEL

STACKPOLE
BOOKS

Published by
STACKPOLE BOOKS
5067 Ritter Road
Mechanicsburg, PA 17055
www.stackpolebooks.com

Printed in the United States of America

10 9 8 7 6 5 4 3 2 1

FIRST EDITION

Library of Congress Cataloging-in-Publication Data

Castel, Albert E.
Articles of war: winners, losers, and some who were both during the Civil War / Albert Castel.—1st ed.
p. cm.
Includes index.
ISBN: 0-8117-0005-4
1. Generals—United States—Biography. 2. Generals—Confederate States of America—Biography. 3. United States—History—Civil War, 1861–1865—Campaigns. 4. United States—History—Civil War, 1861–1865—Biography. I. Title.

E467 .C43 2001
972.7'3'0922—dc21

00-054748

Contents

PREFACE

The "articles of war" in this collection were written over a span of nearly fifty years, with the oldest having been penned in its original form in the spring of 1952 and the newest during March/April 2000. Many were motivated, to be frank, by a desire to keep my wine cellar stocked in the style to which I wished to become accustomed. Even so, and despite most of them having been published in "popular history" magazines, most were either based on primary sources or derived from books I had authored that were as scholarly as I could make them. Only when the subject matter was too large for that type of research—such as, for examples, McClellan, Sherman, or Grant's Vicksburg Campaign—did I rely on secondary sources, and even then I employed memoirs, letters, and firsthand accounts.

As for the literary aspect, the sole difference between how I write for a magazine aimed at a general audience and a journal intended for professional historians is that articles for the latter are more analytical, whereas those submitted to the former are predominantly narratives. Otherwise I write the same for both, simply because that is the way I write. Whatever my subject and potential readership, I strive for clarity and readability, in the belief that history should be enjoyable as well as informative. That this collection of articles has been published long after the majority of them, so I assumed, had died a natural death would seem to indicate that perhaps I have not been altogether unsuccessful in realizing this goal.

I would, though, be the first to acknowledge that the unique popularity of Civil War history is the fundamental reason for the resuscitation of these articles, just as it is for all of my Civil War books remaining in print and continuing to enjoy respectable sales. In today's academia, where the not-so-holy trinity of race/gender/class holds sway, Civil War history increasingly tends to be looked upon with disdain because it deals chiefly with—as it must, given what it is—such old-fashioned and hence unfashionable matters as political and military events and the men who figured in them. But, happily, outside the hollow (in the sense of genuine scholarly content) halls of ivy, that history continues to attract an abundance of devotees, and it is to them I direct this collection, although I hope that some Ph.D.-credentialed historians will find what appears herein of interest and use.

More could be said but need not be. So on to these *Articles of War*—a title for which I am indebted, as I am for so many, many things, to my wife.

ACKNOWLEDGMENTS

First and above all I thank *Civil War Times* for permission by it and its publisher, Primedia, to republish herein the articles that have appeared in it and its lamentably defunct sister journal, *Columbiad*. These articles, spanning a third of a century, constitute the foundation for this book.

My thanks also goes to Dr. Roger Rosentreter, editor of *Michigan History*, for permission to publish in this collection the article on Alpheus S. Williams; to *North & South* magazine for authorizing the publication of the article on William Clarke Quantrill that originally appeared in *Civil War: The Magazine of the Civil War Society*, which has ceased to exist and whose rights it succeeded; to the Louisiana State University Press for permission to present an expanded version in these pages of the introduction I wrote for its edition of John Allan Wyeth's *That Devil Forrest*; to Decision Games, publisher of *Strategy and Tactics* wherein appeared the article and accompanying map on Grant's Vicksburg Campaign; and to Forbes, now the publisher of *American Heritage*, for not only enabling me to present here the article on Sam Houston but also to be of financial assistance to it.

As has almost become routine during the past decade, I extend my gratitude to Larry and Priscilla Massie of the Allegan Forest of their beloved Michigan for their invaluable but much-valued assistance in providing many of the illustrations for this book. I am blessed with friends, and I bless few more than Larry and Priscilla.

My gratitude, too, to Leigh Ann Berry, editor for this book at Stackpole Books, and to William C. "Jack" Davis, also a Stackpole editor and, as anyone familiar with Civil War history knows, premier historian of that subject. Together they made this book possible.

So also did Arlan Gilbert, who at a time of crisis in my life did what I was unable to do. I could say more about Arlan, but that already is said in the dedication.

Author's Note

In writing about war authors must, out of literary necessity, employ certain conventions of terminology. One of them is to describe a commander, a single person, doing things that in fact were done by thousands, perhaps millions, of people. Thus we read of "Napoleon conquering Europe," of "Lee winning the Battle of Fredericksburg," of "Eisenhower invading Normandy on D-Day," etc., etc., *ad infinitum*. This is especially true when, as in this book, the focus is on military and political leaders. Hence, both to demonstrate that I am aware of the artificiality of such expressions and to provide readers with a bit of humor before they embark upon the following accounts of grim conflict, I now will quote from a letter that appeared in the July 3, 1864, issue of *The Memphis Appeal,* which then was being published in Atlanta, Georgia. Written by a Confederate soldier fighting Sherman's army as it advanced on Atlanta, it reveals that the men in the ranks knew the reality of war, and that although they resented the glorification of the generals they at the same time could laugh about it—a sarcastic laugh, but nevertheless a laugh.

> EDITOR'S APPEAL: It is strange to me that our brigade had no chronicler during this arduous campaign. In view of its struggles, services, sufferings and achievements, I shall waive that natural modesty which is the most remarkable trait of my character, and endeavor to do the brigade of Gen. Bullie simple justice—only this and nothing more.
>
> A history of all the gallant exploits of this brigade would require volumes. I shall, therefore, give you but one skirmish as a sample of its general conduct. . . .

I select then the affair of "Lietkill Creek" as the episode in our brigade history for present description—an affair which, in brilliancy of execution, has often been surpassed by us on other fields, but I choose that as only a "small bone of the fossil."

On the morning of the 931 ult. Gen. Bullie occupied the most important position in our line—a position upon the holding of which depended, not only the safety of this army, but the salvation of the Southern Confederacy and the freedom of unborn millions.

Gen. Bullie, with that supernal prescience which characterizes all of our commanding officers, knew that on this eventful morning, Sherman had taken twenty-five cocktails and issued a keg of whisky to each one of his besotted followers. . . .

Our preparations for the shock—the fiercest that ever shook this continent—were rapidly, silently and skillfully made. . . . The enemy advanced in one hundred and fifty lines of battle. They were allowed to approach until the left foot of each vandal rested on our outer breastwork. Then the clarion voice of our general gave the orful order, "fire." The first fifty lines of the enemy melted away like frost before several summer suns. The others, however, advanced with sunken courage to the slaughter pen. . . .

For ninety five hours the battle raged with fearful fury. Line after line, column after column, fell before us in their mad assault. At length our efforts for slaughter became ineffectual. This was owning the fact that the piles of dead were heaped so high in front of our works that our men could not get high enough to shoot over them.

Gen. Bullie seeing this state of affairs, with that masterly strategy and intuitive military skill that has ever been his most prominent virtue and has saved this army on several previous occasions, seized a 20 pound parrott gun [a cannon that fired a 20-lb. projectile] and followed by A. A. G. [Assistant Adjutant General] H. Umbug and the rest of the staff similarly armed, climbed to the tops of the surrounding oaks and poured fearful enfilading fires of grape and canister into the retreating enemy. No human nerve could resist such terrible punishment. Such awful slaughter was never before seen since the invention of firearms. The corps of Hooker, Howard, Palmer and several other [Union] generals, too numerous to mention, were totally annihilated. The enemy lost on this occasion some seventeen hundred thousand and nine men, besides a large assortment of officers and other heavy guns.

Our loss was not slight. A shell exploded in the bowels of Gen. Bullie, rendering him uneasy for an hour or so. Fortunately he is now himself again.

Capt. H. Umbug also had several legs taken off, but has entirely recovered. All the staff were more or less killed. The general and the staff lost each two hundred and fifty horses. In fact this furious contest was characterized in the same remarkable manner as all the other battles of this campaign—i.e. the general and his staff did all the fighting and won all the victories, while the privates stood at "parade rest" and looked quietly on the gallant deeds of their officers. . . . Hoping that Bullie's brigade may have simple justice at this publication done them, I am truly yours or anybody elses,

T. Oady

PROLOGUE

How the War Began: Fort Sumter—1861

This article was first published in October 1976 as a special issue of Civil War Times Illustrated *and subsequently reissued as a booklet by the Eastern National Park and Monument Association for sale at Civil War battlefield parks. Basically it recounts the political duel between Abraham Lincoln and Jefferson Davis. The former, as president of the United States, believed that the retention of Fort Sumter by the Federal government was essential to the preservation of the Union. The latter, as president of the Confederate States, believed that securing possession of the fort was necessary to the establishment of the Confederacy as an independent nation and to it being joined by those slave states that had not yet seceded. Consequently, neither Lincoln nor Davis could concede what the other desired. The inevitable outcome was the Confederate bombardment of Sumter and the beginning of the Civil War. This in turn led to Davis gaining the fort and the accession to the Confederacy of four more states; thus for him it was a victory. On the other hand, despite defeat at Sumter, Lincoln also triumphed, in that he achieved—as a result of the South having fired the first shot—a North united in its determination to maintain the Union. After four years of carnage it did so and Lincoln emerged as the winner and Davis, the loser.*

In 1846 Congressman Jefferson Davis of Mississippi presented to the House of Representatives a resolution calling for the replacement of Federal troops in all coastal forts by state militia. The proposal died in committee, and shortly thereafter Davis resigned from Congress to lead the red-shirted 1st Mississippi Rifles to war and glory in Mexico.

Now it was the morning of April 10, 1861, and Davis was president of the newly proclaimed Confederate States of America. As he met with his cabinet in a Montgomery, Alabama, hotel room he had good reason to regret the failure of that resolution fifteen years earlier. For had it passed, he would not have had to make the decision he was about to make: Order Brigadier General P. G. T. Beauregard, commander of Confederate forces at Charleston, South Carolina, to demand the surrender of the Federal garrison on Fort Sumter in Charleston Harbor.

But before Davis made this decision, other men had made other decisions—a fateful trail of decisions leading to that Montgomery hotel room on the morning of April 10, 1861.

In a sense, the first of those decisions went back to 1829 when the War Department dumped tons of granite rubble brought from New England on a sandspit at the mouth of Charleston Harbor. On the foundation so formed a fort named after the South Carolina Revolutionary War hero, Thomas Sumter, was built.

It was built very slowly, however, as Congress appropriated the needed money in driblets. Thirty-one years later it was over 80 percent complete, though without a garrison and with most of its cannons unmounted. Even so, potentially it was quite formidable. Surrounded by the sea, its five-sided brick walls stood 50 feet high and varied in thickness from 12 feet at the base to 8 1/2 feet at the top. Adequately manned, gunned, and supplied, it could—and in fact eventually would—resist the most powerful assaults.

Three and a third miles to the northwest across the harbor lay Charleston. Here on December 20, 1860, a state convention voted unanimously that "the union now subsisting between South Carolina and other States, under the name of 'The United States of America,' is hereby dissolved." During the rest of that day and all through the night, jubilant crowds celebrated.

To South Carolinians the election of the "Black Republican" Abraham Lincoln to the presidency in November had been tantamount to a declaration of war by the North on the South. They had responded by secession, the doctrine so long advocated by their great leader, John C. Calhoun, now lying in Charleston's St. Philip's churchyard beneath a marble monument. Soon, they were confident, the other slave states would join them in forming a glorious Southern Confederacy.

Meanwhile South Carolina would be a nation among nations. For that reason the continued presence of "foreign" United States troops in the forts that controlled Charleston's harbor was more than irritating—it was intolerable. They must go.

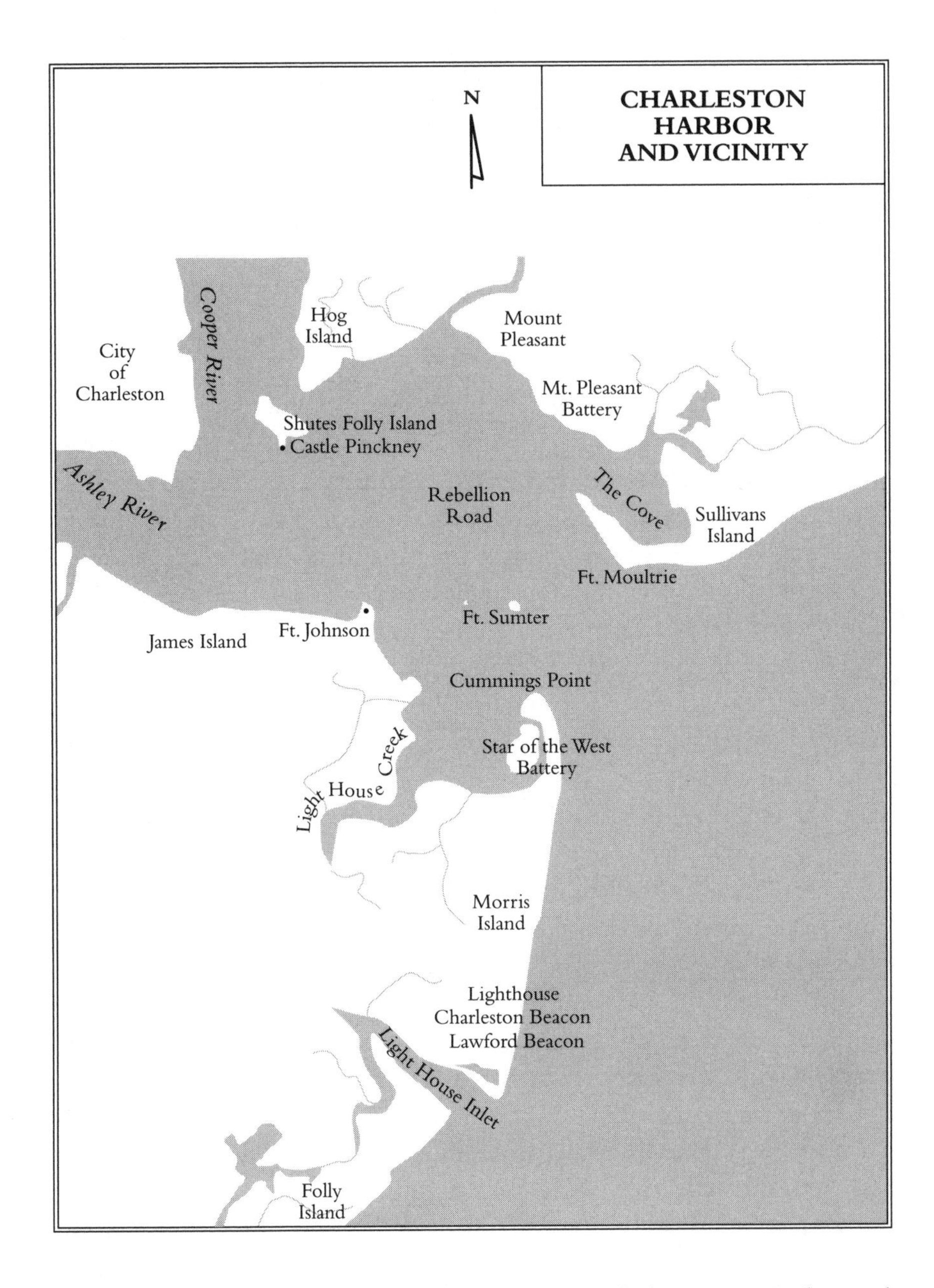

Hopefully the Federal government would pull them out. To that end Governor Francis Pickens of South Carolina appointed three commissioners to go to Washington and negotiate the evacuation of the forts. But if the troops did not leave voluntarily, they would have to be removed.

That did not appear difficult to accomplish. Hundreds of militia, Citadel cadets, and freelance volunteers were gathering in Charleston, spoiling for a fight. In contrast, the United States soldiers numbered a scant eighty-five—nine officers and seventy-six enlisted men, of whom eight of the latter were musicians. Furthermore, nearly all of these troops were stationed in Fort Moultrie on Sullivan's Island. Designed to repel sea attack, this fort was practically defenseless on its land side: Overlooking it were high sand dunes from which riflemen could slaughter the garrison.

In 1780 Major Richard Anderson had gallantly but unsuccessfully defended the original Fort Moultrie against British assault. Eighty years later his son, Major Robert Anderson of the 1st U.S. Artillery, arrived at the new Fort Moultrie and took command of the Federal troops stationed at Charleston.

Secretary of War John B. Floyd of the lame-duck Buchanan administration personally selected him for the post in November 1860. Fifty-five, a West Pointer, and twice promoted for bravery in battle, Anderson was an experienced and competent officer—exactly what was needed at Charleston. Moreover, his background should have been reassuring to the Carolinians. As a Kentuckian he qualified as a Southerner, he had owned slaves, and his wife came from an aristocratic Georgia family. Indeed, it is just possible that Floyd, a Virginian, hoped that the major would do what he himself was already doing: Support secession.

If so, Floyd had picked the wrong man. Anderson may have been a Southerner, but he was dedicated to "Duty, Honor, Country." Above all he was resolved to do everything in his power consistent with those principles to avoid a clash at Charleston that might plunge the nation into civil war.

That is why Fort Moultrie's vulnerability alarmed him. As early as November 23 he reported to the War Department that the Carolinians had "a settled determination . . . to obtain possession of this work." Since then they had made their determination even more evident. Should they attack, duty would compel him, despite the odds, to resist. And that meant war.

Hence he decided to transfer his troops to Fort Sumter. There they would be much more secure, and so would peace. For on being confronted with a target less tempting than Moultrie, presumably the Carolinians would be less bellicose.

To be sure, Floyd had instructed him on December 11 to "avoid every act which would needlessly tend to provoke" the Carolinians. But Floyd had also authorized him to move his command to either of the other two

"Major Robert Anderson [seated, second from left] and the Officers Who Were with Him at Fort Sumter"

forts in Charleston Harbor should he have "tangible evidence of a design to proceed to a hostile act." He ignored a "confidential" letter from Floyd, received December 23, which in effect urged him to surrender the forts rather than "make a vain and useless sacrifice of your life and the lives of the men under your command, upon a mere point of honor." Also he was unaware that on December 10 President Buchanan had informally promised a group of South Carolina congressmen that no change would be made in the military status quo at Charleston.

The transfer to Fort Sumter took place December 26–27. Private John Thompson described how it was managed in a letter to his father in Ireland:

> Our Commander set about fortifying himself in Moultrie, with such unparalelled [*sic*] vigor that our opponents soon became thoroughly convinced that he intended to make a desperate stand in the position he then held, and the duty of watching us was performed with a laxity corresponding to the strength of their conviction. So completely did our Commander keep his own counsel, that none in the garrison[,] officer or soldier[,] even dreamed that he contemplated a move. . . .

> On the night of the 26th Dec. shortly after sun down, we were formed in heavy marching order and quietly marched out of Moultrie leaving only a few men behind on Guard, and embarking on board a number of small boats . . . were safely landed in Sumter.

Several schooners carrying food, munitions, medical supplies, and forty-five army wives and children followed the soldiers. In the morning the rear guard also made the crossing after spiking Moultrie's cannons and setting fire to their carriages.

The column of smoke that rose from Moultrie merely confirmed what had been reported in Charleston by the crew of a harbor patrol boat:

The Federals had slipped away to Sumter. The Carolinians fumed with anger and chagrin, and Governor Pickens promptly sent Colonel J. Johnston Pettigrew to the fort.

Pettigrew accused Anderson of breaking Buchanan's December 10 promise to maintain the existing military situation at Charleston. Anderson replied, truthfully enough, that he knew of no such promise, that he had every right to move to Sumter, and that he had done so to protect his men and prevent bloodshed. "In this controversy between the North and South," he added, "my sympathies are entirely with the South"—but his duty came first.

"Well, sir," said Pettigrew with a bow, "however that may be, the Governor of the State directs me to say to you, courteously but peremptorily, to return to Fort Moultrie."

"I cannot and will not go back," answered Anderson.

Pettigrew left. Soon afterward, at noon, Anderson assembled his troops on Sumter's parade ground. Chaplain Matthias Harris delivered a prayer of thanksgiving; then to the accompaniment of the band playing "Hail Columbia," Anderson personally raised the United States flag that he had brought from Moultrie to the top of a pole, where it waved above the fort.

In Charleston Pickens, on learning that Anderson refused to return to Moultrie, ordered the state troops to seize that fort, Castle Pinckney, and the Federal arsenal, treasury, customs house, and post office. He believed that he was carrying out justified retaliation against aggression. Instead he committed a bad blunder.

Buchanan would retain the constitutional powers of the presidency until March 4, 1861. He no longer possessed its moral and political authority, however; he was old and tired, and his overriding desire was to finish out his term in peace—and with the nation still at peace.

To that end he sought to appease the South and thus prevent war. The North, he declared, was to blame for the sectional crisis. Secession, he announced, was unconstitutional—but so would be any attempt of the Federal government to resist it by "coercion." He refused to reinforce the tiny garrison at Charleston and even ordered it to return muskets and ammunition it had drawn from its own arsenal. This was in keeping with his December 10 promise to the South Carolina congressmen, which, along with the instructions sent to Anderson, he hoped would keep the Charleston powder keg from exploding.

On December 26 the three commissioners appointed by Pickens to negotiate the evacuation of the Charleston forts arrived in Washington. William Trescot, a South Carolinian who was acting as an intermediary, informed Buchanan of their arrival and purpose. Buchanan replied that he would see them "as private gentlemen" and that he would submit to Congress their proposal that the forts and other Federal facilities in Charleston be turned over to South Carolina in exchange for a fair monetary compensation.

The following morning the commissioners were discussing matters in the mansion Trescot had rented for them when a burly, bearded man came slamming through the door. He was Senator Louis T. Wigfall of Texas, a native South Carolinian and fanatical secessionist. A telegram, he announced, had just arrived from Charleston: Anderson had spiked his guns at Moultrie and moved his troops to Sumter.

The commissioners refused to believe it. So did Secretary of War Floyd, who also showed up. Then came another telegram from Charleston confirming the first.

Trescot, accompanied by two top Southern leaders, Senators Jefferson Davis of Mississippi and Robert M. T. Hunter of Virginia, hastened to the White House. Davis told the president the news from Charleston. Buchanan was dumbfounded. "I call God to witness," he exclaimed, "this is not only without but against my orders. It is against my policy."

The Southerners urged him to order Anderson back to Moultrie. Otherwise, they warned, South Carolina almost surely would seize the other forts, attack Sumter, and begin civil war. But he refused to do so until he had consulted with his cabinet.

At the cabinet meeting Floyd charged that Anderson had disobeyed orders. Secretary of State Jeremiah S. Black, a Pennsylvanian, disagreed. To settle the issue, Buchanan and his secretaries examined a copy of Anderson's December 11 instructions. There it was, the authorization to leave Moultrie "whenever you have tangible evidence of a design to proceed to a hostile act." Obviously what constituted "tangible evidence" had to be determined by Anderson—and he had so determined.

Nevertheless, Floyd (who had been asked several days previously by Buchanan to resign for having misappropriated $870,000 of government funds) insisted that Anderson be ordered back to Moultrie. Unless this was done, he argued, Buchanan would be guilty of breaking his "pledge" to the South Carolina congressmen.

Attorney General Edwin Stanton, backed by the other Northern cabinet members, took a different view. "A President of the United States who would make such an order," he asserted, "would be guilty of treason."

"Oh, no! not so bad as that, my friend!" cried Buchanan in dismay. "Not so bad as that!"

The cabinet meeting ended without a decision. Several days later Floyd finally resigned. Eventually, as commander of Confederate forces at Fort Donelson, he would render great service—to the Union cause.

On December 28 the South Carolina commissioners visited the White House. They demanded that Anderson's troops be removed from Charleston Harbor, "as they are a standing menace which renders negotiations impossible and threatens a bloody issue." They also pressed for an immediate reply to this ultimatum.

Again Buchanan refused to commit himself: "You don't give me time to consider; you don't give me time to say my prayers. I always say my prayers when required to act upon any great State affair."

As Trescot shrewdly noted, Buchanan had "a fixed purpose to be undecided." Yet he could not avoid making a decision much longer. What would it be?

His impulse was to grant the Carolinians their demand: Anything to forestall war. But he felt countervailing pressures. The North cheered Anderson's action and hailed the pro-Southern major as a hero. To repudiate what he had done by ordering him to evacuate Sumter would raise a storm that might result in impeachment. Moreover, Black, a close friend, declared that he would resign if the Sumter garrison was pulled out—and undoubtedly the other Northern cabinet members would follow suit.

What tipped the balance, however, was Pickens's seizure of Moultrie, Pinckney, and the other Federal installations in Charleston. This was, Black pointed out, an act of aggression that could not be justified. It was also something which could not be ignored by a president of the United States without violating his oath of office.

Hence on December 30 Buchanan sent a reply, drafted by Black, to the South Carolina commissioners. After referring to the "armed action" taken by South Carolina against Federal property in Charleston, Buchanan stated: "It is under . . . these circumstances that I am urged immediately to withdraw the troops from the harbor of Charleston, and am informed that without this, negotiation is impossible. This I cannot do: This I will not do." Instead, Sumter would be defended, and "I do not perceive how such a defense can be construed into a menace of the city of Charleston."

Having thus decided, Buchanan next gave the commanding general of the army, Winfield Scott, the go-ahead for a plan proposed by him earlier: To send the warship *Brooklyn* with supplies and 250 troops from Fort Monroe in Virginia to reinforce Sumter.

At Sumter Anderson's soldiers and a number of loyal civilian workers busily prepared to resist attack, which they expected at any time. They had a lot to do. Although the fort contained sixty-six cannons, only fifteen had been mounted prior to their arrival. There was plenty of powder and shot, but it lay scattered about the parade ground amidst piles of bricks and sand. Means for repelling a landing on the wharf, which lay outside the wooden gate on the south or gorge wall, were practically nonexistent.

Fortunately for the garrison, the Carolinians thought the fort impregnable. "Twenty-five well-drilled men could hold it against all Charleston," warned the *Charleston Courier* on December 31. "Its batteries could level Fort Moultrie with the ground in a few hours, and shell the city effectively. . . ." Besides, the South Carolinians were confident that Buchanan would evacuate the fort, thus making an attack unnecessary.

Hence they concentrated on building up their own defenses. They removed the soft iron nails with which the Federals, for lack of anything better, had spiked Moultrie's cannons, then remounted the big guns on new carriages. At the same time they constructed a battery on the east shore of Morris Island parallel to Charleston Harbor's main channel. Hundreds of black slaves and white volunteers did the work. Among the latter was sixty-seven-year-old Edmund Ruffin of Virginia. For years he had dreamed and preached secession. Now he had come to Charleston to "commit a little treason."

While the Carolinians labored, so did the garrison. By early January, Anderson was able to report to the War Department that he could "hold this fort against any force which can be brought against me," and that therefore the government could reinforce him "at its leisure."

This was exactly what the government was doing. First Buchanan postponed sending the *Brooklyn* to Sumter until the South Carolina commissioners replied to his rejection of their ultimatum. Then General Scott had some second thoughts—he feared that the deep-draft *Brooklyn* would have trouble crossing the bar of Charleston Harbor and that Virginia secessionists might seize Fort Monroe if its garrison was reduced. So with Buchanan's approval he arranged to charter the unarmed paddle wheeler *Star of the West* at New York, where several days were consumed loading her with supplies and 200 troops. He and Buchanan also hoped that a vessel of this type would be less provocative to the Carolinians than a warship.

Because of this shilly-shallying the relief expedition did not set forth until January 5. Worse, not until that date did the War Department get around to dispatching a letter to Anderson informing him that the *Star of the West* was on the way with reinforcements and instructing him to aid the ship if she was attacked. Furthermore, instead of sending this vital message by special courier, it entrusted it to the regular mail, apparently oblivious to the possibility that the South Carolina authorities might be intercepting all letters to Sumter—which in fact they had been doing for a week.

Consequently Anderson and his men remained unaware that a relief expedition was on the way. In fact, they were about the only ones in the Charleston area who did not know. Despite efforts by Buchanan and Scott to keep the *Star of the West*'s voyage secret, Southern sympathizers in Washington and New York provided ample advance warning. Panic gripped Charleston, and the South Carolina forces frantically prepared to beat back the Yankee ship when it appeared. Their commander, however, openly doubted that his ill-trained artillerists could hit a fast-moving steamer and predicted that Sumter's guns would blast Moultrie off the face of the earth.

At dawn on January 9 the *Star of the West,* with 200 soldiers below deck, entered Charleston's main channel. When she was two miles from Sumter, the Morris Island battery, which had been alerted by a patrol boat, opened fire. George Haynesworth, a Citadel cadet, touched off the first cannon. He missed. So did most of the other rounds from the battery's two cannons. Soon the *Star of the West* passed by, having suffered only minor damage.

From the ramparts of Sumter, Anderson watched the approaching ship through a spyglass. The normally calm major appeared "excited and uncertain what to do." He could see that the Carolinians were shooting at an unarmed vessel flying the United States flag, and only the day before he had read in the *Charleston Mercury* that the *Star of the West* was heading for Sumter with reinforcements. That rabidly secessionist paper was notoriously unreliable, however, and in any event he had no official information or instructions concerning the ship. Besides, the Morris Island battery was beyond the reach of Sumter's guns.

Then the *Star of the West* came within range of Fort Moultrie, which opened up on her. Anderson's gunners eagerly expected his order to return the fire. One of his officers, Lieutenant Richard K. Meade of Virginia, however, pleaded with him not to give the order: "It will bring civil war on us." In contrast, Captain Abner Doubleday, the New York–born "inventor of baseball," stamped his feet in frustration, and a soldier's wife attempted by herself to fire a cannon aimed at Moultrie.

Meanwhile, shot and shell rained about the *Star of the West* and an armed schooner approached her. Concluding that he could expect no assistance from Sumter, and fearful of sinking or capture, the *Star of the West*'s captain turned his ship about and headed back to sea.

On seeing the ship retreat, Anderson decided not to fire on Moultrie. Instinct and training urged him to do so, but while there remained the slightest chance of peace he would not strike the blow that could lead only to war.

By all precedents of law and history the Federal government would have been justified in employing the full power of its armed forces against South Carolina for having fired on the *Star of the West*. It did nothing of the kind, nor did Buchanan even consider such action. First of all, the armed forces of the United States were not very powerful. To be sure, the navy probably could have bombarded Charleston in retaliation, but the bulk of the army was scattered throughout the West, barely holding its own against the Indians.

More importantly, the free states were not ready for a showdown over secession. Most Northerners hoped for, even expected, another great sectional compromise like the ones in 1820, 1833, and 1850. Many of them believed that South Carolina was merely "throwing a tantrum," that the talk of a Southern Confederacy was simply a bluff designed to extract concessions. Others, mainly Democrats, sympathized with the Southerners, whom they viewed as defending themselves against Republican radicalism. Thus Democratic congressman John Logan of Illinois compared the Dixie secessionists to the patriots of the Revolution. At the opposite ideological extreme, such prominent abolitionists as William Lloyd Garrison, Wendell Phillips, Charles Sumner, and Horace Greeley expressed a willingness to "let the erring sisters go in peace." That way the United States would rid itself of the sin of slavery.

Hence, as George T. Strong, a disgusted New Yorker who favored retaliation against South Carolina, wrote in his diary, "The nation pockets this insult to the national flag, a calm, dishonorable, vile submission."

The attempt to reinforce Sumter incensed the Southern secessionists, who saw it as coercion. At the same time, the repulse of the *Star of the West* and the failure of the North to react to it made them all the more confident that the money-grubbing Yankees would not dare fight to keep the South in the Union. Senator Judah P. Benjamin of Louisiana sneered that the Federal government in effect had relinquished all claim to sovereignty. Jefferson Davis met with other Cotton State senators in Washington to plan a convention at Montgomery, Alabama, for the establishment of an independent confederacy. During January Georgia, Florida, Alabama, Mississippi, and Louisiana seceded, and Texas prepared to do the same.

As these states pulled out, their militia took over Federal arsenals, forts, customs houses, and post offices. Nowhere did they encounter resistance. Thus on January 12 semisenile Commodore James Armstrong surrendered the Pensacola Navy Yard to Florida and Alabama troops. Two days before, however, 1st Lieutenant Adam Slemmer, anticipating such an eventuality, had transferred forty-six soldiers and thirty sailors from nearby Fort Barrancas to powerful Fort Pickens on Santa Rosa Island in Pensacola Bay.

Following the seizure of the naval yard, representatives of the governors of Florida and Alabama demanded the surrender of Fort Pickens (named after the grandfather of the South Carolina governor). Slemmer replied, "I am here by authority of the President of the United States, and I do not recognize the authority of any governor to demand the surrender of United States property,—a governor is nobody here."

Thanks to Slemmer's initiative, the Federal government now held another fort off the coast of a seceded state. Like Sumter it was too strong for the secessionists to seize immediately, but unlike the Charleston fort its location made reinforcement easy.

Anderson had refrained from blasting Fort Moultrie. Nevertheless, he was angered by the firing on the United States flag. As soon as the *Star of the West* steamed out of sight he dispatched a note to Governor Pickens. In it he threatened to close Charleston Harbor—which he could readily do—unless Pickens disavowed the attack on the ship as having been made without his "sanction or authority."

Pickens answered that the attempt to reinforce Sumter was a deliberate act of hostility, and that to close the harbor would be to impose on South Carolina "the condition of a conquered province"—something it would resist. In effect he countered Anderson's threat with a threat of his own: All-out war.

Since this is what Anderson hoped to avoid, he agreed in subsequent negotiations to a *de facto* truce while one of his officers, Lieutenant Theodore Talbot, went to Washington for instructions. For his part Pickens allowed mail to enter Sumter and the women and children to leave. Moreover, the garrison could purchase bread, meat, and vegetables (but not flour) in Charleston, and a South Carolina officer sent over several cases of claret.

Notwithstanding these friendly gestures, Pickens was anxious to attack Sumter. Two factors restrained him. First, a number of other Southern leaders cautioned him that precipitate action at Charleston might produce war before a confederacy could be organized. Thus Jefferson Davis wrote him on January 20 that the "little garrison" at Sumter "presses on nothing but a point of pride . . . you can well aford [*sic*] to stand still . . . and if things continue as they are for a month, we shall then be in a condition to speak with a voice that all must hear and heed. . . ."

The other and more basic factor was that Pickens lacked the means to assault Sumter successfully. Time was needed to furnish these means, the truce supplied the time, and the governor made the most of it. At his orders four hulks crammed with stones were sunk in the main channel in order to block future relief ships (though the tide soon swept the sunken hulks away). Working day and night, militiamen and slaves added more guns to Moultrie, strengthened the "Star of the West Battery," established an "Iron Battery" on Cumming's Point due south of Sumter, built batteries at Fort

Johnson on James Island, implanted additional cannons at various other places, and constructed an ironclad "Floating Battery."

The garrison watched as the "enemy" surrounded Sumter with a circle of fire. Captain Doubleday, who was second in command, proposed to Anderson that he tell the Carolinians to cease work, and that if they refused, to level their still-vulnerable fortifications. But the major rejected his advice. Even had he been willing personally to accept it, he could not. His orders from the new Secretary of War, Joseph Holt, echoed those from Floyd: He was to "act strictly on the defensive."

Furthermore, the Carolinians represented no immediate or direct danger to the fort. By January 21 the garrison had fifty-one guns in position, among them two 10-inchers planted in the parade ground as mortars. Also the soldiers and the forty-three remaining civilian workers had closed the open embrasures and prepared a variety of devices calculated to inflict ghastly casualties on storming parties. Some cannoneers, experimenting with one of the 10-inchers, discovered that Charleston itself could be bombarded: Using only a small powder charge, they splashed a cannonball near the city's waterfront.

What worried Anderson—and all of his men—was the long-range prospect. Despite purchases in Charleston, food stocks were dwindling steadily. At the same time, the ever-increasing strength of the Carolina batteries, Anderson notified the War Department, "will make it impossible for any [relief expedition] other than a large and well-equipped one, to enter this harbor. . . ." In short, unless relieved or evacuated soon, the garrison would starve.

Buchanan realized Anderson's predicament. But after the *Star of the West* fiasco he returned to his basic policy of appeasing the South—which probably was for the best, given the fragmented and fluctuating state of public opinion in the North.

Hence when Lieutenant Talbot returned from Washington to Sumter on January 19, he brought instructions from Secretary of War Holt, which boiled down to this: The government did not "at present" intend to reinforce or supply the fort. An "attempt to do so would, no doubt, be attended by a collision of arms and the effusion of blood—a national calamity which the President is most anxious, if possible, to avoid. . . ." But if Anderson decided he needed more troops and supplies, he was to inform the War Department at once, "and a prompt and vigorous effort will be made to forward them."

In other words, the peace-seeking major was asked to decide whether there would be war. It was a decision that he was not prepared to make.

At about the same time that Talbot reported back to Sumter, Buchanan agreed to let General Scott send the *Brooklyn* with a company of Regulars to Fort Pickens. As already noted, the Florida fort differed from Sumter in that there was no way the secessionists could block access to it, thus there was little risk of an armed clash. Meanwhile three other United States warships took stations in Pensacola Bay.

Former United States senator Stephen R. Mallory of Florida, soon to be the highly competent Confederate Secretary of the Navy, assessed the situation at Pensacola and found it inauspicious. Therefore, through Washington intermediaries, he proposed a deal: If the Federal government promised not to reinforce Fort Pickens or try to retake the naval yard, he pledged that no attack would be made on Slemmer's garrison. Buchanan agreed to this *de facto* truce, even though it meant that the government was refraining from doing what it could do easily, whereas the secessionists merely promised not to do what they were incapable of doing successfully. When the *Brooklyn* arrived on February 9, it landed supplies but not troops at Fort Pickens, then joined the other Federal ships nearby. As for the secessionists, they stepped up their preparations for an attack on the fort.

On February 18, 1861, the sun shone brightly over Montgomery, Alabama. Jefferson Davis, standing on the portico of the state capitol, took the oath of office as the first president of the Confederate States of America.

So far, however, the Confederacy consisted of only seven states, all from the Lower South. The Upper South (Virginia, North Carolina, Tennessee, and Arkansas) and the slaveholding Border States (Delaware, Maryland, Kentucky, and Missouri) remained outside the fold. Even worse, a foreign flag, that of the United States, waved over forts in two of the Confederacy's main ports, flouting its claim to independence.

Davis pondered the situation, decided what had to be done, then did it. Late in February he dispatched three commissioners—Martin J. Crawford, John Forsyth, and A. B. Roman—to Washington. He instructed them to seek recognition of the Confederate States by the United States and to settle "all questions of disagreement between the two governments"—that is, induce the Federal government to evacuate Sumter and Pickens.

Next, early in March he sent Brigadier General P. G. T. Beauregard to Charleston and Brigadier General Braxton Bragg to Pensacola. Both had the same orders: As rapidly as possible make all preparations necessary to take, respectively, Fort Sumter and Fort Pickens.

Davis hoped that Crawford, Forsyth, and Roman would succeed in persuading Washington to let the South and the two forts go in peace. But if they failed, time would have been gained for the Confederacy to acquire the means to assert its independence and take the forts by war. Either way, peace or war, the result would be the same: The establishment of a great new nation embracing all of the slave states.

March 4, 1861, was dreary and chilly in Washington, D.C. Standing on a wooden platform in front of the domeless Capitol, Abraham Lincoln donned his steel-rimmed spectacles and began his inaugural address. The crowd listened intently. Since his election nearly five months earlier he had not given the slightest public clue as to what he proposed to do about secession in general and Forts Sumter and Pickens in particular. Now, surely, he would announce his decision on these matters.

He did so. Secession, he said in essence, was unconstitutional and unjustifiable. The seceded states remained in the Union. He would not send troops into any state or interfere with slavery. But he would "hold, occupy, and possess" those places in the South still under Federal control—e.g., Sumter and Pickens. Should they be attacked, they would be defended.

"In your hands, my dissatisfied fellow countrymen, and not in mine, is the momentous issue of civil war. The Government will not assail *you*. You can have no conflict without being yourselves the aggressors. *You* have no oath registered in Heaven to destroy the government, while *I* shall have the most solemn one to 'preserve, protect, and defend' it."

Lincoln thereupon took that oath.

The next morning Joseph Holt, who was remaining on as secretary of war until Simon Cameron arrived in Washington to take over, handed Lincoln a letter from Major Anderson, which had arrived on Inauguration Day. It stated that the Sumter garrison had only forty days' food left and that the Confederate batteries at Charleston were now so formidable that to reinforce and supply the fort would require "twenty thousand good and disciplined men" in order to succeed.

Lincoln was dismayed. His declared intention to "hold, occupy, and possess" the forts was threatened with becoming so many hollow words, at least as it applied to the most important fort of all. Anderson's communication also implied strongly that he believed that his garrison should be evacuated—that indeed there was no alternative.

Did Holt, asked Lincoln anxiously, have any reasons to suspect Anderson's loyalty? None, replied Holt. Had there been any previous indication from the major that he was in such a precarious plight? Again Holt said no—which was not quite accurate. During February Anderson had kept the War Department fully informed about the increasing power of the Confederate armaments at Charleston and the decreasing level of his food reserves. What he had not done was to state explicitly, in accordance with his January 19 instructions from Holt, that he *needed* supplies and reinforcements. He knew that to do so would result in another relief expedition, which in turn would lead to war.

Faced with this unexpected crisis on his first day in office, Lincoln asked General Scott's advice. That night Scott gave it: "I see no alternative but a surrender, in some weeks." He also informed Lincoln of the Buchanan-Mallory "truce" with respect to Fort Pickens—another disturbing bit of news.

Though Scott's opinions on military matters carried great weight, Lincoln, the one-time militia captain, was unwilling to give up on Sumter without further consideration. Therefore he directed Scott to make a thorough study of the problem of relieving the fort.

On March 11 "Old Fuss and Feathers" reported: To "supply and reenforce" Sumter would require such a large force of warships, transports, and troops that it would take six to eight months to assemble it. Thus, "As a practical military question the time for succoring Sumter . . . passed away nearly a month ago. Since then a surrender under assault or from starvation has been merely a question of time."

But even this did not convince Lincoln that Sumter was doomed. There *must* be some way of relieving it, or at least some alternative to meek surrender. In any case, there was one thing that could be done to affirm his determination to retain possession of the surviving Federal outposts in the seceded states: Reinforce Fort Pickens. To be sure, there was the Buchanan-Mallory truce, but he did not consider himself bound by it, and obviously the Confederates were taking advantage of it to prepare an attack on the fort. So he instructed Scott to order the commander of the troops aboard the *Brooklyn,* Captain Israel Vogdes, to land them as soon as possible and hold Pickens at any cost. Scott sent the order to Vogdes the following day, March 12.

William Henry Seward was the new secretary of state. He believed he should be president. As a senator from New York he had been playing a leading role in national affairs while Lincoln was just a country lawyer in Illinois. Only bad luck had prevented him from getting what he thought should have been his: The Republican nomination in 1860.

But if he could not be president in name he proposed to be so in fact. Twice before he had been the power behind the White House throne—first with William Henry Harrison, then with Zachary Taylor. There should be no difficulty in establishing the same sort of domination over Lincoln. Already the Illinoisan was revealing his inexperience and incompetence by his hesitation over what to do about Sumter.

Seward knew what to do: Evacuate the fort immediately. Indeed, do everything possible to avoid an armed showdown with the secessionists. For he was convinced—utterly convinced—that the majority of Southerners remained in their hearts loyal to the Union, and that sooner or later their latent patriotism would assert itself, thereby setting the stage for North-South reconciliation. On the other hand, for the Federal government to employ force against the Confederates, or even threaten to do so, would only intensify and spread the secessionist distemper and result ultimately in civil war.

From the vantage point of historical hindsight it is easy to condemn Seward for underestimating Lincoln and overestimating Southern Unionism. But it should be remembered that few people sensed Lincoln's greatness in the spring of 1861, and that Seward himself was among the first to recognize it. Also it should be pointed out that some of the seven original Confederate states approved secession by very narrow margins, that the other slave states either rejected it or refused even to consider it prior to the actual outbreak of hostilities, and that many knowledgeable people in the South as well as in the North shared Seward's belief that the secessionist fever would ultimately burn itself out. Indeed Lincoln himself hoped that the South's love of Union would prevail over its hatred of the North and had sought to appeal to this in his inaugural address.

Nevertheless, the fact remains that Seward's unrealistic view of Lincoln's ability and of Southern attitudes led him to pursue a course that was morally dubious and nearly disastrous for the Union cause.

First, via pro-Southern former senator William Gwin of California, he assured Confederate commissioner Crawford, now in Washington, that Lincoln's announced intention to "hold, occupy, and possess" the forts actually meant only "so far as practicable." Next he implied to Crawford and another of the commissioners (again through Gwin) that the evacuation of Sumter was being delayed only by "the difficulties and confusion incident to a new administration." At the same time he told his good friend James Harvey, Washington correspondent of the *New York Tribune,* that the government had decided to withdraw Anderson. As he no doubt anticipated, Harvey, a native of South Carolina, telegraphed this intelligence to Charleston on March 11—the same day that Scott, who also had close personal ties with Seward, reported to Lincoln that it was impossible to relieve Sumter.

Seward said and did these things without Lincoln's knowledge, much less approval. But he believed that sooner or later the president would abandon Sumter. He would have no other choice.

But there was another choice, declared Postmaster General Montgomery Blair. When on March 11 Lincoln informed him and the other cabinet members that Scott had stated that Sumter could not be relieved and so must be evacuated, he telegraphed his brother-in-law Gustavus Vasa Fox in Massachusetts to come to Washington immediately.

Blair was more than just a postmaster general—the lowest ranking cabinet post. His father, Frank, had been Andrew Jackson's right-hand man; his brother Frank Jr. was a congressman from Missouri. Together the three Blairs constituted the most politically influential family in America.

Nor was Gustavus Fox an ordinary brother-in-law. Thirty-nine and an Annapolis graduate, he had served with distinction in the navy before entering the textile business. Back in February he had submitted to Scott a scheme for relieving Sumter. Now on the morning of March 13 he arrived at the White House, accompanied by Montgomery Blair, to present his plan to Lincoln.

Organize, he said, an expedition of two warships, a transport, and three tugboats. When it arrives outside Charleston Harbor, transfer troops and supplies from the transport to the tugs, then at night run the tugs in to Sumter. Darkness would protect them from the Confederate shore batteries and the warships from naval attack. It all could be done within a few days and Fox would be proud to command the operation.

Here was an alternative to the impossibly large force of ships and soldiers deemed necessary by Anderson and Scott. But would it work? And would it not put the Federal government in the role of the aggressor? As Lincoln had declared in his inaugural, if war came, it would have to be by an act of the South.

On March 14 Lincoln informed his cabinet of Fox's plan, then the following day asked each member to give a written answer to the question: "Assuming it to be possible to now provision Fort Sumter, under all the circumstances is it wise to attempt it?"

Later in the day Seward promised Supreme Court Justice John A. Campbell, a Virginian who had replaced Gwin as his go-between with the Confederate commissioners, that Sumter would be evacuated in three days. Exactly three days later the cabinet members submitted their replies to Lincoln's question. Five of them—Seward, Secretary of War Cameron, Secretary of the Navy Gideon Welles, Secretary of the Interior Caleb Smith, and Attorney General Edward Bates—advised withdrawing the garrison. Only Blair and Secretary of the Treasury Salmon P. Chase favored making an effort to maintain it—and the latter did so with many qualifications.

Obviously Seward had expected this outcome—hence his promise to Campbell. But to his dismay Lincoln still refused to order an evacuation. Instead he adopted a suggestion from Blair and sent Fox to Sumter for an on-the-spot investigation. He also had two of his Illinois friends, Stephen Hurlbut and Ward Hill Lamon, go to South Carolina to sound out Unionist sentiment.

While Lincoln's three agents were away, Davis's three commissioners repeatedly asked Seward (via Campbell) when the promised evacuation of Sumter would occur. Seward repeatedly assured them that it was just a matter of time. The commissioners hoped, but did not fully believe, that what he said would prove true. In any case, for the time being it did not make much difference. Davis had instructed them to "play with Seward"—that is, hint to him that the seceded states would voluntarily return to the Union if the Federal government gave certain guarantees regarding slavery. That way additional time would be gained for the Confederacy to arm.

On March 25 Fox returned to Washington and reported to Lincoln. During a quick visit to Sumter, Anderson had told him that relief from the sea was impossible. After studying the situation himself, however, he was more confident than ever that his plan was feasible. Anderson had also stated that by putting his men on short rations he could hold out longer than previously estimated. Possibly because he distrusted the major's loyalty, he made no arrangements with Anderson for supplying or reinforcing the fort, nor did he reveal his plan for doing such.

Two days later Lamon and Hurlbut likewise came back from Charleston. The former had accomplished worse than nothing. Having been led by Seward to believe that Lincoln intended to evacuate Sumter, he had so told Anderson and even Governor Pickens. Hurlbut, on the other hand, brought valuable information. A native of South Carolina, he had talked with many intelligent and informed people there. All agreed that Unionism in the Lower South was as good as dead. Furthermore, even "moderates" in South Carolina would approve resisting any attempt to provision Sumter.

Throughout the night of March 28 Lincoln lay in bed sleepless, his mind churning. A decision on Sumter could not be postponed any longer—in two, at most three weeks, the garrison would be starving. But what should it be? An attempt to supply the fort would certainly result in war and probably the secession of most, perhaps all, of the slave states still in the Union. On the other hand, evacuation would discredit him, undermine the already sagging authority of the Federal government, demoralize the North, and increase the prestige and strength of the Confederacy. Moreover, it would not settle anything. The crisis would merely be transferred to Fort Pickens or to some other issue.

When Lincoln got up in the morning he felt depressed—but he had made his decision. That afternoon he proposed it to his cabinet: A relief expedition to Sumter. Governor Pickens would be informed that it was on the way and that if it met no resistance, supplies only would be landed. Otherwise, troops as well as provisions would be sent into the fort under cover of cannon fire.

Every member of the cabinet approved except Seward. And even he based his opposition on the grounds that it would be better to have the war start at Pickens than Sumter. His stated reasons for so contending were deficient both in logic and sincerity.

Having made his decision, Lincoln proceeded to implement it. He ordered the Navy Department to assemble ships and the War Department 300 troops and supplies at New York, then sent Fox there to take charge.

Seward, however, was far from abandoning his effort to impose his leadership and policy on Lincoln. On the evening of March 29 he went to the White House, accompanied by Captain Montgomery C. Meigs of the Army Corps of Engineers, for the purpose of discussing the situation at Fort Pickens. Two days earlier Lincoln had learned from a newspaper report that the *Brooklyn,* which he had sent to reinforce Pickens early in March, had appeared at Key West (which the Union also retained) with troops still aboard. Obviously, as Lincoln put it, the Pickens expedition had "fizzled out." Would Meigs, he asked, prepare a plan for relieving and holding the fort?

Meigs said he would and left to do so. Seward was pleased. He was hopeful now that Lincoln would call off the Sumter expedition in order to concentrate on holding Pickens. In addition, Seward had influenced certain New York businessmen to withhold the assistance needed by Fox to acquire ships and supplies.

On March 31 Meigs presented his Pickens plan to Lincoln, who approved it and instructed Scott that "he wished this thing done and not to let it fail." He adopted this peremptory tone toward the ancient general because several days before Scott had shocked him with a proposal to evacuate the Florida fort as well as Sumter.

On April 1 confirmation that the order to reinforce Pickens had not been executed reached Lincoln in a letter from Captain Vogdes, commander of the troops on the *Brooklyn.* Vogdes neglected to explain this failure, but did speak of "uncertain" communications with Washington and warned that the Confederates might attack Pickens "without a moment's notice."

This alarming news hastened preparations for the Pickens expedition. All through the day Meigs and Navy Lieutenant David D. Porter sat in a White House office drawing up orders for Lincoln to sign. Seward, who in a sense was sponsoring the expedition, personally handed many of the orders to Lincoln. One of them was a telegram to the New York Naval Yard to "Fit out *Powhatan* to go to sea at the earliest possible moment." Meigs and Porter planned to use this warship to support the landing of men and stores at Pickens.

Pickens, however, was not the only thing on Seward's mind that day. There was still Sumter. On March 30 he had promised Justice Campbell that on April 1 he would give him definite word about the government's intentions, concerning that fort, to pass on to the Confederate commissioners. Now Campbell came to Seward for that word.

Seward excused himself, visited Lincoln, then returned and wrote a message to be delivered in Campbell's name to the commissioners: "I am satisfied the government will not undertake to supply Fort Sumter without giving notice to Governor Pickens."

Campbell protested that this was a betrayal of Seward's oft-repeated promises, which Campbell had personally guaranteed, that Sumter would be evacuated. Seward, however, somehow persuaded him that this was not so, with the incredible result that Campbell reported to the commissioners that Seward's promise still held good.

But the commissioners themselves were not so easily fooled. They telegraphed Robert Toombs, the Confederate secretary of state, that Lincoln would not issue an order to evacuate Sumter because he feared the North's reaction. Instead, they reported, he intended to "shift responsibility upon Major Anderson by suffering him to be starved out."

Meanwhile, on this same eventful April Fool's Day Seward, during one of his frequent calls at the White House, handed Lincoln the most remarkable memorandum ever submitted by a cabinet member to a president. Entitled "Some Thoughts for the President's Consideration," it stated that the government was "without a policy either domestic or foreign." Regarding the former, it proposed abandoning Sumter but defending Pickens. This, for reasons unexplained, would "change the question before the Public from one upon Slavery . . . for a question upon Union or Disunion." As for foreign policy, let the government initiate war with France (which was meddling in Mexican affairs), or with Spain (which had occupied Santo Domingo), or with both. Then, faced with a common alien foe, the people of North and South would forget their differences and the Union would be restored.

Seward concluded the memorandum by declaring that "whatever policy we adopt, there must be an energetic prosecution of it. . . . I neither seek to evade nor assume responsibility."

In brief, Seward offered to take command.

Lincoln would have been perfectly justified in demanding his resignation both for insubordination and incompetency. Instead, later in the day he sent a reply to Seward which calmly, tactfully, and firmly said: No.

Seward now realized that he could not dominate Lincoln. But he still hoped to influence him—and to head off the Sumter expedition.

The president, he knew, was especially anxious to keep Virginia in the Union, for should she pull out, the rest of the Upper South soon would follow.

Therefore on the morning of April 4 he brought to the White House John B. Baldwin, a leading Unionist member of the Virginia Convention, which had been called to consider secession. His object was to arrange a deal whereby Lincoln would agree to evacuate Sumter in exchange for the adjournment of the Virginia Convention.

Lincoln and Baldwin conversed long and earnestly—but to no avail. Baldwin somehow got the impression that Lincoln was simply asking for the disbandment of the convention. Lincoln, on the other hand, concluded that Baldwin had contemptuously rejected his offer to give up Sumter in return for the nonsecession of Virginia. Following the interview he denounced Virginia Unionists as nothing but "white crows." Again Seward experienced frustration.

That afternoon Lincoln and Fox, who had returned to Washington, made final preparations for the Sumter expedition. Despite the Seward-inspired obstacles he had encountered in New York, Fox had obtained the passenger steamer *Baltic* and three tugboats. In addition, he had authority to employ the warships *Pawnee* and *Pocahontas* and the revenue cutter *Harriet Lane.* Lincoln instructed him to rendezvous this flotilla outside Charleston Harbor, then to send an unarmed supply boat toward Sumter. If the Confederates opened fire, the boat was to turn back at once, and Fox would endeavor to land troops and provisions at Sumter by means of tugboats covered by the cannons of his warships and of the fort.

In order to make sure that *this time* the fort's cannons would fire, Lincoln also had Secretary of War Cameron send Anderson a letter (by regular mail) notifying him of the relief expedition and urging him to hold out, "if possible," until it arrived, Should surrender become a necessity, however, he was "authorized to make it."

Before returning to New York, Fox asked Secretary of the Navy Gideon Welles for another and more powerful warship for use in repelling Confederate naval attack and transporting 300 sailors, with howitzers and landing boats. Welles, who had been kept totally in the dark about the Pickens expedition, promptly sent orders to Captain Samuel Mercer to take command of the *Powhatan* as part of the Sumter expedition.

The result was a farce. On April 5 Captain Meigs and Captain Mercer both showed up at the New York Naval Yard, where the *Powhatan* was berthed. Meigs insisted that his authority to assume control of the ship took precedence because it was signed by the president. No, maintained Mercer—his order from Welles bore a later date. Finally Meigs telegraphed Seward asking him to settle the dispute.

Feeling rather embarrassed, Seward notified Welles of the mix-up. Welles, understandably enough, was angry over not being informed of the Pickens expedition. Together he and Seward hastened to the White House, arriving shortly before midnight.

Lincoln apologized to Welles, explaining that he had confused the *Powhatan* with the *Pocahontas*. Welles asked him to confirm his order assigning the *Powhatan* to Mercer. Seward, however, insisted that the ship go to Meigs—possibly he hoped even yet to thwart the Sumter expedition by denying it the means for success.

In any case, Lincoln supported Welles; Sumter was more urgent and important than Pickens. He instructed Seward to telegraph the New York Naval Yard to deliver the *Powhatan* to Mercer. Seward did so, but (perhaps deliberately) signed the message "Seward," not "Lincoln" as he should have.

As a consequence the officer in charge of the New York Naval Yard, Commander Andrew H. Foote (whose gunboat operations on the Tennessee and Cumberland Rivers soon would make his a household name), decided to turn over the ship to Meigs's colleague Captain Porter (who also would become a Union naval hero). After all, the president's authority was supreme.

And so it was that on the afternoon of April 6 the *Powhatan,* unknown to Lincoln and against his desire, left New York as part of the Pickens expedition. By the same token, two days later Fox, confident that the *Powhatan* soon would do the same, headed for Charleston aboard the *Baltic,* which carried 200 troops, sixteen launches, and supplies. The three tugboats were to follow him, and he expected to meet the *Pawnee, Pocahontas,* and *Harriet*

Lane outside Charleston Harbor. Strangely, no one thought to inform him that the *Powhatan* had been turned over to Porter, nor did he bother to check on the ship despite the fact that she and her landing boats and sailors were now a key element in his plan to relieve Sumter.

As Fox steamed out of New York, Lincoln dispatched Robert Chew, a State Department clerk, to Charleston with the following unaddressed and unsigned message to Governor Pickens:

> I am directed by the President of the United States to notify you to expect an attempt will be made to supply Fort Sumter with provisions only, and that if such attempt be not resisted, no effort to throw in men, arms or ammunition, will be made, without further notice, or in case of an attack upon the Fort.

By thus giving advance notice of his intention to supply Sumter, Lincoln created a situation in which there was at least a chance that the Confederates would decide to withhold their fire. If they so decided, fine—Sumter would be relieved and United States sovereignty upheld. But if not, then they would have been maneuvered into firing the first shot.

Lincoln did not know it and many historians have failed to realize it, but Jefferson Davis already had decided to shoot first.

His reasons were a mirror image of Lincoln's motives for sending the relief expedition to Charleston. As long as the United States flag flew over Sumter and Pickens, the Confederacy's claim to independence was a self-evident fiction. Unless that flag came down, the authority of the Confederate government would melt away with the coming of the hot Southern summer. On the other hand, by forcing the Federal government to relinquish the forts the Confederacy not only would establish itself but grow in power as the other slave states flocked to join it.

So the question was when and where to use force. By April "when" could be soon, for the preceding weeks had been put to good use in raising, organizing, equipping, and deploying troops. As for the "where," on April 3 Davis addressed an "unofficial" letter to General Bragg at Pensacola: Was he ready yet to take Fort Pickens? If so, he was to take it.

On April 8 Bragg's reply arrived. If ordered, he would attack Pickens. Unfortunately, however, he could not guarantee success—and casualties would be severe.

That same day another message reached Davis. It came from Governor Pickens. Chew had delivered Lincoln's message. A relief expedition was heading for Sumter.

Now Davis had an answer to "where." It would be at Charleston. Immediately he had his secretary of war, Leroy P. Walker, telegraph Beauregard: "Under no circumstances are you to allow provisions to be sent to Fort Sumter."

The previous day, April 7, Davis's commissioners had demanded, through Campbell, that Seward make good on his assurances that Sumter would be evacuated. On April 8 Seward replied: "Faith as to Sumter fully kept; wait and see. . . ." Even now he was unwilling to admit that he had promised what was not his to promise. But later in the day he followed this message with an official memorandum, delivered to Campbell at the State Department, in which he flatly denied Confederate independence and refused to negotiate with the commissioners. The game he had been playing with them, and they with him, had ended.

The commissioners, who meanwhile had learned of Lincoln's note to Governor Pickens, were incensed by what they deemed to be Seward's duplicity. On April 9 they addressed to him a letter which asserted that Lincoln's announced intention of supplying Sumter "could only be received as a declaration of war." They also telegraphed Davis that the Federal government "declines to recognize our official character or the power we represent."

Davis, on reading this message, perceived that there was no longer the slightest possibility of establishing Confederate independence by negotiation. It would have to be done by war. And so it was that late on the morning of April 10 Davis laid before his cabinet a proposal that Beauregard be instructed to demand the surrender of Fort Sumter and to attack it if the demand was rejected. Citing in support a telegram just received from Beauregard himself, Davis declared that Sumter had to be taken before the Federal relief expedition arrived, for once supplied and reinforced the fort would be practically impregnable.

All the cabinet concurred except Secretary of State Toombs: "The firing upon the fort will inaugurate a civil war greater than any the world has yet seen. . . ."

Davis realized that this probably would be the consequence. Yet it would have to be risked. He saw no alternative if the Confederacy was to survive. Consequently he had Secretary of War Walker telegraph Beauregard to demand Sumter's evacuation, "and if this is refused proceed . . . to reduce it."

At 3:30 P.M. on the afternoon of April 11 a small boat flying a white flag tied up to the wharf of Fort Sumter. Three men climbed out—Captain Stephen D. Lee, Lieutenant Colonel A. R. Chisholm, and Colonel James Chesnut, a former U.S. senator from South Carolina. All were members of Beauregard's staff.

They handed Anderson a letter from Beauregard demanding the surrender of the fort. In it Beauregard, who as a cadet had studied artillery tactics at West Point under Anderson, stated that means would be provided for the removal of the garrison, and that "The flag which you have upheld so long and with so much fortitude . . . may be saluted by you on taking it down."

Anderson had been awaiting—and dreading—such an ultimatum since April 7. On that date he had received Cameron's message that Fox's expedition was on the way and that he was to hold out as long as possible. Until then he had both expected and hoped for an order to evacuate: Expected it not only because of Lamon's assurance but also because he considered it impossible to relieve the fort; hoped for it because he believed it was the only way to avert the calamity of civil war, his prime objective from the start. Consequently, in the words of one of his officers, Cameron's letter "deeply affected" him.

In responding to it, however, he wrote: "We shall strive to do our duty, though I frankly say that my heart is not in the war which I see is to be thus commenced." And in keeping with that statement he gave Beauregard's aides a reply which read:

> General: I have the honor to acknowledge the receipt of your communication demanding the evacuation of this fort, and to say, in reply thereto, that it is a demand with which I regret that my sense of honor, and of my obligations to my Government, prevent my compliance.

The aides, without a word, headed for the wharf. Anderson accompanied them. As he did so, he suddenly thought of something which might even yet stop civil war from beginning at Fort Sumter. For the past week the Confederates had not permitted the garrison to purchase fresh food in Charleston. The fort had only a few barrels of salt pork remaining.

"Will General Beauregard," he called to the aides, "open his batteries without further notice to me?"

"No, I can say to you that he will not," replied Chesnut after some hesitation.

"Gentlemen," said Anderson, "if you do not batter the fort to pieces about us, we shall be starved out in a few days."

Surprised by this important admission, Chesnut asked if he might repeat it to Beauregard. Anderson gave him permission to do so. In effect he was telling the Confederates: Wait a few days—if the relief expedition does not show up, Sumter will be yours without a shot.

Less than an hour later Beauregard sent a telegram to Montgomery in which he described Anderson's remark and asked for further instructions. Davis pondered, then had Walker telegraph Beauregard:

> Do not desire needlessly to bombard Fort Sumter. If Major Anderson will state the time at which, as indicated by him, he will evacuate, and agree that in the meantime he will not use his guns against us, unless ours should be employed against Fort Sumter, you are authorized thus to avoid the effusion of blood. If this, or its equivalent, be refused, reduce the fort as your judgment decides to be most practicable.

This meant that unless Anderson agreed to a prompt surrender he was to be attacked at once. Davis did not intend to risk the relief of Sumter. One way or another it must be occupied before Fox's expedition arrived. And above all, he was determined to assert the power and independence of the Confederacy.

Forty-five minutes past midnight, April 12, Chesnut, Chisholm, and Lee again docked at Fort Sumter. Remaining in their boat was Colonel Roger Pryor, a former congressman from Virginia and ardent secessionist, also a member of Beauregard's staff. Anderson read the message they brought from Beauregard: "If you will state the time at which you will evacuate Fort Sumter we will abstain from opening fire upon you."

While the three Confederates waited with growing impatience, Anderson conferred with his officers for over two hours. All of them rejected immediate surrender—even Lieutenant Meade of Virginia, who later joined the Confederate army. In two more days, April 14, the garrison's food supply would be exhausted, however. Accordingly Anderson wrote a letter to

Beauregard stating that he would "evacuate Fort Sumter by noon on the 15th instant . . . should I not receive prior to that time controlling instructions from my Government or additional supplies."

Beauregard's aides, who had been authorized by him to determine whether or not Anderson met the terms of his ultimatum, read the reply. Chesnut pronounced it "manifestly futile:" Then, standing in a casemate, Captain Lee (who was twenty-seven and destined to become the youngest lieutenant general in the Confederate army) wrote the following, which both he and Chesnut signed before giving it to Anderson:

> Fort Sumter, S.C., April 12, 1861, 3:20 A.M.—Sir: By authority of Brigadier-General Beauregard, commanding the Provisional Forces of the Confederate States, we have the honor to notify you that he will open the fire of his batteries on Fort Sumter in one hour from this time.

Anderson read these words, displaying great emotion as he did. Then he escorted the Confederates to the wharf, where he shook hands with them and said, "If we never meet in this world again, God grant that we may meet in the next."

Instead of proceeding directly to Beauregard's headquarters in Charleston, Chesnut's party went to Fort Johnson. There, at 4:00 A.M., Chesnut ordered the fort's commander, Captain George S. James, to fire the gun which would signal the other batteries trained on Sumter to open up. Chesnut acted under authority previously given him by Beauregard and obviously felt no need to check with the general. The prospect of civil war did not unduly disturb him. Back in November he had declared, "The man most averse to blood might safely drink every drop shed in establishing a Southern Confederacy."

Captain James offered Colonel Pryor, the Virginian, the "honor of firing the first gun of the war." But Pryor, who two days before had made a speech urging the Charlestonians to "strike a blow," declined. "I could not fire the first gun of the war," he said huskily.

Chesnut and his companions thereupon returned to their boat and continued across the bay toward Charleston. At 4:30 they heard James's cannon boom. They turned and saw a shell burst one hundred feet directly above the fort.

The Civil War had begun.

Soon nearly all of the Confederate batteries were blazing away. According to many historical accounts, the elderly Virginia secessionist Edmund Ruffin, now an honorary member of the Palmetto Guard, fired the first shot directed at the fort and struck it. Support for this contention comes from his own diary, in which he wrote:

> The night before, when expecting to engage, Capt. [George B.] Cuthbert had notified me that his company [the Palmetto Guard] requested of me to discharge the first cannon to be fired, which was their 64 lb. Columbiad, loaded with shell. By order of Gen. Beauregard, made known the afternoon of the 11th, the attack was to be commenced by the first shot at the fort being fired by the Palmetto Guard, & from the Iron Battery. In accepting & acting upon this highly appreciated compliment, that company had made me its instrument. . . . Of course I was highly gratified by the compliment, & delighted to perform the service—which I did. The shell struck the fort, at the north-east angle of the parapet.

It seems in fact, however, that Ruffin merely fired the first shot from the Iron Battery on Cumming's Point, and that he did not do so until after other batteries had opened up. In his official report of April 17, 1861, Captain Cuthbert stated:

> The mortar battery at Cummings Point opened fire on Fort Sumter in its turn, after the signal shell from Fort Johnson, having been preceded by the mortar batteries on Sullivan's Island and the mortar battery of the Marion Artillery. . . . At the dawn of day the Iron battery commenced its work of demolition. The first shell from columbiad No. 1, fired by the venerable Edmund Ruffin, of Virginia, burst directly upon the parapet of the southwest angle of the fort [a more likely place for it to strike than the northeast angle referred to by Ruffin].

Other Confederate accounts, official and unofficial, confirm Cuthbert's statement.

If the signal shell from Fort Johnson be considered the opening shot of the Civil War, as it should, then Lieutenant Henry S. Farley fired it. He commanded the mortar that lobbed the shell over Sumter and according to his own testimony, which is supported by two eyewitnesses, he personally yanked the lanyard.

Beauregard's guns—thirty cannons and seventeen mortars—pounded the fort during the rest of the night and on into the dawn. Thousands of Charlestonians—men, women, and children, many in nightclothes—crowded the Battery, rooftops, and wharves to watch the pyrotechnics. In her excitement Mary Chesnut, wife of the colonel, sat down on a chimney atop the Mills House with the result that her dress caught fire. Friends beat out the flames before much more than her dignity was damaged.

Sumter's cannons remained silent. This disappointed the spectators and caused some of the Confederate soldiers to feel like bullies hitting a man who will not fight back. Ruffin was "fearful that Major Anderson, relying on the security of his men in the covered casemates . . . did not intend to fire at all. It would have cheapened our conquest of the fort, if effected, if no hostile defence had been made—& and still more increased the disgrace of failure."

Ruffin need not have worried. Anderson intended to fire back—but not until daylight. His guns lacked breech sights, and although Captain Doubleday and another officer had devised notched sticks as imperfect substitutes, they could not be aimed accurately in the dark. Moreover, he had a stockpile of only 700 powder bags (the cartridges used to discharge the cannons), which his men had made out of sheets and shirts. It would be foolish to squander them in nocturnal potshots.

At 6:00 A.M., their regular time, the soldiers assembled in the bombproofs for reveille, ate a quick breakfast of pork and water, and then manned the guns on the lower tier. To the irritation of many of them, Anderson previously had decided not to operate the pieces on the more exposed upper tier (the parapet) because he feared excessive casualties to the small garrison, which would leave it with insufficient strength to repel a landing attempt (something, however, which the Confederates did not plan, as they considered it a hopeless enterprise). It is possible, too, that he wished to save these guns to cover Fox's relief expedition.

Anderson offered Doubleday, his second-in-command, the honor of firing (at least in the figurative sense) the first Union shot of the war. The

New Yorker gladly accepted it. As far as he was concerned, the war was "simply a contest, politically speaking, as whether virtue or vice should rule" in America.

Shortly before 7:00 A.M. Doubleday aimed a 32-pounder at the Iron Battery, then stepped back and shouted "Fire!" The gunner (apparently his name has gone unrecorded) yanked the lanyard, and the cannon belched forth an iron ball, which whizzed across the bay and bounced off the slanting roof of the Iron Battery.

Following this shot the other gun crews went into action. At first they concentrated their fire on the Iron Battery and the Floating Battery, which had been anchored off the western tip of Sullivan's Island. The musicians and most of the workmen assisted by carrying ammunition to the casemates. Also some of the latter sewed up more powder bags, handicapped because only six needles were available. Owing to the lack of manpower and powder bags, the garrison after a while employed but six cannons. On at least one occasion a group of workers took the place of the soldiers in serving a piece.

When it became apparent that no damage was being done to the Floating Battery, Anderson authorized a shift of fire to Fort Moultrie. Most of the projectiles directed against it, however, merely buried themselves harmlessly in piles of sandbags. Equally futile were the few shots aimed at the mortars on James Island. As for the Iron Battery, a Union cannon ball put one of its guns out of action by jamming the steel shutter protecting its embrasure, but the Confederates soon repaired the shutter.

The Federals' fire would have been more effective, especially against Moultrie, had they been able to use shells, but they lacked the fuses necessary to explode the shells, and an attempt to improvise them failed. Likewise the 8-inch and 10-inch Columbiads on the parapet almost certainly would have made things rougher on the Confederates. Not only did they shoot projectiles weighing 65 and 128 pounds, but their angle of fire was superior. Frustrated by the ineffectiveness of the 32-pounders that were being used, Private John Carmody ignored orders and went to the top parapet where he single-handedly fired a number of the big guns, which already were loaded and trained on Moultrie. In addition, two sergeants managed to get off a couple of shots from a 10-inch Columbiad aimed at the Iron Battery. No one, however, attempted to drop a cannonball on Charleston from one of the guns mounted as mortars in the parade ground.

Initially the Confederates tended to fire too high. But with daylight they soon got the range, with the result that numerous mortar shells exploded inside the fort and solid shot riddled the walls. On three different occasions the supposedly fireproof barracks began burning. The first two times parties of workmen headed by Peter Hart, a former sergeant serving as Anderson's personal aide, put out the flames. The third time, however, only the coming of an evening rainstorm completely doused the blaze.

Despite the hurricane of shot and shell, none of the garrison was seriously injured. The same held true of Sumter itself. Although the parapet and gorge wall were badly battered, its defensive capacity remained substantially unimpaired. On the other hand, the closest the Confederates came to suffering some casualties was when Doubleday put a couple of 42-pound balls through the roof of the Moultrie House, a resort hotel located near Fort Moultrie. These, a Charleston newspaper reported, caused the men inside to scatter "miscellaneously." Doubleday's excuse for firing on the hotel was that prior to the bombardment it flew a secessionist flag. As a joke, he told a Confederate officer that once he had received poor service there.

At nightfall Anderson ordered firing ceased in order to conserve the fast-dwindling supply of powder bags. The Confederates for their part slackened off to an occasional shot designed to prevent the garrison from resting. Most of the weary Federals, however, could have echoed Private Thompson, who wrote "I for one slept all night as sound as ever I did in my life."

April 13 dawned bright and sunny, and some people in Charleston witnessed what they hailed as an omen of victory: A gamecock alighted on the tomb of Calhoun, flapped its wings, and crowed. Beauregard's batteries resumed a heavy barrage; the fort responded sporadically. At midmorning flames again engulfed the barracks. Desperate efforts to extinguish them proved futile. Moreover, they threatened to reach the powder magazine, which as a result of very bad planning was located on the ground floor of one of the buildings. Falling embers prevented the removal of more than a small portion of the powder.

By noon, wrote Doubleday later, "The roaring and crackling of the flames, the dense masses of whirling smoke, the bursting of the enemy's shells, and our own which were exploding in the burning rooms, the crashing of the shot, and the sound of masonry falling in every direction, made the fort a pandemonium." According to Private Thompson, the "only way to breathe was to lay flat on the ground and keep your face covered with a wet handkerchief." Yet Anderson's gunners still managed occasionally to fire a cannon as a token of continued resistance. Each time they did so the Confederates gave forth with a cheer in admiration of the garrison's gallantry.

Since early afternoon on April 12 both the garrison and the Confederates had observed ships lying off the bar of the harbor. They were Fox's. At 3:00 A.M. on April 12 he had arrived in the *Baltic,* having been delayed by gales. He found the *Harriet Lane* waiting for him, and three hours later the *Pawnee* showed up. None of the three tugboats appeared. A storm had driven one into Wilmington, North Carolina, and chased another past Charleston to Savannah, and the owner of the third had refused to let it leave New York. During the rest of the day Fox waited, then searched for the *Pocahontas* and the all-important *Powhatan.* Not until the morning of April 13 did he learn from the commander of the *Pawnee* that the *Powhatan* had been detached from the expedition. Without the tugs and without the *Powhatan's* supplies, launches, and 300 sailors, his whole plan for relieving Anderson fell through.

Frustrated but undaunted, Fox then considered trying to reach Sumter in longboats from the *Baltic,* but the heavy sea forced him to reject this idea. Next he proposed to use a commandeered ice schooner to make a run for the fort at night, even though he realized that such a venture would be suicidal: "I should certainly have gone in, and as certainly been knocked to pieces," he subsequently reported. Fortunately, however, he did not have an opportunity to make the attempt.

At 12:48 P.M. a shell cut Sumter's flagstaff. Peter Hart, assisted by several others, quickly replaced it and the banner it bore. But not long after he did so Louis Wigfall of Texas, now (like seemingly all Southern politicians) a colonel on Beauregard's staff, appeared outside one of the fort's embrasures waving a sword with a white handkerchief tied to its point. Having seen the flag go down, on his own initiative he had crossed the harbor to Sumter in a small boat to demand that Anderson surrender.

Anderson agreed to do so on the same terms Beauregard previously had offered. Flames were raging out of control through the fort. At any time the magazine might blow up. Nearly all the powder bags—including two dozen pairs of Anderson's socks—had been expended. The main gate had been blasted away and the fort lay open to a storming party. Above all it appeared obvious that no help could be expected from Fox. Hence there was no point in subjecting his hungry, exhausted, and half-suffocated men to further pounding. They had done their duty. So had he.

The flames in the fort burned down before blowing up the magazine. On the afternoon of April 14, a Sunday, the garrison marched out with drums playing "Yankee Doodle" and boarded a Confederate boat, which transferred it on the following day to one of Fox's ships. That morning Anderson's soldiers, who had made additional powder bags out of scraps of blanket and even paper, had begun firing what he intended to be a hundred-gun salute to the flag before lowering it. Midway in the ceremony, however, a cartridge exploded prematurely. Five cannoneers were wounded, one mortally, and another killed outright. His name was Daniel Hough. He was the first soldier to die in the Civil War. Four years and some weeks and days later, more than 600,000 others would also be dead.

On April 15 Lincoln issued a call for 75,000 volunteers to put down the Southern rebellion. Promptly Virginia, North Carolina, Tennessee, and Arkansas seceded; Maryland, Kentucky, and Missouri threatened to do likewise. At the same time the vast majority of Southerners rallied enthusiastically behind the Confederacy, confident of victory and independence. Davis's decision to force a showdown at Sumter appeared justified by the outcome.

But the attack on the fort had outraged the North. There, too, men flocked to the colors, and crowds cheered them as they marched off to do battle for the Union. On May 1, 1861, Lincoln was able to state quite accurately in a letter to Fox consoling him for the failure of his expedition: "You and I both anticipated that the cause of the country would be advanced by making the attempt to provision Fort Sumter, even if it should fail; and it is no small consolation now to feel that our anticipation is justified by the result."

In years to come historians would debate the question: Who caused the Civil War to begin at Fort Sumter—Lincoln or Davis?

The answer is simple: Both.

Lincoln as president of the United States had a duty to preserve a nation. Davis as president of the Confederacy had a mission to create one. Each decided to do what had to be done. The difference is that Lincoln's decision ultimately led to the success of his cause.

The firing on Fort Sumter decided that war would determine whether the North and South would be two or one. In the war itself the fort did not play a decisive part. Yet its role was prominent. To both Federals and

Confederates it symbolized the Confederacy. Hence the former resolved to take it, the latter to keep it.

On April 7, 1863, nine Union ironclad ships tried to blast their way into Charleston Harbor. Sumter's cannons helped repulse them. In August 1863 the Federals opened on the fort with dozens of huge siege guns implanted on Morris Island. Their navy joined in. By September Sumter was a ruin, its cannons silenced. Yet when on the ninth 500 sailors and Marines tried to storm it, 320 Confederate defenders drove them back with heavy losses.

In December a second "Big Bombardment" took place. This, combined with an explosion in the powder magazine, reduced Sumter to a "volcanic pile." Nonetheless the gray garrison held on, crouching in bombproofs, its musicians defiantly playing "Dixie" whenever there was a lull in the shelling.

In July 1864 the Federals made a third and last attempt to pulverize Sumter into submission. It was no more successful than the first two. In fact, the fort emerged stronger than ever. As a later generation of American soldiers were to learn at Monte Cassino, rubble makes good defense.

Sumter did not fall into Northern hands until February 1865, when the approach of Sherman's army forced the Confederates to evacuate Charleston. By then the "Cradle of Secession" was a ruin, a "city of ashes." First there had been a devastating accidental fire in December 1861—the anniversary of secession. Then during 1863 and 1864 shellfire smashed and burned what was left. Even Calhoun's tomb was empty; the Charlestonians had reburied the coffin in an unmarked grave to prevent the Yankees from getting hold of it.

Shortly before noon, April 14, 1865, a Good Friday, Robert Anderson, now a general on the inactive list, returned to Fort Sumter. With him were his six-year-old son and Peter Hart. The latter carried the same flag that had been hauled down there four bloody years before. A large crowd stood around a newly erected flagpole; many other people watched from boats in the harbor.

Hart attached the flag to the halyards of the pole; Anderson made a short speech, then seized the halyards and pulled the flag to the top of the pole. Sumter no longer was the symbol of the Confederacy. It now was the symbol of the victorious Union.

That night in Washington, D.C., the last important shot of the Civil War was fired. It came from a derringer aimed at the back of Abraham Lincoln's head.

Part One

Some Winners

CHAPTER ONE

Grant Takes Vicksburg

This article comes from Strategy and Tactics Magazine, *where it appeared in the September–October 1985 issue under the title of "The Road to Vicksburg: Grant's Masterpiece in the Mississippi Valley." By the nearly unanimous consensus of Civil War and military historians, Grant's Vicksburg Campaign was indeed a masterpiece, in conception and execution the most brilliantly successful invasion of enemy territory conducted by any army commander during the Civil War. In contrast Lee's forays into the North ended, after victorious beginnings, in failures that would have turned into disasters had he faced a more aggressive foe: Rosecrans, despite matching Grant's maneuvering skill in capturing Chattanooga in September 1863, lacked the strength and the luck needed to secure the fruits of that skill; and Sherman's seizure of Atlanta a year later, although a decisive achievement, could and should have been more decisive still, in that he squandered numerous opportunities along the way to Atlanta to crush the Confederate army opposing him.*

My argument that the strategic impact of the fall of Vicksburg has been exaggerated does, however, depart from the standard view of Grant's accomplishment. Since Grant's success, like all success in warfare, depended on what the enemy did and did not do, I appended to the article as it appeared in Strategy and Tactics, *a short discussion of "Confederate Strategic Options" and have done so again herein.*

THE CONFEDERACY, BY SUMMER 1862, HELD ONLY TWO STRONGHOLDS ON the Mississippi River: Vicksburg and, 240 river miles to the south, Port Hudson. Of the two, Vicksburg was by far the more important. Its formidable batteries, located on a steep hill overlooking a hairpin turn in the Mississippi, blocked the passage of Northern shipping. At the same time, Vicksburg's river and rail connections made it the main supply and communication channel between the western and eastern sections of the Confederacy. Finally, it represented the last major bastion of Confederate power in

UNION POSITIONS
AND MOVEMENTS
DECEMBER 1862
Confederate Defense at
Vicksburg and Jackson
N
TENNESSEE
Jackson
Ft. Pillow
Ft. Randolph
Bolivar
Memphis
Shiloh
Grand Jct.
Corinth
ARKANSAS
Holly Springs
Iuka
Grant's Retreat
Oxford
Arkansas River
Tupelo
Ft. Hindman
Mississippi River
Grenada
Greenville
MISSISSIPPI
Sherman's Route
to Vicksburg
Yazoo River
Pearl River
Monroe
Vicksburg
Jackson
Meridian
Grand Gulf
Bayou
Pierre
Port Gibson
LOUISIANA
Natchez
Port Hudson
Baton Rouge
David Laforce

the Mississippi Valley (Port Hudson was doomed if it fell); thus it had a symbolic importance second only to that of Richmond. For these reasons, if the North captured Vicksburg, the Union would move much closer to victory; if the South lost Vicksburg, the Confederacy would move much closer to defeat.

There were three obvious ways for the North to capture Vicksburg. One, the most obvious, was a direct assault from the river. Accordingly, on the night of June 27–28, 1862, eleven Union warships under Captain David G. Farragut, the captor of New Orleans, pounded the town's defenses for three hours. When they finished, they had done no serious damage, whereas the Union had three ships put out of action. And Farragut's ships could not elevate their cannons sufficiently to hit the Confederate hilltop batteries, which for their part could fire plunging shot at them.

The second obvious way was to march down from the Memphis area through northern Mississippi and take Vicksburg from the rear. In November 1862, Major General Ulysses S. Grant, at the head of 40,000 Union troops, set out to do precisely that. Early in December and still 150 miles from his objective, the Rebel cavalry of Nathan Bedford Forrest and Earl Van Dorn cut his railroad communications and destroyed his forward supply base at Holly Springs. Believing that to continue would be to starve, Grant retreated back to Memphis.

The third obvious way was to load troops on boats, move them up the Yazoo River, and have them seize the Walnut Hills a few miles northeast of Vicksburg, from where they could then either besiege or take the town from its landward side. On December 29, 1862, Major General William T. Sherman, acting on orders from Grant (whom he thought was still advancing toward Vicksburg), attempted to secure a lodgment in the Walnut Hills at Chickasaw Bayou with 30,000 men. Only one of his divisions and a few brigades, however, were able to make the actual attack; a single, well entrenched Confederate brigade repulsed them easily and inflicted heavy losses.

Thus, at the end of 1862, the North had tried to take Vicksburg by all three of the obvious ways and had failed miserably each time. Was, then, Vicksburg unconquerable? Many Northerners feared, and many Southerners hoped, that this was the case.

Grant thought otherwise. Having undertaken the task of capturing Vicksburg, he was determined to keep at it until this was accomplished. Therefore, during the first three months of 1863, he attempted four different

FRANCIS TREVEYLAN MILLER, ED. *THE PHOTOGRAPHIC HISTORY OF THE CIVIL WAR.* 10 VOLS. NEW YORK: THE REVIEW OF BOOKS, 1911.

Ulysses S. Grant, 1863

solutions to the Vicksburg problem—namely, finding a way to get at the place by land with a sufficiently strong enough force to besiege or seize it. Roughly in chronological order, these potential solutions were tried.

First, the construction of a canal through a low-lying peninsula directly across the Mississippi from Vicksburg was begun, in hopes that the river would flow into it, thereby creating a channel through which ships could pass; Grant's Army of the Tennessee could then land on the east bank of the river to strike at Vicksburg from the south. This project came to naught, however, when the rising waters of the Mississippi simply obliterated the canal without changing course.

Second, Grant attempted breaking through the west bank levee of the Mississippi near Lake Providence in Louisiana to create a waterway to that lake, which in turn was connected by a 200-mile-long chain of rivers and bayous to the Red River. From there, it would be easy to proceed to the Mississippi and land below Vicksburg. For a time the Lake Providence approach promised to be the solution, but then difficulty in clearing away underwater tree stumps in the bayous to make them navigable, plus a shortage of shallow-draft transports, forced its abandonment.

Third, Grant tried to cut the Mississippi's east bank levee at Yazoo Pass to the north, thus opening a passage by which ships could move southward via various streams until they reached the Yazoo River at Greenwood, Mississippi. There, Union troops could be put ashore to attack the Walnut Hills defense line from the rear. Using this route, and in spite of many natural obstacles, Union gunboats made their way down the Tallahatchie River; it emptied into the Yazoo near Greenwood. But at this point, they encountered an unnatural obstacle—a newly built Rebel fort and its cannons, which brought the Union force to an immediate halt.

Fourth, Grant moved up the Yazoo River to Steele's Bayou, proceeding northward via this and a network of connecting waterways to the Sunflower River. He then headed down it back to the Yazoo in order to outflank the Walnut Hills. Just as it seemed that the Union gunboats might reach their goal, however, the Confederates blocked up the Sunflower by cutting down giant cypresses; Union forces were lucky to escape back to the Mississippi.

By late March, the Union armies were no closer to taking Vicksburg than they had been in late December. It seemed, therefore, that Grant was left with only two options: To return to Memphis and try marching overland through northern Mississippi, or to attempt to seize the Walnut Hills by an all-out assault with his entire army. Though Sherman favored the first alternative, Grant rejected it because he feared a pullback to Memphis would adversely affect the morale of his troops as well as Northern public opinion. As for the second option, he believed that it would result in a bigger and bloodier fiasco than Sherman's December attack at Chickasaw Bayou.

Grant once again studied the problem of taking Vicksburg. As he did so, a new, daring yet simple solution took form in his mind: The gunboats and transports could run by Vicksburg on the river to below the city and then meet the troops marching down the Louisiana shore; the ships could then meet them and transfer them to the other side of the river, where they could then operate against Vicksburg on land. Of course, there were a few weaknesses with this strategy: Could the ships, or enough of them, make it by Vicksburg? And how would the troops be supplied, once they were on the east bank? Since Farragut's ships and a number of lone vessels already had run by Vicksburg's batteries without serious damage, Grant believed that his own naval support units could do likewise, as did their commander, Rear Admiral David D. Porter. Regarding supplies, Grant had learned something in northern Mississippi back in December that, if need be, could be applied to the central part of that state.

Late in March, Major General John A. McClernand's XIII Corps, soon to be followed by Major General James B. McPherson's XVII Corps, began moving southward along the Louisiana shore, while Major General William T. Sherman's XV Corps remained north of Vicksburg at Grant's base, Milliken's Bend, in order to keep the Confederates uncertain as to Union intentions. Because his route was as much swamp as it was land, McClernand made slow progress, but by the second week of April, he reached New Carthage, well below Vicksburg. Next, on the night of April 16, seven ironclads, three transports, and a ram ran by Vicksburg with the loss of only one transport. Six nights later, six transports made the run, and again only one was sunk. Grant now had the means to put his army across the Mississippi.

He had planned to cross from New Carthage, but on closer inspection decided that this was impracticable. Consequently, he ordered McClernand's and McPherson's corps to resume their southward march. Meanwhile, in a successful effort to further distract the Confederates, Grant had Sherman fake an assault on the Walnut Hills and sent Colonel Benjamin Grierson's cavalry on a raid that swept through central Mississippi all the way to Baton Rouge.

On the morning of April 29, after McClernand and McPherson reached Hard Times, the Union ironclads attacked Grand Gulf in hopes of securing it as a landing place. Though they temporarily silenced the Confederate batteries, the Union ships failed to destroy them. Grant thereupon moved on to Deshoon's Landing. The next morning, the transports began ferrying the XIII Corps and XVII Corps across the river to the undefended village of Bruinsburg on the east bank.

As they landed, Grant felt, as he later wrote in his *Memoirs,* "a degree of relief scarcely equalled since . . . I was now in the enemy's country, with a vast river and the stronghold of Vicksburg between me and my base of supplies. But I was on dry ground on the same side of the river with the enemy. All the campaigns, labors, hardships, and exposures from the month of December previous to this time that had been made and endured were for the accomplishment of this one object."

Anxious to get over the Bayou Pierre (the first natural obstacle between him and Vicksburg) before the enemy could concentrate his army, Grant set out for Port Gibson late in the afternoon and kept marching all evening and through the night. Early on the morning of May 1, McClernand's corps, leading the advance, encountered Confederate forces west of Port Gibson. They belonged to Brigadier General John S. Bowen's division, which had gone there from Grand Gulf on learning of the Union landing at Bruinsburg. Though Bowen had only 5,500 men, he occupied a strong position and was able to hold against McClernand until evening. Grant then threw in two brigades from Brigadier General John A. Logan's division of XVII Corps, whereupon Bowen retreated back to Grand Gulf, having suffered 832 casualties, while inflicting 875.

The next day Grant entered Port Gibson and pushed on to the north branch of Bayou Pierre at Grindstone Ford. Here, he halted while his soldiers, working all night, built a bridge to replace one destroyed by Bowen. On May 3, the main Union column headed north toward Hankinson's Ferry on the Big Black River in order to seal it off against a Rebel counterthrust while Grant himself, accompanied only by one brigade, swerved west and occupied Grand Gulf, which Bowen had evacuated for fear of being cut off from Vicksburg. The seizure of Grand Gulf gave Grant a much better base of operations and ended the first major phase of the campaign.

What next? Grant's alternative plan had been to remain in the Grand Gulf area and send McClernand to help Major General Nathaniel Banks, Union army commander in Louisiana, to take Port Hudson. From there, McClernand and Banks would join up with Grant, and then the combined Federal forces would advance on Vicksburg, amply supplied by ships coming up the Mississippi, which they could not safely do while the Rebels held Port Hudson. Upon arriving at Grand Gulf, however, Grant learned that Banks had gone off into western Louisiana and that it would be weeks before he could attack, much less take, Port Hudson. This meant that, if Grant stayed at Grand Gulf, the Rebels would have plenty of time to build up their forces in Mississippi and then move against him in superior strength.

Grant, therefore, adopted an alternative plan that he had had in mind all along: He would strike northeast from Grand Gulf toward the railroad between Vicksburg and Jackson, thereby forcing the Confederate Army of Mississippi in Vicksburg to sally forth to defend its main supply line to the east; defeat and, if possible, destroy it; and then turn west and take Vicksburg. As to how his army would feed itself so far inland from its base at

Grand Gulf, that was simple: His men would live off the land. Back in December, while retreating to Memphis after an enemy cavalry raid had cut his supply line, Grant's troops had obtained more than enough food from the farms and plantations along their route; now they would do the same while advancing on Vicksburg.

During the next nine days Grant's men scoured the countryside, collecting wagons, buggies, carriages, and animals to pull them. Into these vehicles they piled the basic necessities—ammunition, hardtack, salt, and coffee—and drove them to their advance base at Rocky Springs. Then, on May 12, Grant, his strength up to 48,000 troops with the arrival of most of Sherman's corps, started marching, his objective Edwards's Depot on the Vicksburg-Jackson Railroad.

Lieutenant General John C. Pemberton, Confederate commander of Mississippi and northern Louisiana, had about 40,000 troops available—enough, if concentrated, to make it very difficult for Grant. The trouble was that Pemberton felt that he dare not concentrate them. At least 8,000 men had to be kept near Vicksburg to guard it and the Walnut Hills, he figured; he stationed another 4,000 men at Jackson in order to prevent a Union raid from cutting his rail communications with the rest of the Confederacy. And, Confederate president Jefferson Davis himself objected to bringing Port Hudson's 7,000-man garrison to Vicksburg—both Port Hudson and Vicksburg must be held, Davis declared, to preserve the Confederacy's Trans-Mississippi connections. Thus, Pemberton could put into the field an army of no more than 19,000 men, and even some of this number would have to be detached to protect various crossings along the Big Black River.

The Richmond authorities, however, did begin sending some 12,000 promised infantry troops to Mississippi from South Carolina and Tennessee, and they also ordered General Joseph E. Johnston, overall Confederate commander in the West, to go there and take personal charge of operations. These actions encouraged Pemberton to view the military situation with hope, even optimism. Should Grant advance against Vicksburg, Pemberton reasoned, his first goal would be the Walnut Hills and the Yazoo River, the only area where he could establish what many military theorists thought was vital if Grant was to have any chance at all of taking Vicksburg: a direct logistical link with the North. But in attempting to reach the Yazoo, Pemberton thought, Grant of necessity would expose his flank and rear, whereupon the Rebel forces under Johnston, bolstered by the troops on the way from the East, could pounce on Grant's forces and compel them to fight a battle resulting in their destruction.

Shortly before noon on May 12, McPherson's XVII Corps, advancing on Grant's right, encountered Confederate resistance outside of Raymond. This was the Rebel force of 4,000 troops Pemberton had stationed at Jackson and whom he had ordered to cover the southwest approach to that town. The commander of this force, Brigadier General John Gregg, thought he faced only a "brigade on a marauding excursion" and so stood and fought. Indeed, he fought so well that he held his position against Logan's division until late afternoon. Then, realizing that he was up against an entire corps, he fell back toward Jackson, having suffered 514 casualties while inflicting 442.

Grant, on learning of the encounter at Raymond, decided to alter his plan of operations. Instead of advancing north to Edwards's Depot, he would swing east and drive the Confederates out of Jackson. That way he would eliminate them as a threat and prevent reinforcements from reaching Pemberton via the railroads that bisected Jackson. Accordingly, the next day Sherman's XV Corps pushed on toward Jackson from Raymond, McPherson's XVII Corps moved north to Clinton and then turned east, and McClernand's XIII Corps marched toward Raymond. From there, McClernand was to proceed the following day northwest to Bolton's Depot so as to block any attempt by Pemberton to strike the Union army from Vicksburg.

On the evening of May 13 Johnston, who had traveled from Chattanooga, got off a train in Jackson and was greeted with the news that a large Federal force (under McPherson) was at Clinton, on the railroad between Jackson and Vicksburg. At once he sent a message to Pemberton, who was with his field army near Vicksburg, urging him "if practicable" to march east and attack the enemy at Clinton, whom he estimated to number four divisions, from the rear.

Grant, however, did not give the Confederates time. Late on the morning of May 14, Sherman and McPherson attacked Jackson, which was defended by only 6,000 Rebel troops. After a short, sharp delaying action, Johnston retreated north seven miles to Tugaloo. Grant did not pursue; having accomplished his purpose in marching to Jackson, his target now was Pemberton—and Vicksburg. The next day he turned back west with McPherson's XVII Corps, while Sherman's men remained in Jackson happily executing Grant's instructions to destroy "that place as a railroad center and manufacturing city of military supplies."

Meanwhile, Pemberton, in response to Johnston's plea to attack the Federals at Clinton, was marching toward that place with three divisions totaling 17,500 troops (he left one brigade to guard the railroad bridge across the Big Black River). Near Edwards's Depot, he learned that an estimated five enemy divisions (McClernand's corps, plus a newly arrived division of Sherman's corps) were at Raymond, in position to do any one of three things, all frightening to contemplate: Strike his little army in the right flank as it moved toward Clinton, cut him off from Vicksburg, or dash to Vicksburg and overwhelm its garrison. Understandably, Pemberton promptly halted his eastward march and held a council of war with his division commanders. This resulted in a decision by Pemberton to abandon the move against Clinton and instead turn south toward Dillon's Plantation, with the object of cutting Grant's supply line from Grand Gulf and thereby forcing him to fall back. This plan was in accordance with Pemberton's concept of the situation and was theoretically sound. The flaw in it, of course, was that Grant had no supply line to cut.

Pemberton, however, never had the opportunity to discover this. First, after marching a few miles south, he had to halt in order to bridge a rain-swollen river. Then, during the night, Pemberton received another message from Johnston, whom he had previously notified of his intention to strike at Grant's communications. Johnston disapproved of this move and still wanted Pemberton to go to Clinton, where Johnston would join him; only by uniting their forces, Johnston declared, could Grant be foiled. This message caused Pemberton, who was already having second thoughts about getting so far away from Vicksburg, to return to Edwards's Depot, which he reached early on the morning of May 16. A short time later, as he neared Bolton's Depot, his cavalry scouts informed him that heavy enemy columns were approaching from the east and southeast. At once Pemberton deployed his forces along the crest of Champion Hill, a naturally strong position commanding the road to Vicksburg, and waited for the Federals to attack.

They did so, with McClernand's and McPherson's corps, under the personal direction of Grant. For a time the Confederates beat back their blue-jacketed assailants and even mounted a counterattack that came close to piercing Grant's center. Then, Pemberton's left division, Major General Carter L. Stevenson's, broke under the pressure, whereupon his other two divisions, Bowen's and Major General William W. Loring's, also fell back. Bowen retreated in good order and burned the bridge over Baker's Creek after crossing it, thereby preventing immediate pursuit. Loring, on the other hand, was cut off by the triumphant Federals and so detoured to the south and east, eventually joining Johnston. Union casualties totaled 2,441, while the Confederates lost 3,624 men, not counting the separation of Loring's division. More importantly, Grant was now firmly established between Pemberton and Johnston and, as one of his soldiers wrote home that night, "Vicksburg must now fall."

Pemberton retreated during the night to the Big Black River. Here, on its east bank, and within a horseshoe bend of the river, he had previously prepared a strong, semicircular line of fortifications that covered the railroad bridge. This was where he had intended to resist a Union thrust toward Vicksburg in the first place. He now hoped to hold there long enough for Loring, whom he did not know was heading in the opposite direction, to rejoin him. To that end he posted Bowen's division in the fortifications with Brigadier General John C. Vaughn's brigade, the unit he had detached to guard the bridge; Stevenson's division, badly cut up at Champion Hill, crossed the river to the west bank, where a number of batteries commanded the swampy approaches to the position.

Grant started in pursuit of Pemberton at dawn on May 17, his engineers having rebuilt the burnt bridge over Baker's Creek during the night. A few hours later, he came in sight of the Confederate position on the Big Black River and found it so formidable looking that he decided to outflank it, rather than attack it frontally. Hence, he instructed McClernand and McPherson to feint an assault and sent Sherman's corps, which had just come up, to cross the Big Black River five miles upstream at Bridgeport and then to move against Pemberton's rear. Before this maneuver could be executed, however, Brigadier General Michael Lawler's brigade of McClernand's corps surged forward on its own initiative in a real attack on the Confederate left. Vaughn's brigade, which was opposite Lawler's men, thereupon panicked and fled, as did all the demoralized Southern troops in the position, except for 551 killed and wounded and 1,200 prisoners trapped on the east bank when Pemberton's rear guard set the bridge afire. Grant's loss was a mere 279 casualties; and he had eliminated the last obstacle between him and Vicksburg, twelve miles to the west.

Pemberton retreated to Vicksburg and prepared to withstand a siege. He did so not merely because President Davis had ordered him to hold the town at all costs, but also because it was already too late to follow the course urged by Johnston in a message sent on May 17: Evacuate the place and march northeast to join Johnston. Had Pemberton attempted that, Grant almost certainly would have destroyed his army in the open. On the other hand, if Pemberton could defend Vicksburg long enough, Johnston would have time to gather sufficient strength either to defeat or to drive away Grant. Pemberton believed that he could hold out that long. By withdrawing the forces stationed in the Walnut Hills and at other points, he would have close to 22,000 combat troops to put into the fourteen-mile-long chain of fortifications that ringed Vicksburg's landward side. Pemberton had enough food and ammunition stockpiled in the town to keep them fighting for at least a month and probably longer, if sparingly used. His main worry at present, following the disgraceful Confederate rout at the Big Black River Bridge, was whether his troops would fight.

It was not long before he found out. Grant crossed the Big Black River on the night of May 17, invested Vicksburg the next day, and on May 19 attempted to storm it in the belief that the Confederates were so demoralized by their recent defeats that they would only offer feeble resistance. He was wrong, and Pemberton found he had no cause to worry. Behind their well-built fortifications, and backed by 102 well-sited cannon, the gray-clad soldiers stopped the Union assault cold, and with it 941 Yankees; their own loss was less than 200. Two days later, Grant tried again: His troops, he reasoned correctly enough, would be unwilling to settle down to the long drudgery of a siege unless convinced that there was no quick way to take Vicksburg. What happened convinced them. Though they briefly seized some outlying works, they were ultimately beaten back with even greater casualties than the first time: 3,199 men lost, whereas Pemberton's casualties were far fewer, about 500 men.

The next five weeks were anticlimactic, after the dramatic events of the previous three weeks. Union cannon bombarded Vicksburg from land and water around the clock. Day after day Grant's soldiers dug and burrowed ever closer to the Confederate forts. And each day the food reserves of Vicksburg's defenders and inhabitants dwindled—an inexorable process that could only be slowed, not stopped, by reducing rations to one-fourth and by resorting to mule-meat. Time was what Pemberton was fighting for, but time began to run out. If Johnston did not come soon, then there would be no more time.

Johnston did not come for the simple reason that he could not come. Though his strength increased to 25,000 men by late June, Union reinforcements gave Grant 75,000 troops—more than enough men to keep the pressure on Vicksburg and at the same time to ward off Johnston. The best that Johnston could do was to send a message to Pemberton on July 3 that he intended to "create a diversion, and thus enable you to cut your way out. . . ."

The message never reached Pemberton. That very day he was negotiating terms of surrender with Grant. Many of his soldiers were threatening mutiny unless they got more to eat than "one small biscuit and one or two mouthfuls of bacon per day." Pemberton had lost all hope of being rescued by Johnston; his troops were too physically weak from hunger and privation to break out; and the Federals had pushed their lines to within a few yards of the fortifications—so close, that they could not possibly be repulsed if they attacked (which in fact Grant planned to do on July 6).

On the morning of July 4, Pemberton's Army of Mississippi—29,491 men in all, counting noncombatants—surrendered. As they did so, the U.S. flag went up over Vicksburg. Five days later, Port Hudson fell to General Banks. In Lincoln's words, the "Father of Waters" now flowed "unvexed to the sea," with the Mississippi now under Union control and the Confederacy cut psychologically and symbolically in half. Simultaneously, Robert E. Lee's depleted Army of Northern Virginia retreated from Gettysburg. These twin defeats eclipsed the sun of previous Confederate success of arms. Northern victory was now much closer.

Yet it should be noted that the importance of Vicksburg to the Confederacy is questionable. At no time prior to its fall did the Rebels east of the Mississippi draw large quantities of troops, cattle, or military supplies from the west side of the river. The reason for this is that they simply were not obtainable, given the Trans-Mississippi's sparse manpower, own defense needs, vast distances, and poor transportation system. Thus, the loss of Vicksburg did not seriously impair the Confederacy's physical ability to wage war, especially since nearly all of the Confederate prisoners taken there were paroled, and most returned to service by 1864. The main consequences of the Northern capture of Vicksburg were the great boost it gave to Northern morale and the correspondingly severe blow it gave to Southern morale; the loss of arms and field equipment of one of the three major Rebel armies; and the opening of the river to Northern civilian and military water transportation.

The three main reasons for Grant's triumph at Vicksburg were the superior land and naval power of the North; Jefferson Davis's and General Pemberton's stubborn insistence on trying to hold on to Vicksburg, even after it should have been clear that they lacked the means to do so; and Grant himself. Few commanders in any war, and in the Civil War in particular, displayed more skill, daring, energy, and foresight than did Grant during the month between the running of Vicksburg's batteries and the driving of Pemberton's army from Champion Hill. Grant demonstrated that he was a superior general both before and after the Vicksburg Campaign; but, that campaign proved him to be a great military artist, worthy of high command: It was his masterpiece.

CONFEDERATE STRATEGIC OPTIONS

It is sometimes said that the Rebel government—meaning Jefferson Davis, who in effect functioned as supreme commander—could have saved Vicksburg by keeping Robert E. Lee on the defensive and by transferring Longstreet's corps to the West. Longstreet could have either reinforced Johnston in Mississippi so that he would have had enough strength to relieve Vicksburg or at least enable Pemberton to break out. Or, he could have reinforced Braxton Bragg's Army of Tennessee so that he could send additional troops to Johnston for the same purpose. Or, he could have combined with Bragg to defeat William Rosecrans's Union army in central Tennessee and invade Kentucky, thereby compelling Grant to abandon the siege of Vicksburg in order to defend the North's Ohio River line.

Though this strategy certainly would have spared the Confederacy the defeat at Gettysburg, and though Lee without Longstreet probably would have repelled another Union offensive against Richmond had it been attempted, it is doubtful whether the above strategy in any of its variations could have prevented the fall of Vicksburg.

First, neither Longstreet's corps nor its equivalent from Bragg's army (which was stationed northwest of Chattanooga) could have reached central Mississippi prior to Grant's seizure of Jackson on May 14. After that date, the inadequacy of the Southern transportation system and the destruction of the railroads around Jackson would have made it practically impossible for Johnston to supply a force sufficiently strong enough to break the siege or rescue Pemberton—indeed, Johnston had difficulty obtaining enough food and wagon transport for the 25,000 troops he eventually did assemble.

Second, it is doubtful that Bragg, even if reinforced by Longstreet, could have carried out a successful offensive through Tennessee into Kentucky. The Federal army opposing him was superior in numbers, was ably commanded by Major General William Rosecrans, and possessed strong fortifications at Nashville and Murfreesboro. Furthermore, Longstreet's infantry would have arrived in Tennessee, as they later did at Chickamauga in Georgia, without wagons or artillery; thus, it would have been some time before Bragg could have advanced northward.

Third, the North could have, and presumably would have, countered the movement of Longstreet's corps to the West by also transferring troops there from the East (as it did after Chickamauga) or by launching another offensive against Richmond.

Regarding Pemberton's conduct of operations, probably the best thing he could have done, once Grant established himself on the east side of the Mississippi, was to have followed Johnston's advice: Evacuate Vicksburg and concentrate all of his forces, including the Port Hudson garrison, to defeat Grant in the open field and to protect his communications through Jackson. The second best thing for Pemberton to have done would have been to evacuate Vicksburg after Grant occupied Jackson and to join Johnston in northern Mississippi, thereby at least saving his army. Both moves, however, would have been contrary to Davis's wishes and Pemberton's concept of his mission: Hold Vicksburg above all else.

Given the attitudes of Davis and Pemberton and the manpower and logistical limitations of the Confederacy, Vicksburg and the forces defending it were probably doomed from the moment Grant got his army across the Mississippi. The only thing that could have saved them would have been a major blunder by Grant.

Grant made no blunders during the Vicksburg Campaign.

CHAPTER TWO

"Black Jack" Logan: "Don't He Look Savage!"

During the Civil War the term "political general" became one of contempt and has remained so since. When applied to the likes of Ben Butler, Nathaniel Banks, and Dan Sickles of the North, or to John B. Floyd, Gideon T. Pillow, and George Crittenden of the South, this connotation is amply justified. Yet in both the Union and Confederate armies there were politicians-turned-generals who were, or became, worthy of their rank, and some who equaled and even surpassed in military prowess most West Point–trained wearers of stars. One of them was John A. "Black Jack" Logan of Illinois, who went from a seat in Congress to a seat in a saddle as colonel of a Union regiment. He then rose rapidly, owing to battlefield performance, to brigadier and then major general; by the close of the Vicksburg Campaign, Grant considered him qualified to command an independent army. What follows is the story of Logan's Civil War career and, briefly, the postbellum political career that he built upon it, as related in an article published in Civil War Times Illustrated, *November 1976. At that time I had yet to write* Decision in the West: The Atlanta Campaign of 1864 *(Lawrence: University Press of Kansas, 1992); hence, when I did, I was relieved and gratified to find that my judgment of his capabilities as a general was confirmed by the large number of sources I consulted for that book.*

THE CAPTURED CONFEDERATE SOLDIER GAZED AT THE UNION GENERAL, then whispered, "Don't he look savage!"

That he did. In fact he resembled a barbarian chieftain or a swashbuckling buccaneer. His massive chest and muscular shoulders made him seem gigantic astride his huge black horse, although he was not tall. Thick raven hair hung about his neck, and an enormous black mustache swept below his heavy jaws. His complexion was so swarthy that many believed Indian blood flowed in his veins. But most striking of all were the ebony eyes. They glowed with a warrior's light—the light of battle.

Robert Tomes. *War with the South.*
New York: Virtue & Yorston, 1867.

"Black Jack" Logan

Such in appearance was Major General John Alexander Logan, dubbed by his troops "Black Jack." And in his case, appearance was not in the least deceptive. He was perhaps the best fighting general in the entire Union army, the commander of some of its toughest soldiers, the XV Corps.

Yet prior to 1861 his entire military experience had been limited to a few months as a volunteer officer in the Mexican War—during which the only battle he fought was with measles. By profession he was a lawyer and a politician. Moreover, long after the firing on Fort Sumter it had been uncertain whether he would even support the Union cause, much less fight for it.

In background and upbringing he was a Southerner. His father, Dr. John A. Logan, was a Scotch-Irishman who spent his youth in Maryland and Missouri. His mother, Elizabeth Jenkins Logan, came from North Carolina. He himself was born February 9, 1826, near Murphysboro in southern Illinois. Known as "Egypt," this region had been settled mainly by people from the South. Commercially it looked to St. Louis, Louisville, and New Orleans. Politically it was proslavery and overwhelmingly Democratic.

Logan's father, a well-to-do physician, was a leader of Egypt's Democrats. Thanks to a bill introduced in 1839 by his friend and fellow legislator, Abraham Lincoln, Logan County, Illinois, was named in his honor.

The Logan farm boasted a fine stable and young John became "an expert rider." Also, he learned and loved to play the fiddle while tutors and local academies provided his formal education. Following the outbreak of the Mexican War he joined a local volunteer company as a lieutenant. In the summer of 1847 his regiment marched from Fort Leavenworth to Santa Fe, which it garrisoned until the war ended. Although he saw no combat, he acquired some practical military know-how.

Back to peace and home, he embarked on a career in the allied fields of law and politics. In 1853 he entered the state legislature. At once he gained prominence by pushing through the "Logan Law"—an act excluding free blacks from Illinois. Five years later his fellow Egyptians elected him to the House of Representatives in Washington by a mammoth majority. His fervent support of Stephen A. Douglas and his fiery attacks on Republicans and abolitionists accurately reflected their views. He had no trouble winning reelection in 1860, even though Illinois as a whole went for Lincoln and the Republicans. By then he was the acknowledged spokesman of his region and one of the leaders of the state's Democrats.

Meanwhile, in 1855 he had married. His wife was seventeen-year-old Mary Cunningham, the daughter of a Mexican War comrade. At first the youthful bride found it a strain acting as hostess and performing other duties expected of the wife of a community leader. But, as she wrote later, "Remembering that Logan's wife must be equal to everything, I put aside my timidity. . . ." Her charm, courage, and intelligence made her an important asset to his public career. Their private life was one of mutual devotion.

At the Democratic national convention in 1860 he struggled to preserve the party's unity. When it nevertheless split, he joined the vast majority of Northern Democrats in supporting Douglas's presidential candidacy. Lincoln's election he considered a victory for demagoguery and fanaticism. During the winter of 1860–61 he backed efforts in Congress to bring about compromise between the sections. The South, he declared, had legitimate grievances, and he compared the secessionists to the revolutionists of 1776.

Even after Fort Sumter he continued to hope that a peaceful accommodation could be made. At the same time Egypt wavered between North and South. Many of her people favored the latter, and several dozen of her young men went so far as to join the Confederate army—among them Mary Logan's brother. There was speculation that her husband intended to do the same.

But Logan was far more pro-Union than pro-Southern. When he finally recognized that there was no chance left of restoring the Union peaceably, he concluded that it must be done forcibly. He announced his decision in a most dramatic fashion.

On June 18, 1861, at Camp Yates outside of Springfield, the men of the 21st Illinois assembled in full formation. They had the alternative of re-enlisting for three years or going home. Their commander, Colonel Ulysses S. Grant, feared they would choose the latter. Hence he asked Logan and another influential Democratic congressman, John A. McClernand, to speak to them. He was confident of what McClernand, who already had come out strongly in favor of the war, would say, but he had doubts about Logan's loyalty.

McClernand spoke first and as Grant expected. Then came Logan's turn and Grant held his breath.

"Men!" Logan boomed in a voice that carried across the parade ground. "You can't fall out now. If you go home to Mary, she will say, 'Why Tom, are you home from the war so soon?'"

"'Yes.'"

"'How far did you get?'"

"'Mattoon [a town in central Illinois].'"

The men roared with laughter. Logan then went on to make a speech that, as Grant afterward recalled, "breathed a loyalty and devotion to the Union which inspired my men to such a point that they would have volunteered to remain in the Army as long as any enemy of the country continued to bear arms against it."

A month later Logan demonstrated that his support for the Union was not merely verbal. Along with several other congressmen he accompanied the Federal army as it advanced against the Confederates at Bull Run. The regiment he was with attacked the enemy at Blackburn's Ford. Dressed in a frock coat and wearing a plug hat, he picked up a musket and fired several shots before devoting himself to helping the wounded. It was his baptism of fire and he was proud of it. "I came back," he wrote Mary, "black with powder and bloody from carrying wounded soldiers. . . . I am now glad that I went . . . and safely say that no man who saw me on that field will say that I wanted courage."

Following Bull Run, Logan returned to Egypt and called on its men to fight for the Union. As a consequence many friends turned against him, and even his own mother, now widowed, upbraided him for betraying Southern principles. But the great mass of Egyptians followed his lead: During the war they furnished a higher percentage of recruits than did predominantly Republican northern Illinois. Grant later credited him with saving the region, which was of vital strategic importance, for the North.

Logan had already accepted a colonel's commission. Now he proceeded to raise his regiment, the 31st Illinois, which was made up almost entirely of men from Egypt. He promised them two things: If the war became an "abolitionist crusade," he would lead them home; and, "Should the free navigation of the Mississippi River be obstructed by force, the men of the West will hew their way to the Gulf with their swords."

The hewing began on November 7, 1861. Grant steamed down the Mississippi with transports filled with 3,000 troops, among them the 31st Illinois. Landing near a Confederate post at Belmont, Missouri, he marched to attack it. Another colonel challenged Logan for the right to lead the advance. "I don't care a damn where I am," replied Logan, "so long as I get into this fight." He did so, with his regiment playing a key role in driving the Confederates from their camp. Then, when enemy reinforcements threatened to trap Grant's little army, the 31st cut through them and helped cover a successful retreat to the transports.

The Battle of Belmont was not a victory, but Logan had performed well in it. Besides the common virtue of courage, he had displayed coolness, decisiveness, and above all an ability to inspire troops during combat. It was now that his men began calling him "Black Jack."

A sterner test of both Logan and the "Dirty-First" came three months later in Tennessee. Along with the rest of Grant's army they occupied Fort Henry on the Tennessee River, then marched over to the Cumberland and invested the Confederate stronghold of Fort Donelson. On February 15 the Rebels tried to break out. Blocking them was McClernand's division, of which the 31st was a part. After several hours of fierce fighting, the regiments on McClernand's right fell back, their ammunition exhausted. In so doing they left the 31st exposed to the enemy's main onslaught. Should the regiment break, the entire Federal line would be in danger of dissolving.

Logan drew back his right to form a 90-degree angle with his left. Then, with blood streaming from a bullet wound in his left shoulder, he galloped up and down the line shouting in a voice that could be heard above the din of battle: "Boys! give us death, but not dishonor!"

For an hour the 31st, practically unaided, fought off the Confederate charges. It suffered heavy casualties and began to run out of ammunition. Hit by another bullet in his thigh, Logan was barely able to stay in his saddle. Finally he sent word to the regiment on his left that he would have to withdraw. As he did so the other regiment took over and held the position.

The battle raged for several more hours before Grant organized a counterattack that drove the enemy back into Fort Donelson, which on the following day surrendered. The Confederates' breakout attempt would have succeeded, however, had not their commander, Major General Gideon J. Pillow, lost his nerve and ordered a retreat after knocking a hole in McClernand's line. That he did so was at least in part attributable to Logan's stubborn stand. "Had it not been for that regiment of regulars clothed in short blue jackets," Pillow later declared in an inaccurate but flattering reference to the 31st, "I would have made a Bull Run of it." Grant in his report praised Logan and recommended him for promotion to brigadier general, a position he had "fully earned . . . on the field of battle."

Logan received the promotion but did not recover from his wounds in time to participate in the Battle of Shiloh. During the subsequent advance on Corinth, Mississippi, several members of his brigade, railroad men in civilian life, brought him word that by putting their ears to the tracks they could tell that the Confederates were evacuating the town—empty cars were entering it, full ones leaving. He promptly reported this information to the top Union commander, Major General Henry W. Halleck, but "Old Brains" scoffed at it and the enemy slipped away unscathed.

Late in 1862 Logan led a division during Grant's attempt to take Vicksburg by marching south through Mississippi. Forced to retreat when Confederate cavalry cut the Union supply line, he angrily denounced Mississippi and swore that "he would burn every damned home in it if he had command of it a couple of days." And although he privately thought that Lincoln's Emancipation Proclamation was "foolish," he did not carry out his promise to lead his men home if abolition became a war aim. Instead he argued that the South itself had already killed slavery by its rebellion, and urged his soldiers to accept not only emancipation but the enlistment of blacks: "We must hurt the rebels in every way possible. Shoot them with shot and shells and minie balls, and damn them, shoot them with Niggers. . . ." Having at the beginning of the war drawn his sword with reluctance, by the middle of it he was prepared to wield it with savage ferocity.

In March 1863 he became, at Grant's urging, a major general—a promotion that his soldiers acclaimed. "Logan," wrote one of them, "is brave, and does not seem to know what defeat means. We feel that he will bring us out of every fight victorious. . . ."

During Grant's brilliant Vicksburg Campaign of May 1863, Logan, whose division formed part of the XVII Corps, was outstanding. At Raymond, Mississippi, on May 12, while leading Grant's advance, he encountered a large and well-posted enemy force. Acting on the suggestion of a private, he outflanked and routed the Confederates, thereby opening the way for the capture of Jackson, the state capital.

Grant then swung west toward Vicksburg. On May 16 he attacked the main Confederate army under Lieutenant General John C. Pemberton at Champion's Hill. Ordering McClernand's corps to pin down Pemberton's center and right, he sent Logan and Major General Marcellus M. Crocker (whom he considered his best division commanders) to strike his left. Once again Logan managed to turn the enemy flank. More than that, he reached a position from which he could have cut off Pemberton's line of retreat had not Grant (who did not realize this) ordered him to go help one of McClernand's hard-pressed divisions. As a consequence the Confederates, although badly defeated, escaped total destruction and made their way back into the fortifications of Vicksburg.

Logan clearly was the hero of Champion's Hill, considered by some to be the decisive battle of the Civil War in that it drove Pemberton into Vicksburg, sealed the fate of that fortress, and so doomed the Confederacy. Yet if an account written thirty-some years later by Charles A. Dana, special emissary from the War Department accompanying Grant's army, is correct, after the fighting ceased "Logan declared that the day was lost, and that he would soon be swept from his position." Further inquiry by Dana revealed that this postbattle pessimism was "simply a curious idiosyncracy of Logan's. . . . It did not in the least impair his value as a soldier or commanding officer."

During the grueling siege of Vicksburg, Logan's division occupied the key position on Grant's line and Logan himself established his headquarters in a blockhouse at the most exposed point on the front. Here during the day he shared the danger and hardships with his men. At night, however, he rode to Grant's headquarters for some convivial relaxation. Newspaper correspondent Sylvanus Cadwallader recalled seeing him on one occasion "with nothing on him . . . but his hat, shirt, and boots, sitting at a table on which stood a bottle of whisky and a tin cup." Several blacks danced while Logan played a violin, stopping frequently to pass around the cup from which he took large gulps himself. Yet, stated Cadwallader, who had a passion for sniffing out drunkenness among Union generals, "he was not intoxicated from the beginning to the end of the war, so far as came to my knowledge."

When Vicksburg fell, Grant honored Logan by assigning his division to occupy the city. In his opinion, Logan, along with Crocker, "ended the campaign fitted to command independent armies."

Following several months of much-needed rest at home—during which, however, he campaigned for pro-war candidates and raised recruits for the army—Logan returned to service as commander of the XV Corps. This corps, formerly Sherman's, consisted of battle-hardened veterans from Iowa, Wisconsin, Minnesota, Missouri, Indiana, Ohio, and Logan's own Illinois. They considered themselves the best fighters in the Union army—an opinion many Confederates shared.

When Grant went to take on Lee in Virginia, Sherman became overall commander in the West. Early in May 1864 he began moving through northern Georgia toward Atlanta with a 110,000-man host consisting of George H. Thomas's Army of the Cumberland, John M. Schofield's Army of the Ohio, and James B. McPherson's Army of the Tennessee, of which the XV Corps formed a part along with Grenville Dodge's XVI Corps and Frank Blair's XVII Corps. Facing them were 60,000 toughened Rebels under General Joseph E. Johnston.

Sherman tried for a quick knockout by sending McPherson on a sweep around the Confederate left to capture Resaca, thereby severing Johnston's railroad connection to Atlanta. Sherman's vague orders, McPherson's consequent hesitation, and the inopportune arrival of Confederate reinforcements foiled the maneuver, however. A newspaper reporter accompanying the Federal army claimed many years later that Logan was "thoroughly disgusted" by McPherson's failure to assault Resaca and pleaded to be allowed to take the town with his corps alone—something he probably could have done had the move been made soon enough.

During the rest of May and most of June, Sherman steadily forced Johnston back by flanking marches carried out by the "whip-snapper" Army of the Tennessee. On May 28 near Dallas the Confederates sought to forestall a repetition of this strategy by attacking McPherson's troops just as they began pulling out of their trenches. The brunt of their assault fell on the XV Corps, overrunning a battery and scattering several regiments. Logan, "growling and waving his sword," galloped to the front. "Damn your regiments! Damn your officers!" he shouted at soldiers who were milling about trying to re-form in proper ranks. "Forward—and yell like hell!" Personally he led a counterattack (during which he was wounded slightly in the left arm) that recaptured the battery and hurled back the enemy with heavy loss. Soon afterward he proudly wrote Mary: "Since the fight of Saturday, the men are all enthusiasm and think I am all they want to command them."

On June 27 Sherman again tried a shortcut to victory by ordering a frontal assault on Johnston's practically impregnable position atop Kennesaw Mountain. Logan did not think the attack could succeed—an opinion shared by his troops. Nevertheless, they climbed up the mountainside through a hurricane of fire and seized two outlying lines of rifle pits, before Logan, "finding that . . . many gallant men were being uselessly slain," ordered them to halt and entrench.

Sherman now reverted to his flanking tactics, with the result that late in July he reached the outskirts of Atlanta. At this point John B. Hood replaced Johnston as the Confederate commander. At once Hood came out slugging. On July 20 he hit Thomas's Army of the Cumberland along the banks of Peach Tree Creek north of Atlanta. Thrown back but undaunted, two days later he lashed out again. This time Hood's target was the Army of the Tennessee, which he attempted to crush with a flank attack east of Atlanta.

Hood very nearly succeeded. McPherson, who had been told by Sherman that the Confederates were retreating, was caught badly off balance. Hood drove back Dodge's XVI Corps on the left. And when McPherson rode forward to find out what was happening, some Rebel soldiers shot and killed him.

Sherman directed Logan as senior corps commander to take charge of the Army of the Tennessee. Logan's first act was to recover McPherson's body and to order reinforcements to the XVI Corps, after which he hastened to Dodge's headquarters. An officer who accompanied him subsequently wrote: "I shall not easily forget the ride I had with him as he made his way to the point of danger. . . . Although whizzing balls sped about our ears as we entered the open ground near Dodge's position, and shells now and then exploded overhead, General Logan moved in the most direct line. . . ."

He found that Dodge had already stabilized his front. On the right, which was held by the XV Corps, however, the Confederates had charged up a railroad cut, captured a battery of Parrott guns at the Troup Hurt house, and sent an entire division reeling. Informed of this new crisis, Logan rushed back across the battlefield, followed by a brigade from the XVI Corps.

Astride his horse, "Old John," he galloped along the line of the XV Corps, waving his hat and shouting "McPherson and revenge!" The troops rallied, then chanted "Black Jack! Black Jack!" as they surged forward in a well-executed counterattack, which regained the lost guns and forced the Confederates to retreat.

During the remainder of that long, hot July afternoon and on into the evening, Hood's men charged again and again. Each time—and sometimes just barely—Logan's troops beat them off. At one stage in the struggle Blair's XVII Corps was assailed from the rear, then on the flank, and at last on the front. Not until midnight did the Confederates finally quit. Their losses totaled more than 3,000—as did those of the Army of the Tennessee.

The Battle of Atlanta was the biggest and the hardest of the Atlanta Campaign and also the most decisive. It gutted Hood's army and practically assured the ultimate fall of Atlanta. More than anyone else Logan, by his skillful handling of his troops, his coolness and determination, and above all his inspiring presence, won it. Understandably he and the rank and file of the Army of the Tennessee expected him to be named that army's permanent commander.

Instead, Sherman appointed Major General Oliver Otis Howard, whose main achievements up to that time had been to be routed by Stonewall Jackson at Chancellorsville and by Dick Ewell at Gettysburg. Then and afterward Sherman gave many reasons for his choice. But they all boiled down to this: He considered Logan a politician, a potential troublemaker, and—despite his talents as a combat leader—a soldier lacking in the skills needed to maneuver and administer an army. Howard on the other hand was a West Pointer, congenial and cooperative, and—despite his lackluster record—a competent professional.

Logan never forgave Sherman. In a letter to Mary he wrote: "West Point must have all under Sherman who is an infernal *brute*." But he made no public protest. Instead he continued to fight and to fight well. At Ezra Church on July 28 the XV Corps, to whose command he returned, defeated Hood's third and last sortie from Atlanta practically unaided. Then, after a month of siege warfare, it forced Hood to evacuate Atlanta by seizing and holding a position that cut that city's last rail link to the Confederacy.

Shortly thereafter Logan, at Lincoln's behest, took leave of absence and returned to Illinois, where he campaigned for the Union (Republican) party. Thanks in large part to his efforts the state, even Egypt, voted with the rest of the North to reelect Lincoln, an outcome previously considered unlikely.

Following the election Logan went to Washington to confer with Lincoln, then visited Grant's headquarters in Virginia. Meanwhile Sherman set out from Atlanta on his famous March to the Sea, and Hood advanced northward to the gates of Nashville, where he dared a much larger army under Thomas to come out and attack him. Grant, overestimating the danger from Hood and underestimating Thomas's problems, became unjustly impatient over the "Rock of Chickamauga's" failure to do exactly that. Since Grant could depend upon Logan to fight, Grant sent him west on December 13 with authority to supersede Thomas if that general had not yet moved against Hood. Unlike Sherman, Grant obviously thought that Logan's lack of West Point training did not disqualify him for high command.

Logan reached Louisville on December 15. That same and following day Thomas crushed Hood. On December 17 Logan telegraphed Grant from Louisville: "People here jubilant over Thomas' success. . . . It would seem best that I return to join my command with Sherman."

He did so at Savannah early in January. During the ensuing three months the XV Corps rampaged northward through the Carolinas with the rest of Sherman's host. Terror preceded it; destruction followed it. Once a detachment of Confederate cavalry fled when told, "You'd better get out, this is the Fifteenth Corps." In Columbia, South Carolina, a resident wrote in her diary: "Two corps entered town . . . one, the diabolical 15th which Sherman had hitherto never permitted to enter a city on account of their vile and desperate character. . . . The devils as they marched past, looked strong and well-clad in dark, dirty-looking blue."

That night Columbia burned. According to some accounts Logan tried to control his men. Others say he did not try at all.

The march continued. In North Carolina on March 21 Logan participated in the closing stages of the Battle of Bentonville—a routine action for him, but his last. Three weeks later came news of Lee's surrender—then of Lincoln's murder. Enraged, several thousand of Logan's troops headed for Raleigh, intending to do to it what they had done to Columbia. Logan ordered them back, but they ignored him. Then he threatened them with canister, whereupon they turned around.

On May 24 Sherman's army paraded through Washington in a final grand review. Sherman, aware that the Army of the Tennessee regarded "Black Jack" as its true commander, asked Howard to let Logan lead it. Howard, the "Christian general," reluctantly agreed. And so, to the accompaniment of thunderous cheers, his "coal-black hair giving him the air of a native chief," Logan rode his big black horse down Pennsylvania Avenue at the head of the men he had led so well on July 22, 1864.

Grant offered Logan a brigadier generalship in the Regular army; he declined, resigned, and returned to politics. In 1866, after formally joining the Republican party, he was elected congressman-at-large from Illinois. After two terms in the House, during which he served on the committee that brought impeachment charges against Andrew Johnson, he went to the Senate. In 1880, according to one dubious source, he could have had the Republican presidential nomination but turned it down out of loyalty to Grant, for whom he sought a third term. Four years later he did become James G. Blaine's running mate, only to share in the "Plumed Knight's" narrow defeat by Grover Cleveland.

A powerful auxiliary to his political ambitions, and to the Republican party as a whole, was the Grand Army of the Republic. He helped form this Union veterans' organization in 1866 and by 1868 was its national commander. His stock-in-trade as a politician was the "Bloody Shirt," to which he gave literary expression in a book, *The Great Conspiracy*. In addition, he took out his grudge against the West Pointers by writing *The Volunteer Soldier of America*.

No Republican blamed him for the 1884 setback; in fact, many favored him as the party's standard bearer for 1888. In 1885 a group of artists from Milwaukee arrived in Atlanta to work on a mammoth circular canvas depicting the Battle of Atlanta of July 22, 1864. Either by intent or coincidence this splendidly executed and highly realistic painting was well calculated to promote Logan's presidential aspirations. In it he was the central figure, depicted in the act of leading the counterattack against the Troup Hurt house. And although it is now known as the Battle of Atlanta Cyclorama and is housed in a building in Atlanta, it was first displayed in the North in 1887 under the title of "Logan's Great Battle."

Logan, however, never saw the completed work or benefited from it politically. Increasingly afflicted in his later years by rheumatism, he died on December 26, 1886, at his Washington mansion. In politics, as in war, he approached, but never quite reached, the top.

Today his deeds in both areas are lost in the passage of time. Yet, as a soldier he probably came closer than anyone in the Union army to being a counterpart of Nathan Bedford Forrest—although perhaps John B. Gordon would be a better comparison. Ironically enough, it was Sherman who, in an interview a few days after Logan's death, gave the best description of his military qualities: "He was a good deal like some of the best division commanders in the Southern Army—a brave, fierce fighter, full of the passion of war. . . . He was perfect in battle."

CHAPTER THREE

Alpheus S. "Ol' Pap" Williams: The Fighting and Writing General from Michigan

Alpheus S. Williams was a politician but not a political general. Instead he belonged to a small yet important group of Northern civilians who had acquired practical military experience in the Mexican War and/or by serving in state militia organizations. Upon the outbreak of hostilities in 1861 he presided over the rapid mobilization of Michigan troops and was deservedly commissioned a brigadier general in the Union army. Unfortunately, he remained at that rank throughout the war (he did not regard a belated brevet promotion to major general as being worth much, for the very good reason that in fact it was worth little). He did this in spite of commanding a division and frequently a corps from mid-1862 onward, consistently performing well in nearly all of the major battles of the Eastern theater during 1862–63 and in the Atlanta Campaign of 1864. The reasons for his inability to obtain promotion are set forth in this article; clearly he never served under a commander who possessed the personal status and professional sense to insist that he receive the rank to which he was entitled.

Along with being a good fighter, Williams was a fine writer. His letters to his daughters, which will be found in Milo M. Quaife, ed., From the Cannon's Mouth: The Civil War Letters of General Alpheus S. Williams *(Detroit: Wayne State University Press and the Detroit Historical Society, 1959), are among the best—if not the best—written by any Civil War general. The letters are filled with vivid descriptions and perceptive observations, all eloquently expressed. They provided the factual foundation for this article, but not without being checked against other, more objective accounts of the campaigns and battles in which Williams participated. Rarely did he exaggerate his accomplishments; more often than not he was too modest.*

This article first appeared in a special issue of the Michigan History Magazine *devoted to the Wolverine state's role in the Civil War and published in the summer of 1998. I welcome the opportunity to make Williams known to a wider audience, and I would be remiss not to note that* Michigan History, *under the skilled editorship of my former student, Roger Rosentreter, enjoys by far the largest readership of any state historical magazine.*

ASK MOST ANYONE WITH A FAIR KNOWLEDGE OF THE CIVIL WAR WHO WAS Michigan's greatest Civil War general, and the answer probably will be George Armstrong Custer. This is understandable. Custer became a brigadier general at twenty-three and a major general at twenty-five; he gained his initial fame as commander of the Michigan Cavalry Brigade; and if you go to Monroe, Michigan, you will find an entire museum devoted to him. No other Civil War general is so commemorated. Even Grant has only a tomb.

But there are two problems with Custer being the Wolverine state's most prominent wearer of a general's stars during the Civil War. One, he was born in Ohio, spent most of his boyhood there, and left for West Point from there. His sole association with Michigan, apart from the fortuitous command of the Michigan Cavalry Brigade, consisted of briefly attending a school in Monroe, often visiting a half sister who resided there, and marrying Elizabeth, "Libbie" Bacon, the belle of Monroe. He never lived in Michigan in the sense of owning or renting a house there, and his grave is at West Point.

Second, there was another Union general who was a Michiganian, who held higher commands and contributed far more to Northern victory than did Custer, and who was superior to Custer in every military talent except the ability to publicize himself and secure promotion. This was Alpheus Starkey Williams, a man who lived and died in Detroit.

Unlike Custer, Williams was not a professional soldier. Born in Connecticut on September 20, 1810, he was orphaned at seventeen and received a $75,000 inheritance. After graduating from Yale in 1831, he used this small fortune (at the time) to study law and to travel. His travels took him twice through the South and from 1834 to 1836 on a tour of Europe with Henry Wikoff, a wealthy idler, and the not-yet-famous actor Edwin Forrest. In 1836, having spent most of his money in this pleasant and no doubt instructive fashion, he returned to the States and began practicing law in the raw but booming frontier town of Detroit. During the next twenty-some years, he prospered, first as a lawyer, then as a bank president, newspaper editor, and holder of various public offices, including postmaster. He also, in 1839, married a young widow who bore him a son and two daughters before dying in 1849 at age thirty. Williams enjoyed a successful but common career. What was uncommon was his active interest in military matters.

MILLER, ED. *PHOTOGRAPHIC HISTORY.*

Alpheus S. "Ol' Pap" Williams

Shortly after arriving in Detroit, Williams joined the Brady Guards, a company of young men who provided their own uniforms and equipment, conducted regular drills, and supplied a martial presence at parades and such. Soon he became a lieutenant and then captain of the company, the position he held when war broke out with Mexico in 1846. Michigan contributed only one regiment to that conflict; Williams was its lieutenant colonel. It reached Mexico too late to participate in any fighting, but it did perform garrison duty, and Williams acquired practical experience in handling a large body of volunteer troops in camp and in the field. Furthermore, following the war, he continued to take a leading role in Detroit's militia. Thus, when the Civil War broke out, Williams was Michigan's premier citizen-soldier.

Like most Northern Democrats, Williams supported Lincoln's policy of preserving the Union by force, an attitude foreshadowed back in 1833, when, after a stay in South Carolina, he wrote with precocious perception in his diary that "there is growing up in that state a generation which will despise our government from earliest childhood and finally effect its ruin without once knowing or entering into its benefits." Recognizing Williams's loyalty and ability, Republican governor Austin Blair placed him in charge of recruiting, organizing, and training the state's volunteers. This he did with such marked efficiency that Michigan became the first Western state to send a regiment to Washington, D.C., causing Lincoln to exclaim, "Thank God for Michigan."

Lincoln, at Blair's behest, appointed Williams a brigadier general on August 7, 1861, with his rank dating from May 17. This gave him the same rank dating from seniority as Ulysses S. Grant and William T. Sherman and placed him far ahead in both categories to dozens of future major generals, including Custer, who at that time was a shavetail fresh out of West Point.

Early in October 1861 Williams reported to Washington for duty with the Army of the Potomac. He hoped, in fact expected, to be given command of a Michigan brigade. Instead he was assigned to General Nathaniel P. Banks's division and placed in command of a brigade consisting of New England and New York regiments. Thus his service in the field began with disappointment. It would not be the last.

When they assembled for inspection by their commander, Williams's New Yorkers and New Englanders beheld a man of medium height; stalwart build; dark, curly hair; a short, graying beard; and unmatchable mustachios. Less impressive were his gold-rimmed glasses and his age; at fifty-one he was much older than most Civil War generals, who tended to be in their thirties and forties. But as every one of his soldiers learned, behind his weak eyes was a strong mind, and despite his age he possessed abundant energy and endurance and a rugged constitution that enabled him to bear every hardship and go through the entire war without serious illness. They also found that he was firm but fair, worked them no harder than he worked himself, looked after their comforts and shared their discomforts, and that although he rarely spoke he always meant what he said. They liked Old Pap, as they called him. The only question they had about him was the same one they had for themselves: How would he do in battle?

The answer came on May 24, 1862, at Winchester, Virginia. There, Banks's small contingent was assailed by a far superior Confederate force under Stonewall Jackson, who, taking advantage of the scattered deployment of the Union army, had launched his brilliant Shenandoah Valley Campaign. Banks gave Williams, who now headed a division, the mission of holding the enemy in check while his large wagon train sought safety across the Potomac River. Although soon forced to retreat in order to avoid being outflanked and cut off, Williams executed his assignment well enough to enable the wagon train and most of Banks's troops to cross the Potomac. He also displayed in his first full-fledged battle good judgment and coolness under fire. As he later wrote one of his daughters, during the fighting he "felt rather exhilarated than depressed. There is a singular fascination and excitement about the banging of guns and the rattling of musketry."

Less than three months later, on August 9 at Cedar Mountain in northern Virginia, Banks and Williams again encountered mighty Stonewall. Ordered to block the road to Culpeper, on which Jackson's corps was advancing, Banks attacked, despite being outnumbered three to one. It was a blunder but a good blunder, for the attack caught Jackson literally napping. In particular, Williams's division was able to do to Jackson what he had done to him at Winchester—strike his flank and roll it up. By personally rallying his troops and throwing in heavy reinforcements, Jackson stopped Williams's assault and then drove back all of Banks's corps. Nevertheless, he suffered a strategic defeat, being compelled to abandon his march to Culpeper and to retreat. Williams's division, which lost over one-third of the 3,000 men it took into action, deserved most of the credit, and Williams showed that his skill on the battlefield matched his courage.

The second phase of Williams's Civil War career began in early September 1862, when he assumed acting command of what was then the XII Corps of the Army of the Potomac, replacing Banks, who, Williams dryly remarked in a letter, "seems to get sick when there is most to do." In that capacity, Williams on September 18 played a key role in one of the major turning points of the Civil War. Two of his soldiers, while poking about in a former Confederate bivouac near Frederick, Maryland, discovered an order revealing that the major units of Robert E. Lee's army, which had invaded Maryland, were widely separated. The order made its way to Williams, who had a member of his staff take it to General George B. McClellan, commander of the Army of the Potomac. Thanks to this "lost dispatch" the super-cautious McClellan moved against Lee faster than he otherwise would have and thus brought on the Battle of Antietam on September 17.

Williams went into battle once more at the head of his division, having been superseded as commander of the XII Corps by General J. K. F. Mansfield. A white-bearded, fifty-nine-year-old West Point graduate, Mansfield had spent forty years in the Regular army as an engineer and staff officer without ever directing a large body of troops in combat. Ordered to join in the Union assault on the Confederate left, he promptly revealed his lack of experience by deploying his regiments in columns thirty ranks deep, a formation guaranteed to produce maximum casualties and little else. Realizing this, Williams, according to one of his letters, "begged him to let me deploy them in line of battle [two ranks] . . . but I could not move him," for although brave, Mansfield had a "very nervous temperament and a very impatient manner."

Fortunately for the XII Corps, five minutes after coming under fire, Mansfield was mortally wounded and Williams resumed command. He quickly realigned the XII Corps and then plunged into the fighting, his antagonist yet again Stonewall Jackson. For several hours he slugged it out with Jackson, giving as good as he got but unable to make any headway, due to lack of support from adjoining Federal units. When another corps finally joined the XII, Williams could only fall back, his troops and ammunition exhausted. The XII's casualties totaled 1,596 out of about 9,000 soldiers engaged—close to one-eighth of the entire Federal loss in what proved to be the war's bloodiest day of fighting. Its sacrifices, however, were not in vain. Following the battle, Lee retreated back into Virginia, thereby providing Lincoln with the occasion for issuing his Emancipation Proclamation, which transformed the war from one being fought solely for the preservation of the Union into one also being waged for the destruction of slavery.

Williams believed, and rightly so, that he had earned a major general's commission at Antietam. Those who bestowed commissions didn't think so. Shortly after the battle, Williams returned to his division with the appointment of General Henry Slocum, a thirty-five-year-old West Point graduate, as commander of the XII Corps. At first miffed at being passed over for a man almost young enough to be his son, Williams soon came to respect the quiet but competent Slocum, who reciprocated with the same attitude toward Williams. For the remainder of the war the two would be closely associated.

The XII Corps escaped the bloodbath at Fredericksburg (December 13, 1862). It more than made up for that by being in the thick of the carnage at Chancellorsville (May 1–4, 1863) and Gettysburg (July 1–3, 1863). In both of these engagements, Williams performed superbly, preventing an even greater Union defeat in the first and clinching a Northern victory in the second.

At Chancellorsville it was Williams's division that, fighting from behind log barricades, brought Jackson's great flanking attack, which had swept all before it, to a halt. Moreover, and in the long run much more important, Williams's stout stand caused Jackson to search for a weak point in the Federal front; it was while he did this that some of his own troops, mistaking him and his staff for Yankee cavalry, shot him. The subsequent death of Jackson—Williams's opponent in every fight so far—provided him with his sole consolation for Chancellorsville, where his 5,000-man division lost one-third of its number and the Army of the Potomac a battle it should have won. "I am not much of a military genius," he wrote his daughters, "but if I could have commanded the Army of the Potomac at Chancellorsville I would have wagered my life on being in Richmond in ten days."

At Gettysburg Williams took charge of the XII when Slocum was placed in command of the Union right wing. Williams again found himself opposing Jackson's veterans as he struggled to hold onto Culp's Hill, the loss of which would have rendered the entire Union position at Gettysburg untenable and turned the battle into a Confederate victory rather than defeat. This he achieved brilliantly. According to Edwin Coddington's *The Gettysburg Campaign,* the most authoritative study on the subject, "Williams' well-conceived battle plans were much more effectively executed than his opponent's" and his "tactics in protecting a naturally strong position offered excellent use of manpower and increased the effectiveness of the infantry by the proper use of artillery."

When the firing ceased at Gettysburg, no general in the Army of the Potomac not already possessing that rank deserved a major general's commission more than Williams. Despite his record and efforts by Slocum, Governor Blair, and Senator Jacob Howard of Michigan to secure his promotion, Williams remained a brigadier. And, adding insult to ingratitude, others claimed and received the credit, both in newspapers and official reports for what he in fact had accomplished.

Small wonder that he felt "disgusted and chagrined" or that in October 1863, when the XII was sent to Tennessee along with the Army of the Potomac's XI Corps to reinforce the beleaguered Army of the Cumberland at Chattanooga, he welcomed the transfer. Perhaps in the West he could obtain what had been denied him in the East.

Williams spent the first six months guarding the railroad between Nashville and Chattanooga and on leave in Detroit, the only one he ever took. In early May 1864 he returned to the battlefield. He did so as commander of the First Division of General Joseph "Fighting Joe" Hooker's XX Corps, Army of the Cumberland. Composed mostly of veterans of the XI and XII Corps, which had been consolidated, the XX Corps numbered over 21,000 as it marched into Georgia with the rest of Sherman's army—the objective: Atlanta. Four months later, when it entered that city, its strength had been reduced by nearly one-third, having had more hard fighting, suffered more casualties (7,387), and put out of action more Confederates (at least 10,000) than any of the other six Union corps.

From May into July Williams's division participated in the worst of the fighting and sometimes did most or all of it. At Resaca on May 14 it executed a counterattack in which just one of its brigades drove back a full enemy division that had swept around Sherman's left flank and threatened to gain his rear. The following day the XX stopped cold another Confederate attempt to turn the Union left. Ten days later at New Hope Church, Williams's men spearheaded an assault by the XX Corps, losing 745 men merely to demonstrate what everyone knew except Sherman—that a strong force of Rebels held the position. On June 22 at Kolb's Farm, Williams's men avenged this bloody repulse by inflicting an even bloodier one on two Confederate divisions, a victory largely achieved by Williams's skillful use of artillery, the fire of which was so effective that it stopped many of the gray-clad assailants before they came within rifle range. Then on July 20 at Peachtree Creek, north of Atlanta, Williams's division joined the XX's other two divisions in beating off a fierce attack by two enemy corps, despite being caught in the open and by surprise as a result of assurances from Sherman that they faced little or no opposition. "My veteran division," wrote Williams to a friend after the encounter, "has been sadly cut up, so that it is reduced in number to a brigade."

Fortunately, Peachtree Creek proved to be the last battle fought by the XX Corps during the Atlanta Campaign, it having been posted in a sector where the fortifications on both sides were so formidable that neither side dared attack. On July 27 Williams again became an acting corps commander when he replaced Hooker, who left the army because of what he saw as a personal insult by Sherman. Recently, Sherman had put another brigadier general in permanent charge of a corps but that brigadier, although not a West Point graduate, had been a Regular army officer prior to the war and

Williams had not. Hence, after a month commanding the XX with his usual efficiency, Williams gave way to Slocum, whom Sherman brought from Mississippi, where he headed the Vicksburg District. Williams was pleased to be back under Slocum, or so he wrote his daughters, adding, "I am satisfied with my old division and I have long since given up all hope of promotion from the present powers."

On the evening of September 1, the Confederates, their last railroad supply line cut by a Union flanking move, evacuated Atlanta and the next day the XX Corps occupied the city, which it garrisoned until Sherman set off in mid-November on his famous March to the Sea. During that "promenade militaire," as he called it in a letter, Williams once more headed the XX, with Slocum in command of the left wing. Apart from some skirmishing on the outskirts of Savannah, Williams engaged in no combat, but his troops perpetrated their share of plundering and destroyed seventy-some miles of railroad as they tramped through Georgia.

In January 1865, after the capture of Savannah, Williams at long last received a promotion—to brevet major general. Basically, this was an honorary rank and its only practical purpose was to give him the right to wear two stars, which he did. Otherwise, it was meaningless and he continued to resent not being a real major general.

From Savannah Sherman swung north, continuing his march of devastation through the Carolinas. This was especially true in South Carolina, where the soldiers, wrote Williams, "impressed with the idea that every South Carolinian was an arrant Rebel, spared nothing but the old men, women, and children. All materials, all vacant houses, factories, cotton-gins and presses, everything that makes the wealth of the people, everything edible and wearable, was swept away." Sherman's "bummers," he continued, "put the flames to everything and we marched with thousands of columns of smoke marking the line of each corps. The sights at times, as seen from elevated round, were often terribly sublime and grand."

In North Carolina the Federals for the first time encountered serious resistance in the form of a small but spunky Rebel army headed by General Joseph E. Johnston. On March 19 near Bentonville, Johnston, in a well-conceived maneuver, pounced with his full force of 20,000 men on Slocum's left wing. The blow struck the XIV Corps, taking it by surprise and threatening to smash it until Williams came to the rescue. Rapidly deploying his infantry and artillery, he joined with the XIV Corps in a series of counterattacks that halted the Confederate onslaught. The next day the other wing of the army arrived on the field, giving Sherman such an overwhelming preponderance of numbers that Johnston had no choice other than to retreat in order to avoid destruction.

By what historian Nathaniel C. Hughes Jr. calls Williams's "timely and competent" action, he saved Sherman at Bentonville from an embarrassing defeat. So what was his reward? Several days afterward Sherman again relegated him to division command and turned over the XX Corps to General Joseph Mower, a full-fledged major general and personal favorite. "This," commented Williams in a letter to one of his daughters, "is about the fortieth time that I have been hoisted up by seniority to be let down by rank!"

Less than three weeks after Bentonville, Lee surrendered at Appomattox Court House and the war, for all practical purposes, was over. On May 24, 1865, Williams rode at the head of his division as Sherman's army paraded through Washington in the Grand Review. This would have been a perfect way to conclude his army career. Instead, at the behest of General George H. Thomas, he performed occupation duty in Arkansas until January 1866. He then resigned his commission and returned to Detroit. But not for long. He was sent to San Salvador, where he served as minister-resident until he was removed from office in 1869 by Republican president Ulysses S. Grant. Although he had voted for Lincoln in 1864, Williams remained a Democrat. Back in Detroit, Williams ran unsuccessfully for governor in 1870 and successfully for Congress in 1874 and 1876. On December 21, 1878, he died, leaving behind his second wife, whom he married in 1875. Following an impressive funeral, he was buried in Detroit's Elmwood Cemetery.

Without doubt Williams was a superior division commander and excellent corps commander and was capable by 1863 of being a successful army commander. He himself attributed his failure to attain higher rank and command to his refusal to "pander to the paid puffers of the press." This surely was a factor, but there were other factors, such as his age, his not being a West Point graduate, his lack of political clout, and, above all, the ridiculous rank system of the Union army, which had no full generals, only one lieutenant general (Grant) and where, by late in the war, it was common for brigadiers to lead divisions and colonels to lead brigades.

In any case, historian Jeffrey Charnley is absolutely correct in stating that Williams "commanded more troops in more important battles than any other Michigan general." And in so doing he contributed more to Union victory than any other Michigan general both by the battles he helped win and the defeats he helped prevent turning into debacles. This, furthermore, would be true even if Custer had been a genuine Michiganian. Although a dashing cavalry commander during the Civil War, Custer's great fame derives not from what he achieved but from his failure at the Little Big Horn. Take that away and he would not be what he is—the subject of more books and movies than can easily be counted. (Just try it.)

Today, an equestrian statue of Williams, erected in 1921, stands on Detroit's Belle Isle. Probably few passersby notice it, and most of those few neither know nor care who Williams was. But this makes no difference. Williams's true monument is more lasting than a statue and he created it himself. It is his Civil War letters, which were published by Wayne State University Press in 1959 under the title *From the Cannon's Mouth*. Both from a literary and historical standpoint, they are among the finest, if not the finest, letters written by any Civil War general. To read them is to have an enjoyable and at times entrancing experience, to learn much that is definitely worth knowing about the Civil War, and to become acquainted with that remarkable man—Old Pap Williams, Michigan's top Civil War general.

CHAPTER FOUR

Nathan Bedford Forrest: Born to Fight

I close this section devoted to "winners" with a brief essay on a general who, no one would deny, deserves to be placed in that category, even though he became a "loser" when the cause for which he fought so brilliantly became the Lost Cause. By then he was recognized by Northerners and Southerners alike as possessing a natural genius for war that made him the most formidable cavalry commander of the Civil War. Since then his reputation has grown until now it is surpassed among Confederate military leaders only by that of Robert E. Lee and Stonewall Jackson. This article, which I wrote as a foreword to a new, abridged edition of John Allan Wyeth's classic biography of Forrest, That Devil Forrest *(Baton Rouge: Louisiana State University Press, 1989), assesses the reasons for Forrest's success and addresses the question of whether he would have been equally successful commanding a large army. I have added for this book a short account of Forrest's postwar career and some comments on what today are in the eyes of many the two great stains on his reputation—the Fort Pillow Massacre and his alleged leadership of the Ku Klux Klan.*

SHERMAN CALLED NATHAN BEDFORD FORREST A "DEVIL" AND PROMISED A brigadier general promotion to major general if he killed him. Two generations later the southern Agrarian writer Andrew Lytle described him as the "spiritual comforter" of his people because during Reconstruction he headed the Ku Klux Klan. Today blacks in Memphis regard the equestrian statue of him as an offense to their race and are demanding that it be removed. On the other hand, to Civil War buffs, the vast majority of whom are white, he is a hero with a status rivaling that of Lee, Grant, and Stonewall Jackson. Hated and admired, feared and glorified when alive, he remains more than a hundred years after his death a controversial figure and no doubt will continue to be.

Miller, ed. *Photographic History.*

Nathan Bedford Forrest

About one thing, however, everybody always has agreed: He was a remarkable man and an outstanding military commander. The man was born dirt poor in 1821 on a backwoods Tennessee farm. He had only a few months of formal schooling, and though he learned to read with fair facility, he never looked at a pen, as he once put it, "without thinking of a snake." These educational deficiencies were not insuperable handicaps in the semifrontier society of his time and place, and by 1861 he had made a fortune as a slave trader, planter, and speculator. His appearance reflected his background. In the words of one of his officers, "Without a uniform, and this did not much change him, he looked like an old country farmer," and his "manner was mild, his speech rather low and slow." Battle, or its approach, transformed him. "His face flushed," wrote another of his officers, "till it bore a striking resemblance to a painted Indian warrior," his eyes blazed "with the intense glare of a panther springing upon his prey," and his voice became "shrill," "piercing," and "electrifying." Perhaps no commander since the age of the armored knight killed more foes in personal encounters than he—at least thirty—or had more horses shot out from under him—twenty-nine. Yet he himself suffered, throughout the entire war, only two serious wounds—and one of those was inflicted by a disgruntled officer in his own command who shot him in the hip at point-blank range with a large-caliber pistol. Forrest's instantaneous reaction was to disembowel the officer with a pocketknife. Moreover, twelve days later he was back in action.

By all odds and all logic he should never have become a military leader, much less an outstanding one. Not only was he totally devoid of military training and experience, he had opposed secession until it took place, and when he joined the Confederate army in June 1861, a month shy of his fortieth birthday, it was as a private. To be sure, he soon received a lieutenant colonel's commission and authorization to raise a cavalry battalion, but numerous other wealthy, upper-class Southerners started their war careers the same way, only to remain at their original rank, or close to it, and little known then and since. Forrest, in contrast, at once displayed a natural knack for warfare and did it, furthermore, in such a way and at such places as to make him famous quickly.

At Fort Donelson and Shiloh early in 1862 he distinguished himself for daring, skillful fighting, and enterprise. Starting in the summer of 1862, he made slashing raids through western Tennessee and Kentucky, harried the Federals in Middle Tennessee, and in northern Mississippi helped turn back Grant's first attempt to take Vicksburg. In the spring of 1863, now a brigadier general, he pursued Colonel Abel Streight's Yankee raiders through northern Alabama and captured them all, despite being outnumbered nearly three to one. Following the Battle of Chickamauga in September 1863, when he again performed superbly, he became so disgusted with the petty-minded General Braxton Bragg that he refused to serve under him. Ordinarily such insubordination would have brought a court-martial, but in Forrest's case it resulted in his reassignment to Mississippi with the rank of major general, for even Bragg recognized his value to the Confederacy. There was, however, a catch to this transfer and promotion: He was permitted to take along fewer than 300 veterans of his old command and thus would have to acquire a new one. In December 1863, going into Union-occupied western Tennessee, he did exactly that, coming back with 2,000 recruits.

Thus he made ready for 1864. Three times during that year he repulsed vastly superior Federal forces that set out from Memphis to destroy him, and on two of those occasions (Okolona and Brice's Cross Roads) he routed them. Then, faced by a fourth enemy expedition of overwhelming strength, he turned it back too by striking directly at Memphis itself. Following the defeat of the first invasion, he raided deep behind Union lines, penetrating all the way to the Ohio River, capturing forts, and in one case (Fort Pillow, Tennessee, April 12) wiping out most of an enemy garrison. In the autumn he swept northward twice more, each time to attack Sherman's supply line in Tennessee. But though he devastated an entire railroad, demolished depots, burned transport ships, and even captured and used Yankee gunboats, he was, through no fault of his own, too late to prevent what many believed then and believe now he could have prevented had he been unleashed sooner—Sherman's capture of Atlanta.

Finally, as a climax, in November he joined General John Bell Hood's army as it invaded Tennessee in a desperate attempt to undo the calamitous consequences of the fall of Atlanta by smashing Federal forces in that state before they could concentrate, seizing the immense military storehouse in Nashville, and then pushing on to the Ohio or to Virginia. At Spring Hill he gave Hood a chance of success, supposing he had any chance at all, only to have him muff it. At Franklin he gave Hood advice that would have enabled him to at least postpone failure, but Hood disregarded it and proceeded to murder his own troops. And after what was left of Hood's army was routed at Nashville on December 15–16, Forrest commanded the rear guard that prevented annihilation. Throughout the entire war no general, Northern or Southern, came close to matching, much less surpassing, the level of activity and intensity that Forrest achieved in 1864.

The spring of 1865 found him a lieutenant general in charge of the Alabama-Mississippi remnant of the Confederacy. On April 2 he fought his last battle and lost it—a hopeless defense of Selma against an immensely stronger force of Union cavalry armed with repeating rifles. Yet he remained in the field, undaunted and deadly, and Sherman worried that he would join John S. Mosby and Wade Hampton—both, like him, nonprofessionals who had fighting in their blood—in waging guerrilla warfare. When, following the surrenders of Lee and Johnston, Forrest obeyed the order of his departmental commander and also surrendered, Sherman and other Northern generals could feel much easier about the future.

No one illustrates better than Forrest the truth of what the Union general Jacob D. Cox, himself a civilian who became an excellent soldier during the Civil War, declared in his *Reminiscences,* namely, that "a bold heart, a cool head, and practical common sense were of much more importance than anything taught at school" in determining success as a commander. Or, as one of Forrest's veterans put it more succinctly and colorfully, Forrest's "commission as General was signed not only by Mr. Jefferson Davis, but by the Almighty as well."

What were the components of the spectacular success of what one author has called this "untutored military genius"? One, certainly, was his enormous energy, endurance, and determination. To quote another of his soldiers, "He never seemed to be satisfied with any amount of success so long as there remained anything else to do, and he never let a chance to strike the enemy go by if there was any possibility of defeating him or doing him damage, and never seemed to get tired or sleepy or discouraged." At Okolona in February 1864, he routed a Union force that outnumbered his own three to one largely because, wrote one of his officers, he was able to "inspire every one with his terrible energy, more like that of a piece of powerful steam machinery than a human being." Four months later, following eight hours of fierce fighting against heavy odds at Brice's Cross Roads, he pursued the defeated Federals relentlessly for two days, not stopping until his troopers were falling out of their saddles and their horses collapsing from exhaustion.

He also possessed a talent for improvisation, an almost incredible ability to adapt to the unexpected, the element that Clausewitz terms the essence of war. Thus during an engagement near Franklin, Tennessee, in April 1863, a courier galloped up to him with the alarming news that the enemy had gotten into his rear. Forrest instantly replied, "That's where I've been trying to get him all day, damn him! I'll be in *his* rear in about five minutes!"—and proceeded to do exactly that. Afterward he admitted that he had been taken totally by surprise and had thought his whole command had "gone up."

Yet he was no hell-for-leather berserker, wading into battle without foresight or forethought. On the contrary, he planned and prepared carefully whenever he had the opportunity. General Richard Taylor, a highly competent Confederate commander, relates in his memoirs, *Destruction and Reconstruction,* how he met Forrest for the first time in September 1864 to plan the latter's raid into Tennessee against Sherman's supply line. To his surprise, Forrest "suggested many difficulties, and asked many questions"—so many that Taylor "began to think he had no stomach for the work." But then, "having isolated the chances of success from causes of failure, with the care of a chemist experimenting in a laboratory," Forrest's "whole manner" abruptly changed and in "a dozen sharp sentences" he outlined what he would do and how, then declared that he would "march with the dawn, and hoped to give an account of himself in Tennessee."

Last but far from least, Forrest had that power that all great commanders have, which, perhaps more than anything else, makes them great commanders—the ability, so to speak, to read the mind and sense the mood of an opponent and to act accordingly. The best, most telling example of this knack comes from the Okolona campaign of February 1864. Brigadier General William Sooy Smith, at the head of a large and well-equipped Union cavalry expedition, moved deeper and deeper into Mississippi, encountering practically no resistance from Forrest's much smaller force. Suddenly—and correctly—he perceived that he was walking into a trap and was in danger of being destroyed. Therefore he sent several regiments to fake an attack on Forrest so as to conceal the retreat of his main body. Forrest was not deceived. "I think," he told one of his generals, "they are badly scared" and launched an all-out pursuit that overtook and routed Smith.

Complementing Forrest's personal strengths—indeed, making possible their full development—was the qualitative superiority of the Confederate cavalry. The Southern troopers were not braver than their Northern counterparts; certainly they did not surpass them in discipline; and—legend to the contrary—they were not necessarily better riders, at least in the West. There, a large portion of the Union cavalrymen were themselves Southerners from Kentucky and Tennessee, or else farm boys from the Midwest who by no means were strangers to either horses or the hunt. The Southerners, with their cavalier tradition and self-image, believed they were superior, and because this belief was not mere conceit, it helped make them so in actuality. More important, from the very beginning of the war the Confederates had a larger number of capable cavalry commanders than did the Federals, who failed to produce comparable leadership until much later; and the spectacular exploits of these commanders—notably Stuart, Ashby, Morgan, and Forrest himself—enhanced the Southern sense (and thus fact) of superiority. Likewise, the Confederate army organized and utilized its cavalry more effectively than did the Union forces, grouping them into large and centrally controlled units that performed important tactical and strategic missions. Northern horse-soldiers, in contrast, long remained scattered in small detachments engaged primarily in scout, picket, and police duties.

Finally, and also paradoxically, the one thing in which the Southerners were inferior—weapons—turned out to be yet another, sometimes decisive advantage. The Confederacy lacked the means to furnish its troopers with the breech-loading carbines that were standard for cavalry at the outbreak of the Civil War. Perforce, therefore, most of them, especially in the West, had to make do with the same long-barreled, muzzle-loading rifle issued to the infantry. Since they found aiming these rifles accurately and reloading rapidly to be virtual impossibilities while on horseback, out of necessity they dismounted to fight. They discovered that a man standing on the ground could shoot faster and truer than could one on horseback while at the same time offering a far less vulnerable target. Moreover, the rifle had a much longer killing range than did the carbine, not to mention revolver and saber. Besides, most of the time the terrain, being densely wooded and brush-covered, made classic cavalry tactics impractical. For example, prior to his ill-fated expedition against Forrest in 1864, William Sooy Smith proclaimed to his men that "on favorable ground a saber charge of our forces upon the enemy, who have laid aside their sabers, must result in most signal and decisive success, if resolutely made." Following his debacle at Okolona he complained that the Rebels were "better armed for fighting dismounted" and that saber attacks failed to "cut them to pieces because of the undergrowth to which they fled." Only in the closing months of the war, when they were armed with Spencer repeaters and themselves usually fought on foot, did the Union cavalrymen match their Confederate opponents in combat effectiveness—and even then their victories owed more to greater numbers than to anything else. Like Alexander the Great, like Napoleon, Forrest benefited from having at his disposal a superior military instrument, one that he improved even more by the skill and inspiration of his leadership.

But the ultimate explanation of Forrest's success lies in his realism—the ability to see things as they are and to do what needs be done. This ability can be found in his attitude toward war in general and the Civil War in particular. Despite all the rhetoric from the South's politicians and editors about "States Rights" and "Southern Nationalism," he had no illusions about its true purpose: "If we ain't fightin' to keep slavery, then what the hell are we fightin' for?" Following the failure to turn the hard-won victory at Chickamauga into a decisive one, he concluded that both the Confederacy and slavery were doomed, and accordingly he freed the forty-five slaves who were serving him as teamsters. Henceforth he fought only out of a sense of duty and honor—and, one suspects, for the sheer joy a master artist derives from doing what he does so well. After the military war was over he helped the South, as head of the Tennessee Klan, to win what was still winnable—the political war—and thus get what it then wanted: "White Supremacy" and "Home Rule."

As for war per se, Forrest stripped it to its basics: "War means fighting, and fighting means killing." Victory goes to the side that does the best job of killing. The secret of victory is to "get there first with the most." To achieve that, he attacked whenever possible: "Fifteen minutes of *bulge* is worth a week of tactics." Yet he was an excellent tactician. Invariably he sought a weak spot in the enemy's line, supported his assaults with close-range artillery fire, and from his first skirmish onward sent part of his force to strike an opponent's flank or, as he put it, "hit 'em on the end." The detachment executing the flanking movement usually was mounted, an exception to his standard practice of fighting his troops on foot, and he himself rode into battle with his escort company, an elite band of fighters, if the issue trembled in the balance or when firepower had prepared the way for shock action. If at all possible, he endeavored not merely to drive back but to rout his foes: "The time to whip the enemy is when they are running." As a matter of policy he threatened fortified garrisons with extermination if he was forced to storm their works, with the result that they generally surrendered—especially after what happened at Fort Pillow. He could be equally harsh with his own men, shooting them down if they broke to the rear during combat and instructing his officers to do the same. Although he hacked down a large number of antagonists with his razor-sharp sword, thanks to his strength, size, and ferocity, he considered revolvers far more effective for hand-to-hand fighting and so retained sabers as a badge of rank in his command only for officers. In contrast, during the spring of 1864, by which time it should have been obvious that "cold steel" was about as obsolete as the crossbow, Major General Joseph Wheeler, head of the cavalry of the Confederate Army of Tennessee, West Pointer, and author of a manual on cavalry tactics, had his troopers practice saber attacks on straw dummies attired in Yankee uniforms because General Joseph Johnston, commander of that army, wanted "cavalry who can charge infantry." In the ensuing Atlanta Campaign, Wheeler's cavaliers did not make a single mounted charge against real Union infantry but did spend considerable time in the trenches serving as infantry themselves.

There can be no doubt that Forrest did everything that could be asked of a cavalry leader and did it supremely well: Scout, screen, raid, and fight effectively both as part of an army and as head of an independent force. The only question that can be, and indeed has been, raised concerning his military talents is whether he could have successfully commanded a large, full-fledged army in major operations. On the negative side, his stormy temper would likely have provoked crippling conflicts with the high command in Richmond and with his subordinate generals. Further, his lack of formal education, intellectual sophistication, and military training would have handicapped him when it came to complex administrative, logistical, and strategic matters. Last but far from least, the history of war is filled with generals who were brilliant so long as they, like Forrest throughout his career, headed a force small enough to direct and supervise personally, but who failed when placed in command of an army so big that they had to rely on others to implement their plans and who faltered under the awful responsibility of fighting a battle or waging a campaign that might determine the outcome of the whole war. On the positive side, Forrest obeyed orders even when, as at Harrisburg, Mississippi, on July 14, 1864, it would have been better had he not. His subordinates, fearing his wrath, would likely have done their best to carry out his instructions, no matter how much they might have disliked or disagreed with him. In addition, any technical or administrative deficiencies he had could have been supplied by competent staff officers, people he was adept at selecting. And, as another Confederate general observed after the war, "Forrest's capacity for war seemed only to be limited by the opportunities for its display." Which point of view is correct cannot, of course, be objectively determined. Furthermore, historically it is a moot question, for not once during the entire Civil War did Jefferson Davis give command of a major Confedrate army to anyone who was not, as he himself was, a graduate of West Point. But at the very least it seems possible that the man who, unlike the West Pointer Simon Bolivar Buckner, refused to surrender at Fort Donelson when it was easy to escape; who at Chickamauga urged the West Pointer Bragg to go after the defeated Federals before they had time to recover; and who at Franklin tried to stop the West Pointer Hood from making an attack that was as unnecessary as it was doomed, had the potential of being a successful army commander, provided he had an army of sufficient strength to perform the mission assigned it. Certainly he could not have done worse than any of the commanders just named.

Following the war Forrest returned to one of his plantations, dabbled in the insurance business, and engaged in railroad promotion with some success but much more failure. He also is alleged to have become the grand wizard of the Ku Klux Klan (KKK) for the entire South—an allegation that all of the numerous biographers writing after his death and many historians have accepted as fact, with the result that he has been both glorified as the "savior" of the White South and vilified as an enemy of blacks.

The truth of the matter would seem to be that, although Forrest held the post of grand wizard of the Klan in Tennessee during 1867–69, he never headed the KKK southern-wide for the very good reason that it did not exist in many of the former Confederate states at that time—and in some of those states never at all, at least under that name. Furthermore, by its very nature the Klan operated at the local level and hence could not be controlled from a central headquarters by a single man, not even Forrest, whose power of leadership was personal, not impersonal.

Last but not least, in 1866 in Tennessee, where it first came into existence, the Klan's primary goal—some would say sole goal—was to gain control of the state government for the Democrats, whose voting strength had been greatly reduced by the disfranchisement of Confederate veterans and the enfranchisement of blacks (something that at that time had not occurred in any other of the Rebel states). But the Republicans were a minority of the population concentrated in East Tennessee. In the 1868 election the Democrats—thanks in large part to KKK terrorism directed against blacks, carpetbaggers, and scalawags—supplanted the Republicans, whereupon Forrest, acting as spokesman for the Klan, which he did not even join until well after its founding, dissolved it. Since Tennessee by then had been readmitted to full membership in the Union, the Radical Republican–dominated Congress in Washington could do nothing about this outcome, and thus the Volunteer State became the sole full-fledged Confederate state to escape Congressional "military reconstruction." This is another reason for doubting what is inherently improbable, that Forrest ever was emperor of the "Invisible Empire."

No doubt making Forrest's putative leadership of an all-South KKK easy to believe for some is the Fort Pillow Massacre, April 12, 1864. According to what can be called the anti-Forrest version of this event, Forrest's troops at his order, or at least with his tacit permission, slaughtered most of the garrison's black soldiers, not to mention (as often it is not) a large portion of its Unionist white Tennessee defenders. That a massacre took place, in the sense that many Federals were killed or wounded while trying to surrender or else ceasing to resist, is not open to reasonable doubt on the basis of factual evidence, Confederate as well as Union. On the other hand, the same evidence provides no basis for concluding that Forrest in any way ordered or intended the massacre, which basically was the spontaneous product of a lethal mixture of racism, battle rage, and resentment by the Confederates, many of whom were Tennesseans, against the "Tory" Tennesseans.

Starting in the early 1870s, Forrest experienced financial frustration, then physical degeneration, ultimately becoming a mere remnant of his once magnificent self. But even before this terrible collapse began he realized that his true vocation was one of warrior. Thus he dreamed of leading a giant filibustering expedition into Mexico to conquer and rule it, and when it seemed that a war with Spain over Cuba might occur, he offered his services as a cavalry commander to Sherman, by then the top general of the U.S. Army. Sherman, who once had placed a price on "that devil's" head, replied by thanking him but rightly pointing out that the navy would determine the outcome of such a conflict. (Which of course did not prevent Theodore Roosevelt from becoming, by a roundabout and accidental route, president of the United States as a result of going to Cuba in 1898 with a regiment of horseless Rough Riders.)

So it was that Forrest's military career ended as it began, with the Civil War. That sufficed. During it he demonstrated a genius for war based on a realistic conception of it and a natural knack for waging it. Of him it can be said that he never lost a battle he had a chance of winning, and won many battles that by all odds he should have lost. He was born to fight.

Part Two

Some Losers

CHAPTER FIVE

George B. McClellan: "I Can Do It All"

McClellan possessed every quality needed to be a victorious general save the most essential one of all: A willingness—more than that, an eagerness—to engage the enemy in battle when there was reasonable prospect of victory. As a consequence he threw away two surefire opportunities to win the Civil War for the Union—first outside of Richmond in June 1862, then at Antietam in September of the same year. The following article, which appeared in Civil War Times Illustrated *in its May 1974 issue under the title of "George B. McClellan: Little Mac," endeavors to explain why McClellan lacked this indispensable attribute of a successful general. Since the writing of it, numerous books about McClellan and his campaigns have been published that contain revealing information unavailable to me in 1974, but I have found nothing in them that compels me to alter my evaluation of him as a man and a general: His greatest foe was himself, not the Confederates.*

PRESIDENT ABRAHAM LINCOLN HAD MET MAJOR GENERAL GEORGE Brinton McClellan before. In fact, on several occasions they had sat together at night by the stove in some Illinois town, Lincoln passing the time telling stories. That was in 1859, when McClellan was an official of the Illinois Central Railroad, Lincoln an attorney representing the same company.

Now it was July 26, 1861. Five days previously the Confederates had routed the main Union army at Bull Run. At once Lincoln had summoned McClellan, the North's only victorious general, and given him command of the demoralized rabble streaming into Washington from the battlefield. When McClellan arrived at the White House for a conference, Lincoln greeted "George" not only as an old friend but as the man he hoped would win the war.

Judged by his record, the young general—he was just thirty-four—seemed a good bet to do exactly that. Born in Philadelphia on December 3,

1826, the son of a prominent physician, he entered West Point at fifteen and graduated second in a class that included the future "Stonewall" Jackson (who finished seventeenth) and George E. Pickett (who came in last). Besides shining in the classroom, he excelled at riding and fencing. A broad-shouldered, deep-chested, five feet eight inches, be could bend a two-bit piece between his fingers.

During the Mexican War he served in Winfield Scott's army along with such fellow engineer officers as P. G. T. Beauregard, George Meade, and Robert E. Lee. Bravery and skill won him promotion to first lieutenant, and following the war he was assigned to Lee's engineer company at West Point. While there he prepared a study of the Russian campaign of 1812 for the Napoleon Club and translated a French manual on bayonet fighting, which the army adopted as a text. He also applied for a professorship at Virginia Military Institute but former classmate Jackson got the job instead.

Next came exploring duty in the Far West, followed by a secret mission to Santo Domingo to locate a site for a possible naval base. In 1855, frustrated by the slow promotion rate in the engineers, he transferred to the cavalry with the rank of captain. At the same time Secretary of War Jefferson Davis sent him to Europe to study recent military developments.

He was abroad a year, during which time he observed the Siege of Sebastopol in the Crimean War. After returning he filed an elaborate report and proposed a new saddle based on the Prussian model. The War Department adopted his design, and as a result the bottoms of three generations of army troopers bounced on the none-too-comfortable "McClellan Saddle."

Early in 1857 he resigned his commission to become chief engineer of the Illinois Central. Two years later he rose to vice president, and in 1860 he moved to Cincinnati as president of the Eastern Division of the Ohio & Mississippi Railroad. That same year he married vivacious, flirtatious, but pious Ellen "Nellie" Marcy, whom he had met while serving under her father in Texas. He had courted her five years. His chief rival for Nellie's hand was Ambrose Powell Hill of Virginia, a former West Point roommate who on a certain September afternoon in Maryland would have some revenge.

Despite his spectacular business success McClellan hoped to return to the military—provided he could do so at high rank. He and close friend Joseph E. Johnston even investigated possibilities in the Mexican Army. Then in April 1861 came Fort Sumter. The governor of Ohio appointed

MILLER, ED. *PHOTOGRAPHIC HISTORY.*

George B. McClellan

McClellan commander of the state militia, and soon afterward the War Department commissioned him a major general and put him in charge of operations in the Ohio Valley. Late in May he marched into western Virginia, defeated the Confederates at Philippi and Rich Mountain, and secured Union control of the area.

"Soldiers of the Army of the West!" he proclaimed. "I am more than satisfied with you. You have annihilated two armies commanded by educated and experienced soldiers entrenched in mountain fastnesses prepared at their leisure. . . ."

Hailed by the press as "The Young Napoleon," he became the hero of the North. No one doubted that he was the right choice to redeem Bull Run and lead the Union cause to victory. From Washington he proudly wrote Nellie:

> I find myself in a new and strange position here—Presdt., Cabinet, Genl. Scott and all deferring to me—by some strange opera-

> tion of magic I seem to have become *the* power of the land. I almost think that were I to win some small success now I could become Dictator or anything else that might please me—but nothing of that kind would please me,—*therefore* I *won't* be dictator. Admirable self denial!

To be sure this was written in a bantering tone. Yet obviously McClellan had been taken to the mountaintop. Already there was talk that he would be the next president, particularly by Democrats, whose 1860 candidate, Stephen A. Douglas, McClellan had supported.

During the rest of the summer he organized and trained the thousands of recruits who poured into Washington. By midautumn the Army of the Potomac, as he named it, was a well-drilled and well-equipped host, high in morale and devoted to "Little Mac," whom they cheered lustily whenever he rode by on his magnificent black stallion Dan Webster—which was often.

But, Northern newspapers, politicians, and people began to ask, when would this mighty military machine roll forward and crush Joseph Johnston's Rebel army in Virginia? It was being held back, McClellan told a group of influential senators, by the seventy-five-year-old general in chief, Winfield Scott. A short time later Scott retired and Lincoln appointed McClellan to his place. "I can do it all," the Young Napoleon assured the president.

Yet he did nothing, except to continue drilling and reviewing his troops. "I will pay no attention to popular clamor," he wrote a friend. "My intention is [to] quietly, and quickly as possible, make this army strong enough . . . to give me a reasonable certainty that . . . I will win the first battle—I know full well the capacity of the generals opposed to me, for by a singular chance they were once my most intimate friends. . . . But of one thing you may rest assured—when the blow *is* struck, it will be heavy, rapid and decisive."

December found the Army of the Potomac still in its camps—and its commander in bed with typhoid. He soon recovered, but despite what amounted to orders he refused to divulge any definite plans for taking the offensive, arguing that the president and his cabinet were incapable of understanding them or keeping them secret! He had no sympathy for Lincoln's concern over Northern morale, nor did he feel a sense of obligation to the civilian heads of the government. They were, he wrote Nellie, a bunch of "rascals" and "incompetents," whereas he had been chosen by

God to restore peace and unity to the land. Indeed, "I receive letter after letter, have conversation after conversation, calling on me to save the nation, alluding to the presidency, dictatorships, etc." Once he openly snubbed Lincoln, who had come to visit him at his headquarters, sending an aide to tell the president (whom he called the "original gorilla" in a letter to Nellie) to come back at some more convenient time. Lincoln ignored the insult—"I will hold McClellan's horse if only he'll win the war."

Lincoln's deep patience, however, was wearing thin: "McClellan's a great engineer, but has a special talent for stationary engines." Furthermore the powerful Radical Republicans, suspicious of McClellan's Democratic affiliations and conservative views on slavery ("Help me," he wrote a prominent New York Democrat, "dodge the nigger—we want nothing to do with him"), were becoming increasingly critical of the general's inactivity, going so far as to hint that he did not really want to suppress the rebellion.

Finally, in February Lincoln virtually forced McClellan to produce a plan of operations. It called for the Army of the Potomac to move by ship down the Chesapeake Bay, land at Fort Monroe on the tip of the Virginia Peninsula, and go fifty miles to Richmond. Lincoln, who favored advancing from the north, reluctantly approved it, but only after extracting a promise that Washington would be left "entirely secure." In addition, he relieved McClellan of his post as general in chief.

Late in March the Army of the Potomac disembarked at Fort Monroe. This move, strategically outflanking Johnston's army in northern Virginia, was described by a British military writer as "the stride of a giant." But what came next the same author termed "the step of a midget." Instead of ripping through the scant 10,000 graybacks who initially opposed his 100,000 troops, as urged by Lincoln, McClellan stopped to besiege Yorktown, thereby giving Johnston ample time to shift forces to the Peninsula.

For a month, sweating Yankees dragged cannons through swamps in preparation for an assault on Yorktown. Then on May 4, just as everything at last was ready, the Confederates evacuated their fortifications. McClellan pursued, but the following day Johnston checked him at Williamsburg, after which he resumed his retreat. Slowed by rain and mud, McClellan ponderously followed. Not until late in the month did he reach the Richmond area.

Here he halted to await the arrival from northern Virginia of Major General Irvin McDowell's 35,000-man army. This reinforcement, he asserted, was vital to the taking of Richmond; for according to Allan Pinkerton, the detective who headed his intelligence service, Johnston outnumbered him nearly two to one (actually almost the reverse was true). He had requested that McDowell's army be sent by boat; but at the insistence of Lincoln, who wished to keep Washington covered, it marched overland. In order to link up with it, as well as protect his base at West Point on the York River, McClellan extended his right flank northward across the Chickahominy River.

McDowell, however, did not arrive. McClellan's old classmate Jackson saw to that. Sweeping down the Shenandoah Valley, he threatened Washington. Alarmed, Lincoln sent McDowell in futile pursuit of the elusive Stonewall, thereby removing him for the time being from the military chessboard around Richmond.

McClellan was outraged at being deprived of McDowell. To his close friend Major General Ambrose Burnside he wrote, "The Government have deliberately placed me in this position. If I win, the greater the glory. If I lose, they will be damned forever, both by God and man."

Seeking to exploit the division of the Union army by the Chickahominy, Johnston on May 31 suddenly counterattacked. Throwing 40,000 men against 16,000, he threatened to overwhelm McClellan's left in the Seven Pines–Fair Oaks sector. But Federal troops from his right rushed to the danger point across a rickety bridge spanning the flood-swollen Chickahominy. They stopped the Rebel thrust and Johnston himself fell severely wounded. A second Confederate assault on June 1 likewise failed.

Possibly a determined Union push would now have taken Richmond, less than six miles away. But McClellan had been badly shaken by Johnston's attack, which seemed to confirm Pinkerton's estimates. Therefore he decided to hold where he was until McDowell finally arrived. At the same time he bombarded Washington with pleas for reinforcements, even proposing that Union troops be brought from Mississippi. Lincoln responded by sending 20,000 more men, which meant that all told 149,000 soldiers had gone to the Peninsula. Yet on June 20 McClellan reported his "present for duty" strength at 105,000, of which number only 90,000 were "available for combat"! No wonder Lincoln commented that sending troops to McClellan was "like shoveling fleas across a barnyard; half of them never get there!"

Even with McDowell's army added to his own, McClellan did not propose to make an all-out assault on Richmond. Instead he planned to batter his way into the city with siege artillery, as the British and French had done at Sebastopol, as he himself had prepared to do at Yorktown.

Johnston's successor, Robert F. Lee, guessed his former subordinate's intent and took bold action to frustrate it. Leaving a small force to screen Richmond, he deployed the bulk of his army north of the Chickahominy, where it was joined by Jackson's corps coming by train from the Shenandoah. Then on June 26 he moved with 70,000 troops against the 35,000-man Union right wing under Major General Fitz John Porter, planning to seize the bridges across the Chickahominy and cut McClellan's supply line. Jackson, who was to strike Porter's flank from the north, however, failed to execute his assignment. Consequently the Federals beat back a premature Confederate frontal attack at Mechanicsville.

Had McClellan promptly advanced his 70,000-man left wing following Porter's victory, he could have, in the words of one Southern general, "captured Richmond with very little loss of life," for only a meager 15,000 troops manned the city's sketchy fortifications. At the very least he could have reinforced Porter while feinting toward the Confederate capital—a strategy that probably would have compelled Lee to abandon his offensive.

But he did neither of these things. Instead he ordered a retreat, or as he termed it "change of base," to Harrison's Landing on the James River. Claiming that the enemy outnumbered him two to one, his only thought was to save his army—not defeat Lee or take Richmond.

During the next five days the Union forces fought as many battles as they fell back to the James. Each time, except at Gaines's Mill on June 27, they held off fierce Confederate attacks, and even there the enemy's success cost him 8,000 casualties and was barren of strategic result. The climax came late on the afternoon of July 1 at Malvern Hill. Frustrated by his failure to gain decisive victory, and mistakenly believing the Federals to be demoralized, Lee hurled his tattered troops forward in a mass frontal assault. The Northern cannons, standing hub to hub, slaughtered them: "It was not war—it was murder!" declared a Confederate commander.

Conceivably a Union counterthrust on the following day would have defeated, or at least hurled back, Lee's decimated, disorganized, and exhausted army—several Federal generals urged that one be made. But McClellan, who had not been present at Malvern Hill, nor for that matter at any of the preceding battles, again retreated from victory. That night his troops marched in torrential rain to Harrison's Landing, where they camped under the cover of the gunboats offshore.

During the Seven Days' Battles the Army of the Potomac inflicted 20,000 casualties while losing 15,000, and it won or held its own in every engagement. In other words, not it but its commander had been defeated.

McClellan, however, blamed the politicians in Washington. On June 28, following Gaines's Mill, he sent this remarkable message to Secretary of War Edwin Stanton:

> I feel too earnestly tonight. I have seen too many dead and wounded comrades to feel otherwise than that the government has not sustained this army. If you do not do so now the game is lost.
>
> If I save this army now, I tell you plainly that I owe no thanks to any other person in Washington.
>
> You have done your best to sacrifice this army.

Shocked by the last two sentences, the supervisor of the military telegraph in Washington deleted them before passing on the message to Stanton and Lincoln. Had they remained, possibly Lincoln would have removed McClellan from command—which was the penalty he deserved for his tantrum. As it was, Lincoln hurried all available troops to the Peninsula, making good the Army of the Potomac's losses.

But that did not satisfy McClellan. He demanded 100,000 reinforcements. Once he got them, he promised, he would advance up the James and take Richmond from the south. Moreover, when Lincoln visited Harrison's Landing on July 9, McClellan handed him a memorandum stating that emancipation of the slaves should not become a purpose of the war—otherwise the army would refuse to fight. Lincoln pocketed it without comment. McClellan's presumption was exceeded only by his naiveté. A defeated general, he attempted to impose his policy views on the president while the Republican press and politicians were denouncing him as an incompetent, even a traitor, and calling for his dismissal.

After much pondering, Lincoln decided to abandon the Peninsula Campaign: "If I could send McClellan 100,000 reinforcements, the General would claim that the Confederates had 400,000, and that to advance he would need still more men." Accordingly, on August 3 Major General Henry W. Halleck, the new general in chief, instructed McClellan to ship his troops to Major General John Pope's army in northern Virginia. He complied, as usual, slowly. Lee, as soon as he saw that the Army of the Potomac was leaving the Peninsula, swung about and routed Pope at the Second Battle of Bull Run, August 29–30.

With great reluctance Lincoln again turned to McClellan to salvage the situation. He believed (mistakenly) that McClellan had deliberately delayed reinforcing Pope, and he even considered the general "a little crazy." Yet, as he explained to his cabinet when it protested placing McClellan in charge of the defense of Washington, "There is no man in the Army who can lick these troops of ours into shape half as well as he."

The disorganized, discouraged Union soldiers broke into cheers upon learning that "Little Mac" once more was at their head, for despite the failure of the Peninsula Campaign they retained their faith in him. And as Lincoln foresaw, he soon had them back in fighting trim. Meanwhile Lee marched into western Maryland, hoping thereby to draw McClellan out of the impregnable fortifications of Washington and into the open field.

Lee's strategy worked, as the reconstituted Army of the Potomac began moving cautiously towards Frederick, Maryland. Then on September 13, McClellan had one of the most extraordinary bits of luck in the history of warfare. Two Indiana soldiers accidentally found a copy of a Confederate dispatch, which revealed that Lee had divided his army, with one part under Jackson going to Harpers Ferry to capture the Union garrison there while the rest deployed around Hagerstown to the north.

"Here is a paper," McClellan exclaimed gleefully, "with which if I cannot whip Bobbie Lee I will be willing to go home!"

He set his troops in motion, intending to cross South Mountain and get between the Confederate halves and defeat each separately. He moved fast—but not quite fast enough. Alarmed by McClellan's unexpectedly and uncharacteristically rapid advance, Lee attempted to hold the South Mountain passes. On September 14 the Federals fought their way through the passes but needed all day to do it. Even worse, McClellan relapsed into his customary timidity on coming into contact with the enemy. Not until the evening of September 16 did he bring his 70,000-man army into position to attack the Confederates, who had retreated to Sharpsburg near the Potomac. By then Lee had regrouped all of his forces, except A. P. Hill's division still at Harpers Ferry, behind Antietam Creek. He had fewer than 40,000 men.

At dawn on September 17 McClellan's right wing under "Fighting Joe" Hooker surged forward. Just barely Jackson's men held. Next "Bull" Sumner's divisions pounded Lee's center, bending it but not breaking it at "Bloody Lane." Last Burnside belatedly crossed the Antietam and rolled through the Confederate right, which had been stripped of troops in order to beat back Hooker and Sumner. Then panting up from Harpers Ferry, A. P. Hill's division struck Burnside's left flank and sent him reeling back across the Antietam. The fighting stopped.

Antietam was the bloodiest single day of the Civil War: 11,426 Northerners, 11,724 Southerners lay dead or wounded. It was also one of the great "what if" battles of all time. Almost surely McClellan would have defeated Lee, and probably ended the war, had he (1) advanced his entire army simultaneously in assault; or (2) posted his cavalry on the Harpers Ferry Road, thereby blocking or delaying Hill, instead of stationing it uselessly in his center; or (3) attacked the exhausted Confederates, following Burnside's repulse, with the 24,000 fresh troops he had for no good reason held in reserve. Moreover, he threw away two more excellent opportunities to win decisive victory by failing to renew the battle on September 18 (incredibly, he spent the day expecting Lee to attack), and by not making any attempt to pursue the Confederates when they retreated across the Potomac on the nineteenth.

Lincoln was grateful for Antietam. Not only was the Southern invasion of the North repelled, it probably prevented British recognition of the Confederacy and provided the occasion for the Emancipation Proclamation of September 22. On the other hand, he was profoundly disappointed that Lee's army was not destroyed, as it should have been. Hence he urged McClellan to advance promptly into Virginia. But Little Mac, who asserted that he had won a great victory against great odds at Antietam, refused to budge. He needed, he declared, more men, more horses, more wagons, more everything. In addition, he in effect called on his troops, to repudiate the Emancipation Proclamation.

Not until late in October did he enter Virginia. According to plan he was to move rapidly down the east side of the Blue Ridge and seize Richmond before Lee's army in the Shenandoah Valley could intercept him. Needless to say, his march was anything except rapid—a mere six or seven miles a day. Consequently Lee had no trouble blocking him in front while Jackson menaced his rear.

Lincoln had seen enough. On November 7 he relieved McClellan of command. Twice the general had rescued the North from defeat, but obviously he was not the man to lead it to victory. He had, said Lincoln succinctly, "the slows."

So at age thirty-five McClellan's military career ended. He still, however, had one major role to perform in the Civil War. In 1864 the Democrats nominated him for president on a platform that denounced the war as a failure and called for immediate peace. To his credit McClellan repudiated these planks. Even so, had he won the presidency, the Union cause probably would have been lost. Fortunately the victories of Sherman in Georgia and of Sheridan in Virginia assured Lincoln's reelection and with it the defeat of the Confederacy.

After the war McClellan made a lucrative living as a consulting engineer, travelled a great deal in Europe, and from 1878 to 1881 was governor of New Jersey. On October 29, 1885, he died of a heart attack, leaving behind an autobiography, which was published two years later under the title of *McClellan's Own Story.* In it he steadfastly defended his generalship and blamed all failures on Lincoln, Stanton, Halleck, and various former subordinates. The most he conceded was that "while striving conscientiously to do my best, it may well be that I have made great mistakes that my vanity does not permit me to see."

McClellan commanded nineteen months. During that time his armies fought thirteen battles, won eleven, and lost two—Gaines's Mill and Antietam—and even they were strategic successes. In addition he was an exceptional organizer, trainer, and inspirer of troops—qualities that twice helped save the Union cause.

He must, however, be judged—and he has been judged—not for what he did but for what he should have done. As a result his name is a synonym for military futility. The efforts of a few apologists and revisionists to rehabilitate his reputation have been as unavailing as they are unconvincing. Thus, to cite one of their favorite arguments, Lee may (it is doubtful) have said in 1870 that McClellan was the best general he ever faced. But what is certain is that Lee in 1862 felt that he had little to fear from McClellan and acted accordingly.

The "slows," as Lincoln observed, was McClellan's outstanding defect. But why did he suffer so from them? One explanation is that his conservative political view of the war resulted in his adopting a conservative approach to fighting it—he wanted to assemble such an overwhelming force that the South, realizing the futility of resistance, would lay down its arms and the Union would be restored with a minimum of bloodshed and without radical change (such as the abolition of slavery). If this was the case, then the Republicans who charged that he did not really want to whip the Rebels were in a sense correct. In addition, and quite ironically, by prolonging the conflict through his delays and overcaution, he helped make inevitable the emancipation policy that he opposed.

He also had a false conception of warfare as such. For example, during the West Virginia Campaign, he wrote Nellie that "No prospect of a brilliant victory shall induce me to depart from my intention of aiming success by maneuvering rather than fighting." Apparently he did not learn from his studies of Napoleon that maneuvering and fighting cannot be separated—that the prime object of the former is to maximize the chances of success in the latter—and that in any event, to succeed, maneuvering must be done swiftly.

Joined to his lack of political and military realism was an excessive egotism, which rendered him incapable of evaluating either himself or others objectively. Hence, while constantly berating various superiors and subordinates as "fools" and "villains," he remained purblind to his own faults: After Antietam, for instance, he fatuously informed Nellie that "Those in whose judgment I rely tell me that I fought the battle splendidly and that it was a masterpiece of art."

But the fundamental reason McClellan failed was, paradoxically, fear of failure. Or, in other words, he was so afraid of losing that he was unable to win. This interpretation is supported by many of his actions (as well as non-actions), and by revealing passages in his letters to Nellie, such as "I cannot afford to fail." It also accounts for his reluctance to come to grips with the enemy, his habit of leaving the actual conduct of battles to subordinates, and his quickness to blame others for setbacks. In particular it explains his grotesque exaggeration of Confederate strength: He wanted to believe, or at least have others believe, that he was heavily outnumbered so as to have an excuse to avoid the danger of defeat.

Perhaps his early and easy success engendered this crippling fear of failure: Having rocketed to the top, he may well have been haunted by a vision of plummeting to the bottom. Or possibly, as U. S. Grant suggested after the war, he was crushed psychologically by having such "vast and cruel responsibility" placed on him while still so young and inexperienced, and that had "he gone into the war as Sherman, Thomas, or Meade, and fought his way along and up," he may have won "high distinction." Interestingly enough, McClellan ventured a similar opinion himself in his memoirs. It is most unlikely, however, that prior service at the lower levels would have made him a successful top commander. He lacked the essential quality of all good generals: He was not a fighter.

Even so, there are several things worth pondering before passing final judgment on McClellan: (1) Although young and robust, he suffered at crucial times from ill-health. (2) Circumstances were different, yet Grant took Richmond in 1865 only after achieving the sort of overwhelming numerical superiority over the Confederates that McClellan had sought three years earlier. (3) Had Johnston remained at the head of the Confederate army, McClellan, despite his defects, might well have captured Richmond, won the war, and gone on to become president. After all, Johnston possessed comparable weaknesses. So perhaps McClellan's downfall began when Lee took command—and Lee, as he once remarked, "understood" McClellan.

CHAPTER SIX

Earl Van Dorn: Bravery Was Not Enough

Unlike Union general George B. McClellan, Confederate general Earl Van Dorn liked to fight. In fact, he liked to fight too much, with the result that he sometimes fought when he should not have or persisted in fighting longer than he should. But his greatest deficiency was one for which he was not responsible: He lacked luck, that attribute that Napoleon deemed more important for a general than skill. Because of ill-luck, which took the form of subordinates who either could not or would not perform their assigned missions, he lost whatever chance he had—and at first it was good (or so it seemed to him)—of winning the two most important battles of his career, Pea Ridge on March 7–8, 1862, in Arkansas, and Corinth on October 3–4, 1862, in Mississippi. Worse, when it appeared that he had found his true calling as a cavalry commander, he suffered the irreversible misfortune of being shot and killed by an irate husband.

This article, bearing the title of "Earl Van Don—A Personality Profile," appeared in the April 1967 issue of Civil War Times Illustrated, *the first one that I published in that magazine, and was derived from the manuscript of my book,* General Sterling Price and the Civil War in the West *(Baton Rouge: Louisiana State University Press, 1968; paperback reprint by same publisher, 1994). Because the article followed another one about the Battle of Corinth, it merely mentioned that encounter in passing. Consequently I have added herein a short account of the engagement in order to demonstrate the role that chance and circumstance played in Van Dorn's initial success and eventual failure.*

MAJOR GENERAL EARL VAN DORN, C.S.A., WAS THE VERY INCARNATION of a Southern cavalier: Birthplace, a large Mississippi plantation; graduation from West Point; heroic service in the Mexican War and against the Indians; slim-waisted, broad-shouldered; handsome face with light chestnut hair, mustache, and imperial looks (he was "much admired and much pursued by the ladies"); accomplished amateur poet and painter, but at the same time "the finest horseman in the cavalry of the old United States Army"; and above all a dedicated romantic who cherished honor as the highest value and sought glory as the greatest prize. "What," he wrote his sister Octavia from Mexico in 1846, "does the gambler know of excitement who has millions staked on a card? He can lose but millions, he can win but millions. But here *life* is to lose—glory to win."

The only thing preventing Van Dorn from becoming one of the legendary heroes of the Old South, a paladin ranking with Jeb Stuart and Stonewall Jackson, was just a little luck. This is the story of his lack of that precious commodity and of his consequent failure to win the glory he so earnestly sought.

From earliest youth Van Dorn dreamed of being a soldier. At sixteen he wrote President Andrew Jackson (a distant cousin) stating his ambition, and in return obtained an appointment to West Point. He graduated from the Academy in 1842, fifty-second in a class of fifty-six that included James Longstreet and William S. Rosecrans.

During the Mexican War he distinguished himself for gallantry by raising a flag under heavy fire, was one of the first to scale the walls of Chapultepec, and was wounded storming the Belen Gate at Mexico City. He emerged from the conflict a first lieutenant and fully confirmed in his choice of a military career. "I never could be happy out of the Army," he declared. "I have no other home—could make none that would be congenial to my feelings." By then he had married the daughter of an Alabama planter, and was to have a son and daughter. But his wife spent most of her time at home while "the young lieutenant was often alone at his barracks"—on his desk a bust of Napoleon.

During the late 1850s he served as a captain in Texas with the famous 2nd U.S. Cavalry, which had Albert Sidney Johnston as colonel and Robert E. Lee as lieutenant colonel, and contained among its other officers George H. Thomas, William S. Hardee, Edmund Kirby Smith, John B. Hood, and Fitzhugh Lee. In the fall of 1858 he was badly wounded in an attack on a Comanche camp a few miles east of the present Rush Springs, Oklahoma. On May 30, 1859, he again attacked a Comanche village, this time fifteen miles south of the site of Dodge City, Kansas. This victory led to his promotion to major, and according to Fitzhugh Lee he was "easily the most conspicuous officer of his grade" in the army.

Earl Van Dorn

Then came secession. At once "Buck" Van Dorn, as he was called in the "Old Army," resigned his commission and hastened to Mississippi, where he became commander of the state troops. The imminent prospect of war filled him with frank delight. "Who knows," he wrote his wife, "but that *yet* out of the storms of revolution—the dark clouds of war—I may not be able to catch a spark of the lightning and shine through all time to come, a burning name! I feel greatness in my soul—and if I can make it take a shape and walk forth, it *may* be seen and felt."

Soon he entered the Confederate army as a colonel. Following the firing on Fort Sumter his "strong friend" Jefferson Davis sent him to take charge of the defense of Texas. He carried out the assignment successfully, capturing three Union troopships and becoming "the hero of the day." Promoted to brigadier general, he remained in Texas until August, when he was transferred to the command of a division in Virginia with the rank of major general.

His rise had been rapid but his thirst for glory could be satisfied only by battle. Administrative duties, he complained, "are not congenial to my taste or proclivities. . . . I am as restless as a panther caged, in an office, and have not the patience to attend to the duties required of me. The free air, a brave troop, and a bright sword on the plains, and I breathe again."

In January 1862 Davis placed him in command of the Trans-Mississippi District—Missouri, Arkansas, and Indian Territory. There, despite spectacular early victories, affairs had gone poorly for the South. The Federals held most of Missouri; and the two main Confederate armies, Sterling Price's Missouri State Guards and Ben McCulloch's Confederate forces, were weak, divided, and ill-equipped. Van Dorn's extremely difficult mission was to roll the Federals back and seize St. Louis so as to relieve the pressure on the Confederate armies in Kentucky and Tennessee.

"I am now 'in for it,'" he wrote his wife en route to Arkansas, "—to make a reputation and serve my country conspicuously or to fail. I must not, shall not, do the latter. I must have St. Louis—then Huzza!"

But before he could launch a counteroffensive, a strong Union army under Brigadier General Samuel Ryan Curtis drove Price out of Missouri and invaded northwestern Arkansas. At once Van Dorn telegraphed Price and McCulloch to link up, then set out on horseback across the Ozarks, accompanied only by two aides, to take personal charge of operations. His plan was to attack and smash Curtis, then push on for St. Louis.

On March 2 at Cove Creek he assumed—to the sound of blaring bands and booming cannons—command of the combined Missouri and Arkansas forces, which he named "The Army of the West." The next day, despite a heavy snowstorm, he began marching north up the Telegraph Road, the main highway of the region, hoping to "gobble up" the Federals, who were dispersed through the prairies and hills in quest of food and forage. Curtis, however, realized the danger in time and fell back quickly to Little Sugar Creek near the Missouri border. Here, on March 6, he concentrated his army of 10,500 in a fortified position astride the Telegraph Road and behind Little Sugar Creek.

Van Dorn's 16,000 men heavily outnumbered the enemy. They were tired, cold, wet, and hungry, however, after four days of hard marching over sleet-swept hills. In addition Van Dorn himself was suffering from chills and fever, the consequence of his boat capsizing while crossing an icy river, and had to travel bundled up in an ambulance. Nevertheless he remained determined to strike the Northerners a decisive blow. Indeed the only alternative to attack was ignominious retreat.

At McCulloch's suggestion he resorted to a daring strategy: He left a small force facing the Federals at Little Sugar Creek and with the main part of his army marched under cover of darkness around Curtis's right flank by way of the Bentonville Detour, a dirt trail that branched off west from the

Bentonville Road and joined the Telegraph Road above Pea Ridge. If all went as planned he would be able to make a surprise attack on the Union rear and so place Curtis in a situation where battle meant defeat and defeat meant disaster.

All did not go as planned—far from it. The lead division under Price did not, because of unexpected delays encountered on the Bentonville Detour, reach the enemy rear until long after daylight, ruining all chance of surprise and giving Curtis ample time to shift his forces. Van Dorn, because of the delay, made a fatal change in his battle plan. McCulloch, whose division was following Price's Missourians, was directed to countermarch and pass to the west of Pea Ridge, a rugged plateau. Van Dorn had thus divided his army; Price's troops were to the east of Pea Ridge attacking down the Telegraph Road while McCulloch's division and Brigadier General Albert Pike's Indians were southwest of the ridge. Several miles now separated the two wings of Van Dorn's army.

Early in the afternoon McCulloch was shot, his second in command was also killed, and the third ranking officer was captured. Bereft of leaders, McCulloch's division and Pike's Indians retreated from the field, nullifying the limited success that had been won by Price's Missourians and enabling Curtis on the night of March 7 to deploy his full strength against Price.

Finally, as the culminating stroke of ill fortune, an unknown ordnance officer on the morning of the eighth, when the battle was resumed, through some "strange and criminal mistake" sent the reserve ammunition train back down the Bentonville Detour away from the army. The blunder was a contributing factor in Van Dorn's decision to order a retreat because of empty caissons and cartridge boxes. Many of Price's Missourians, as they withdrew down the Huntsville road, swore that Van Dorn had lost his nerve. Unpursued by the badly battered Federals, his troops made their way back to Van Buren, Arkansas, suffering terribly from cold and hunger, their heavy battle losses enormously increased by straggling and desertion.

Van Dorn was disappointed but not dismayed by the setback at Pea Ridge, which he blamed on the incompetence of his generals and the poor discipline of his soldiers. Even as he retreated he began planning a new advance on St. Louis through southeastern Missouri. But before he could get it underway he received orders to bring the Army of the West to Corinth, Mississippi. He promptly obeyed and during the fourth week of April crossed the Mississippi—too late, however, to participate in the Battle of Shiloh.

In June he left the Army of the West to take charge of the defense of Vicksburg, a key stronghold, which promised ample opportunity to wipe out the stain left on his reputation by Pea Ridge. And, indeed, in the last days of June and first half of July his forces repelled a full-scale naval attack on the river fortress, the powerful ironclad C.S.S. *Arkansas* being the decisive factor. Stimulated by this success, and confident that the *Arkansas* was invincible, he then sent the ship and 5,000 troops under Major General John C. Breckinridge to take Baton Rouge. But nearly half of Breckinridge's force succumbed to fever in the Louisiana swamps, and the *Arkansas* broke her main shaft and had to be scuttled. Thus the victory at Vicksburg was cancelled out by the failure at Baton Rouge.

Much chagrined, Van Dorn blamed the failure of the expedition on "causes which were not only beyond my control, but out of the reach of ordinary foresight"—a less than candid statement, for he had ignored the repeated warnings of the *Arkansas's* captain that the vessel's engines were defective and might break down at any moment.

In September Jefferson Davis ordered Van Dorn to resume command of the Army of the West and invade western Tennessee to support Braxton Bragg's Kentucky offensive. Earlier Bragg had sent him similar instructions, but he had found excuses for persisting in the futile Baton Rouge operation. Now, however, he acted with his usual promptness. On September 29, at the head of 22,000 troops, he moved north, threatened various strongpoints held by Grant's army in West Tennessee, then suddenly swerved southeast towards Corinth, Mississippi, hoping to seize this strategic railroad center before the Union commander there, former classmate William S. Rosecrans, could concentrate his forces. But unfortunately for this plan (which was basically the same one he had employed at the outset of the Pea Ridge campaign), Rosecrans called in his outlying detachments and was fully prepared to meet Van Dorn's onslaught. Furthermore, he had 23,000 men, not the 15,000 Van Dorn believed he had.

Van Dorn assaulted Corinth on October 3, and his troops drove the Federals back into their last line of fortifications. Also, unbeknownst to him, he enjoyed some good luck—a potentially devastating attack on his left flank, craftily arranged by Rosecrans, never took place because the Union general who was to deliver it failed to do so, subsequently claiming that his orders were unclear. But on the morning of October 4, Dame Fortune again frowned on Van Dorn when one of his division commanders, Major General Mansfield Lovell, refrained from obeying instructions to join in an attempt to storm Corinth's defenses, in the belief that it was foredoomed. Perhaps it was, although the fact that one of Price's divisions broke through and swarmed into the streets of Corinth before being expelled by a counter-attack seems to indicate otherwise. In any case, Van Dorn suffered a repulse and nearly 4,000 casualties, which brought his loss for both days to 5,000.

Even though his army had been reduced by close to one-fourth, and the survivors were physically and psychologically exhausted, Van Dorn remained full of fight. While withdrawing from Corinth during the afternoon of October 4, he suddenly halted and issued orders to his generals to turn about and attack the town yet again, this time from a different direction. Astonished, Maury and Price concluded that he had been rendered desperate by misfortune. They hastened to his headquarters and protested that the men were in no condition to fight another battle and that an attempt to do so would result in disaster. Maury, who was a personal friend, added: "Van Dorn, you are the only man I ever saw who loves danger for its own sake. When any daring enterprise is before you, you cannot adequately estimate the obstacles in your way."

Van Dorn sat in silence for a moment, then replied, "While I do not admit the correctness of your criticism, I feel how wrong I shall be to imperil this army through my personal peculiarities. . . . I will countermand the orders."

The next day the Confederates continued their retreat to the Hatchie River, where they found a strong Union force blocking their path. For a while it appeared that they were hopelessly trapped: "We all thought," growled a disgusted Missouri soldier, "that Van Dorn had played hell at Pea Ridge—but *now* he has done it, sure enough." The cavalry, however, discovered another way across the Hatchie, and Van Dorn's army escaped with only minor additional losses.

News of the bloody debacle at Corinth produced a fierce outcry against Van Dorn throughout the South and especially in his native state. Editors, politicians, and ordinary citizens denounced him as a rash incompetent who had squandered the lives of his men in a "mad and hopeless" assault against an "impregnable fortress." Some even declared that he had been drunk during the battle. But most serious of all, one of his brigade commanders formally accused him of gross neglect of duty and of "cruel and improper treatment" of his troops. Van Dorn at once demanded and obtained a court of inquiry. His dreams of fame and glory had now given way to a fight for professional survival.

The court met in November at Abbeville, Mississippi. In a moving opening statement Van Dorn declared: "I have accumulated nothing of the world's wealth, having devoted my whole time and energies to the service of my country; therefore my reputation is all that belongs to me, without which life to me were as valueless as the crisp and faded leaf of autumn." The subsequent hearings demonstrated that the charges against him were untrue or exaggerated, and the court unanimously acquitted him on all counts.

He had escaped disgrace, and he remained in command of Confederate forces in northern Mississippi; but he was subject to close supervision by the newly appointed commander of the Department of the Mississippi and East Louisiana, Lieutenant General John C. Pemberton. Furthermore, he knew that only the continued friendship of President Davis prevented him from being shunted off to some remote post, and that another defeat would mean the end of his military career. In short, his next battle had to be a victory.

In November Major General U. S. Grant's army began advancing on Vicksburg. Too weak to stand, the Confederates fell back ever deeper into Mississippi. Lieutenant Colonel John S. Griffith of the Texas brigade saw a chance for the Confederate cavalry to strike a terrible blow. He and his officers urged Pemberton to place Van Dorn in charge of his cavalry and to "penetrate the rear of the enemy, capture Holly Springs, Memphis, and other points." Pemberton saw the value of this suggestion and gave Van Dorn command of the cavalry. At the head of a column of 3,000 hard-riding Confederate horse-soldiers, Van Dorn took the field on December 17 and made a wide sweep behind Grant's lines toward Holly Springs.

This time his luck matched his daring. The Union commander at Holly Springs, though warned of Van Dorn's approach, neither alerted his troops nor posted sufficient pickets. As a result, on December 20 Van Dorn captured the town and most of its garrison, then burned a million dollars' worth of supplies stored there for Grant's army. Van Dorn's dash on Holly Springs, in conjunction with Brigadier General Nathan Bedford Forrest's sweep into west Tennessee, had immediate repercussions on Grant's plans. He was compelled to abandon his initial plan in his Vicksburg campaign. He ordered his forces to retire behind the Tallahatchie.

Once again Van Dorn had helped save Vicksburg, once again he was the South's hero of the day. Furthermore, he had brilliantly demonstrated his true military vocation: Cavalry. His superiors recognized this, and in January assigned him to the command of a cavalry corps in Middle Tennessee.

He performed capably at his new post, gaining on March 5 a smashing victory at Thompson's Station, where he routed a Union brigade and took more than 1,000 prisoners. Late in April, however, his extreme sensitivity on the subject of personal honor involved him in a heated quarrel with one of his brigade commanders, the redoubtable Bedford Forrest. Both men reached for their swords, and only Forrest's good sense prevented a duel, which, given the character of the two antagonists, would probably have proved fatal for both.

Van Dorn's headquarters in Tennessee was located in a large brick-and-wood house in Spring Hill. On the morning of May 7 he was at his desk conferring with a staff officer. Dr. George B. Peters, a prominent local citizen, entered the room and asked for a passport to Nashville. The staff officer left and Van Dorn began to write out the passport. As he did so Peters pulled out a pistol and shot him. Peters picked up the passport, walked out, mounted his horse, and rode to Nashville. There he declared that he had killed Van Dorn for having seduced his wife—a charge indignantly denied by Van Dorn's friends and family, who claimed that Peters had murdered the Confederate general for personal gain.

Thus, suddenly and tragically, ended the life of Earl Van Dorn. As a man and a general his failings were obvious: Carelessness, rashness, arrogance, stubbornness. Yet in each instance these defects were but the reverse side of his strong points: Love of action, daring, self-confidence, determination. Furthermore, with better luck, his great defeats at Pea Ridge and Corinth could well have been great victories. But he was, as Douglas Southall Freeman wrote of another ill-starred Confederate commander, one of those soldiers "unhappily numerous in military history, who consistently have bad luck."

Only once, at Holly Springs, did fortune truly smile on Van Dorn. Then, as he seemed to have found his proper sphere of action, there came the last, the cruelest blow: He who cherished honor went to his grave with it besmirched; he who lived for glory died at the hands of a jealous husband.

To this day his ghost must weep—he should have died leading a cavalry charge.

CHAPTER SEVEN

In Quest of Glory: George Stoneman's Attempt to Free the Andersonville Prisoners

Like so many Civil War commanders, Northern and Southern alike, Union general George Stoneman, although no doubt patriotic, was motivated primarily by a desire for military glory—a desire that intensified when he was blamed for a failure that he believed, with some justification, had not been his fault. What follows is the story of how he sought to vindicate himself and how that quest led to his making a cavalry raid, which, had it succeeded in its objective, would have been the most sensational exploit of the Civil War—and also, in all probability, produced the greatest disaster of that war. Fortunately it came nowhere close to success, and Stoneman's name became linked to another failure and will remain so. Another name, however, should also be attached to that failure: William Tecumseh Sherman.

This article appears here for the first time, the consequence of it having been written for a periodical that, unbeknownst at the time, had ceased publication. In it I correct, thanks to David Evans's Sherman's Horsemen: Union Cavalry Operations in the Atlanta Campaign *(Bloomington: Indiana University Press, 1996), some factual errors in the account of Stoneman's raid to be found in my* Decision in the West: The Atlanta Campaign of 1864 *(Lawrence: University Press of Kansas, 1992). I also withdraw, as a result of a closer study of the primary sources, the contention made in appendix B of* Decision in the West *that there is good reason to believe that Sherman gave Stoneman informal permission to disregard his formal orders for conducting the raid. In painting a large historical canvas, sometimes the brush slips.*

MAJOR GENERAL GEORGE STONEMAN WANTED GLORY. AND HE HOPED TO find it as the commander of a cavalry division in the army that William T. Sherman was marshaling early in May 1864 for the invasion of Georgia, target Atlanta. So strongly did Stoneman desire glory that he was prepared to die, if need be, to obtain it.

Stoneman had a compelling reason for his quest, for until a year ago he had enjoyed a highly successful military career. Born in 1822 in western New York, he graduated from West Point in 1846, served in the Mexican War, fought Indians in Texas. By 1861 he was a captain in the elite 2nd Cavalry Regiment, the colonel of which was Albert Sidney Johnston, the lieutenant colonel Robert E. Lee, and the majors George H. Thomas and William J. Hardee. Upon the outbreak of war between the North and the South, Stoneman served as a major on the staff of General George B. McClellan, a West Point classmate, and took part in his victorious West Virginia campaign during the summer of 1861. This in turn led to his being promoted to brigadier general and appointed chief of cavalry of the Army of the Potomac when McClellan took command of it toward the end of July 1861. In little more than three months Stoneman had risen from captain to general, from leader of a company to head of the largest mounted force in the Union army.

At this point, though, his rapid ascension came to an abrupt halt. Like all Northern commanders early in the war, McClellan scattered his cavalry in small units throughout his army, leaving Stoneman little to do because he had so few troopers under his actual control. Therefore, when Ambrose Burnside succeeded McClellan in November 1862 and offered Stoneman command of an infantry division, he gladly accepted it, and at the Battle of Fredericksburg (December 13, 1862) Stoneman directed not only his division but the corps to which it belonged as the Federals bravely but futilely assailed the Rebel defenses.

Bumbling Burnside, having manifested his chronic incompetence, gave way to Fighting Joe Hooker, who revived the Army of the Potomac's morale and restored Stoneman to the post of chief of cavalry with the rank of major general. More than that, he also organized the cavalry into a three-division corps, thereby transforming it into a force capable of playing a significant role in the forthcoming campaign. And such a role he had cast it in, instructing Stoneman to swing across the Rappahannock River into the Confederate rear, cut railroad lines, and prevent gray-clad reinforcements from reaching the front—all in preparation for an offensive that he, Hooker, confidently predicted would destroy Lee's Army of Northern Virginia and thus win the war.

When, on April 13, 1863, Stoneman set forth to accomplish his mission, he too felt confident, for he headed close to 9,000 horsemen whereas, according to intelligence reports, Jeb Stuart's cavaliers available for active

WILLIAM A. CRAFTS. *THE SOUTHERN REBELLION.* BOSTON: S. WALKER, 1870.

George Stoneman

service totaled little more than a third of that number. But the next day, on reaching the Rappahannock, he found that heavy rains had so greatly widened and deepened the river that he could not cross. Worse, it continued to rain, rain, rain. Not until April 29 was he able to pass over to the other side. By then the entire Army of the Potomac was advancing; instead of preparing the way for Hooker's victory, Stoneman at best could only assist it.

As it turned out, he was unable to do even that. After a bold start, Hooker grew cautious and went on the defensive in a wilderness area surrounding the one-house hamlet of Chancellorsville. Lee and Stonewall Jackson (another of Stoneman's classmates) took advantage of Hooker's reticence and executed a daring plan whereby Jackson, with the largest portion of the Confederate forces, struck and crushed the Union right flank. Although this blow did not defeat the Army of the Potomac as such—it remained capable of continuing and winning the struggle—it defeated Hooker, who was transformed from Fighting Joe into retreating Joe.

Hooker blamed his failure on various of his generals. One of them was Stoneman, whom he removed from command and charged with having not even attempted to sever the enemy's railroad supply lines. This accusation, to say the least, was excessive. Despite again being hampered by rain, Stoneman's troopers had wreaked enough damage on Lee's main rail link to cause the Confederates to spend two days repairing it, and throughout the Chancellorsville Campaign Lee had received no substantial reinforcement. But Hooker wanted scapegoats and before long Stoneman found himself kicked upstairs to the post of chief of the Cavalry Bureau in Washington. There he sat at a desk, holding a pen—he, who lived to sit astride a saddle brandishing a sword and cutting, with his tall and lithe physique, a dashing figure even if, as historical rumor would have it, he did suffer from hemorrhoids.

Not until the spring of 1864 did Stoneman return to the field as commander of the cavalry corps of Major General John M. Schofield's Army of the Ohio in eastern Kentucky and Tennessee. Actually the "corps" consisted of a hodgepodge of widely dispersed and poorly disciplined horsemen—many without horses—and numbered only a few thousand. During April Stoneman assembled and mounted slightly more than 2,000 of them and endeavored to tighten discipline. He achieved little success with the latter, particularly among the Kentucky contingent: By the time he set out for Georgia to join Sherman's army all except two of the officers in one of the Bluegrass regiments were under arrest.

In Georgia Stoneman's command became one of the four mounted divisions in Sherman's 100,000-man host. As such it reported to, and received orders from, Sherman himself. This arrangement suited Stoneman. Besides sparing him the embarrassment of serving under Schofield, his junior in rank as well as in age, it put him in direct contact with Sherman, who could be counted on to be sympathetic to his desire to wipe away the stain placed on his reputation by Hooker, whom Sherman also detested.

Throughout May, June, and into July Stoneman persistently tried to perform a brilliant feat of arms that would bring him martial glory and personal vindication. Just as persistently he failed. In his first encounter, near Dalton on May 11, a far stronger Confederate cavalry force supported by infantry attacked him; Union ground troops had to come to his aid. Four days later, at Resaca, when he took advantage of an unguarded enemy flank and sent his troopers rampaging through the Confederate rear, they ransacked some hospital tents, captured a few medical attendants, and even shot some Rebel wounded before they were driven away. No glory gained here—if anything, the opposite.

Perhaps this explains the curious dispatch Stoneman sent Sherman on May 17: "I have sent two picked parties, one 250, the other 500 strong, to strike . . . the railroad between Kingston and Allatoona, and if not there, between Allatoona and Atlanta, and if not there, between Atlanta and Augusta, after which they are to take care of themselves." Sherman's reply ignored the "picked parties" and ordered Stoneman to combine with Brigadier General Edward McCook's cavalry division in intercepting the Confederate wagon train, which he mistakenly believed was traveling by way of Cassville to the Etowah River. Stoneman at once recalled the "picked parties"—a fortunate occurrence for them—and on May 18 linked up with McCook. The next day their divisions approached Cassville just as Confederate general Joseph E. Johnston was about to launch an ambush attack on the left wing of Sherman's army. Their unexpected appearance in his rear forced Johnston to cancel the attack. Stoneman's and McCook's interception would prove to be the outstanding accomplishment of Sherman's cavalry during the entire Atlanta Campaign, but no one in the Union army knew about it then or later—not even Stoneman. Again no glory.

In June and early July rain, mud, and the overall military situation prevented Stoneman from attempting anything noteworthy. Finally, on July 9, after Johnston retreated to the outskirts of Atlanta, Sherman instructed his frustrated cavalry general to cross the Chattahoochee River northwest of that city and break the Atlanta & Macon Railroad to the south. The assignment delighted Stoneman. With the campaign (so it seemed) coming to a close, he had a chance to deliver a stroke that, along with other cavalry raids ordered by Sherman, would completely cut off Atlanta from the rest of the Confederacy and compel Johnston to evacuate it.

At first all went well. On July 13 some of Stoneman's Kentuckians surprised and captured the Confederates guarding a bridge over the Chattahoochee before they could set it afire. The planking had been removed but, Stoneman reported to Sherman, it would be relaid during the night and in the morning he would be on the way to the Macon Railroad, a mere ten miles distant. In the morning, however, when his troopers tried to cross the bridge they were greeted by artillery fire. Efforts to cross elsewhere failed despite, so Stoneman notified Sherman, his being "anxious to strike the railroad for personal reasons as well as other considerations." His division remained on the wrong side of the Chattahoochee, eating blackberries. A passing army chaplain noted that the men were "far from presenting a bold appearance."

Had Sherman captured Atlanta as quickly as he had expected, Stoneman's futile attempt to raid the Macon Railroad would have ended his

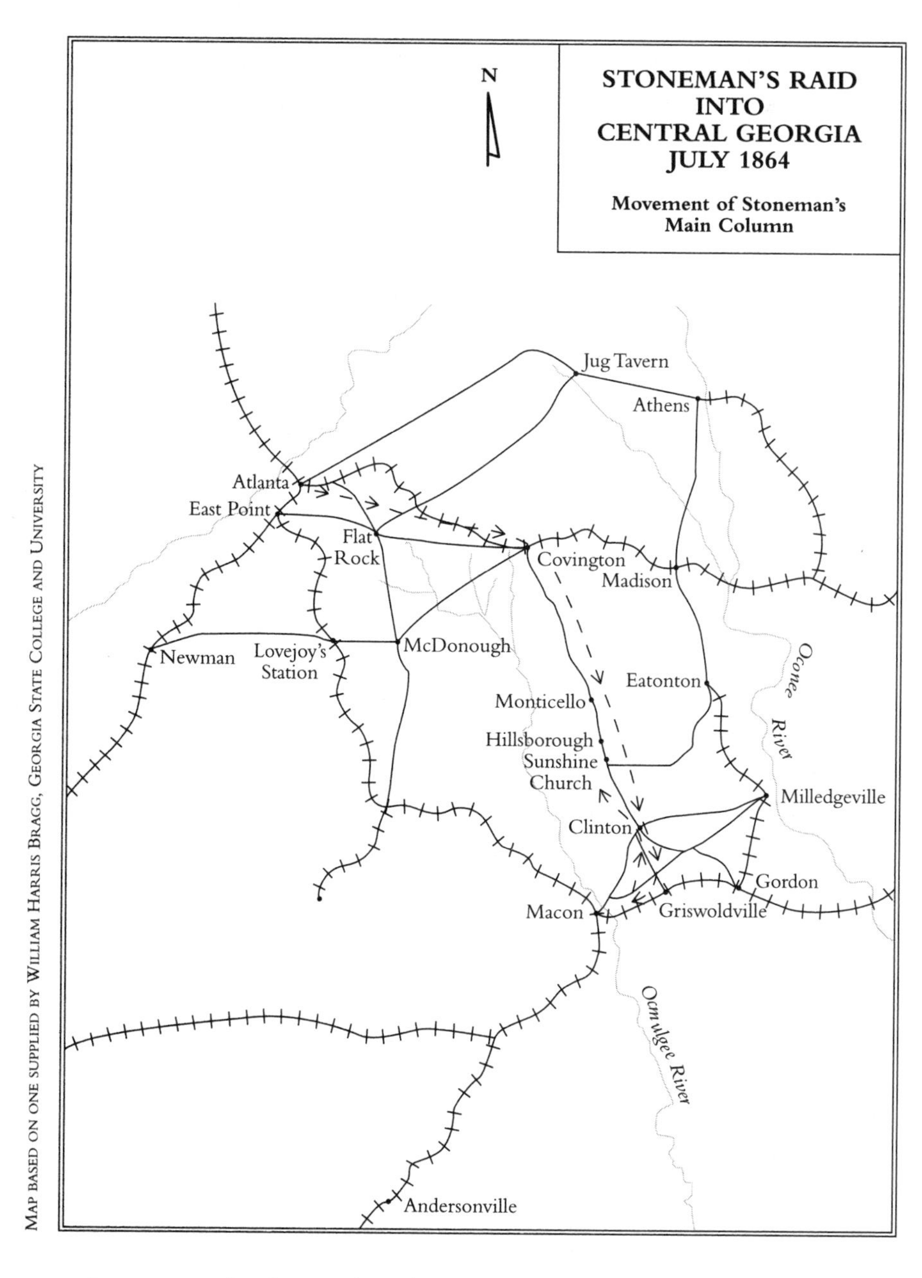

Map based on one supplied by William Harris Bragg, Georgia State College and University

endeavors to gain glory and vindication in the Atlanta Campaign. But Sherman did not fulfill his expectation. On July 17 Confederate president Jefferson Davis, not trusting Johnston to make a determined stand at Atlanta, replaced him with General John B. Hood, who could be trusted to fight, and fight hard, for the city.

This Hood did, lashing out against Sherman's right wing on July 20, then at his left wing two days later. Both onslaughts were repulsed, yet they halted Sherman's advance on Atlanta from the north and east and caused him to switch his offensive endeavors to the west. There his prime goal was to do what Stoneman had failed to do in his aborted crossing of the Chattahoochee—cut the Macon Railroad. Since Union forces already had severed Atlanta's rail connections to the east and west, this railroad now was the sole source of supplies for Hood's army.

On July 25 Sherman issued orders for McCook's and Stoneman's divisions to join in breaking the railroad at a point south of Atlanta, with the former to strike from the west and the latter from the east. Here, then, was another opportunity for Stoneman to engage in an operation that could lead to the fall of Atlanta. But he wanted to do more than that—much more.

On July 26 he wrote Sherman asking permission, once the railroad raid had achieved its objective, to make with his division "a dash on Macon." He would free the 1,500 Union officer prisoners there "by a vigorous stroke" and continue on to Andersonville to liberate the enlisted men being held captive in that death camp. "I would like to try it and am willing to run any risks. . . . Now is the time to do it before the rebel army falls back and covers that country, and I have every inducement to try it. If we accomplish the desired object it will compensate for the loss as prisoners of us all, and I should feel compensated for almost any sacrifice."

Sherman replied the same day with a letter authorizing Stoneman to go on to Macon and Andersonville "after breaking good the railroad." He saw "many difficulties, but, as you say, even a chance of success will warrant the effort." Should Stoneman "bring back to the army any or all of those prisoners of war it will be an achievement that will entitle you and the men of your command to the love and admiration of the whole country."

On July 27 Stoneman, with slightly more than 2,000 men and two cannons, marched southeast of Atlanta to Decatur, accompanied by Brigadier General Kenner Garrard's cavalry division, which had been placed under his command. According to Sherman's still-standing July 25 instructions, from Decatur Stoneman was to turn west toward the Macon Railroad beyond McDonough, leaving behind Garrard as a reserve. Instead, on the morning of July 28 he headed south via Covington toward Macon while sending Garrard to Flat Rock to act as a decoy.

Obviously Stoneman was disregarding Sherman's order to join with McCook in breaking the Macon Railroad. Why? The answer almost surely is that he saw a golden opportunity to gain the glory he craved by freeing the prisoners at Macon and Andersonville, that he believed that he could greatly enhance his prospect of doing this by striking directly and immediately for those places, and that Sherman would forgive his disobedience if he was successful. Should, on the other hand, he fail, then so be it. As he had stated in his letter to Sherman, he was "willing to run any risks." Besides, had not Sherman himself declared that "even a chance of success will warrant the effort"? Now was the chance, and he would take it.

At first all went well. Confederate major general Joseph Wheeler, whose cavalry corps had pursued the Yankee raiders to Decatur, followed Garrard to Flat Rock. There, discovering that Stoneman was heading south, he decided to move with his main body against McCook while detaching three brigades under Brigadier General Alfred Iverson to overtake Stoneman' s force. Assuming that Stoneman would go by way of McDonough, Iverson set out for that village and thus away from his actual path.

On the evening of July 28 Stoneman halted to bivouac about four miles north of Monticello. Since it was little more than forty miles from Macon, had he pressed on until nightfall he could have placed himself in position to reach Macon no later than the early afternoon of July 29. But believing that he was in no danger of immediate pursuit, he saw no need for haste. His belief was correct yet it was to cost him dearly.

In the morning he resumed his march—a leisurely one, during which detachments burned bridges while the troopers in the main column filled their saddlebags with loot and themselves with liquor from plantations along the way. At nightfall they bivouacked some five miles from Macon. Stoneman still assumed that he was not being closely pursued and he still was correct—for the time being. Iverson, on reaching McDonough, discovered that the raiders had not passed through there and so concluded that they were heading toward either Macon or the state capital, Milledgeville. He sent out scouts to ascertain which.

Meanwhile, on the morning of July 29, McCook reached Lovejoy' s Station on the Macon Railroad and tore up a couple of miles of track. Then, perturbed by Stoneman's failure to join him and learning that Wheeler was approaching, he retreated toward the Chattahoochee, intending to cross to safety. He did not make it. Intercepted by Brigadier General William "Red" Jackson's Rebel cavalry and beset from the rear by Wheeler, his division was routed, scattered—in effect, destroyed.

Most of Stoneman's raiders spent the morning of July 30 ripping up track, wrecking trains, and burning bridges and trestles east of Macon. Not until noon did they approach the town in full strength. By then the Confederates had evacuated all but a few hundred of the officer prisoners. Stoneman nevertheless decided to seize Macon, which housed large quantities of military supplies in the town's factories. He first had to overcome two obstacles: the Ocmulgee River, which could be crossed only by a railroad bridge, and 2,500 defenders. Although the latter consisted mainly of over- and underage home guards and some convalescent Confederate soldiers, they were posted behind barricades and supported by artillery.

Stoneman's two cannons bombarded a stockade anchoring the enemy line and lobbed a few shells into the town, which did no significant damage. He then ordered the aptly named Kentucky Independent Brigade to charge on foot and take the railroad bridge. The men advanced, but as soon as they came under fire, retreated. Not only did the Kentuckians dislike Stoneman for his West Point notions of discipline, their enlistments were to soon expire; thus they were more interested in surviving than in fighting. Disgusted, Stoneman abandoned his hope of freeing the prisoners at Andersonville and gave orders to head south, the objective Pensacola, Florida.

Hardly had the raiders started marching when a scout reported—erroneously, it would turn out—that a sizable Confederate cavalry column was entering Macon from the south. Fearing interception by this supposed force, Stoneman at once reversed course and headed northward via the same route by which he had come. At nightfall he reached Clinton, where a road branched off to Union lines. He had planned to take it, but now he changed his mind and, over the protests of his brigade commanders, continued north toward Hillsboro where, so he claimed, there would be a choice of three roads by which they could return to Sherman's army.

This proved to be Stoneman's final and fatal blunder. Two miles from Hillsboro he encountered such stiff enemy resistance that he halted overnight. In the morning (July 31) he resumed his march, only to come upon a large Rebel force—Iverson's three brigades—deployed on foot near Sunshine Church behind a log barricade in the shape of an inverted V.

The Union troopers dismounted, and Stoneman ordered a breakthrough attack. It failed, with the Kentuckians again showing no inclination to close with the foe. During the rest of the morning and on into the afternoon both sides engaged in futile charges and countercharges. Late in the day, two of Iverson's regiments circled around behind the Federals, causing them to think that the Confederate cavalry supposedly seen at Macon had come up in their rear and that they were surrounded. Not wanting to go to Andersonville as prisoners when so many of them were close to returning home as civilians, the Kentuckians remounted their horses and galloped off to the northeast, easily penetrating a thin line of Rebel skirmishers. Large numbers of other Union troopers followed their example.

Only Stoneman and several hundred remaining men continued to fight, deliberately sacrificing themselves, some of them subsequently stated, in order to aid their comrades' escape. For a while, thanks to their two cannons, they held out atop a hill. When the big guns expended their last shots, members of Stoneman's staff urged him to surrender. Reluctantly, he agreed. From the reckless manner in which he had exposed himself during the combat it was clear that he would have preferred to die. A few minutes later he handed his sword to a Georgia colonel after vainly demanding that Iverson come for it in person. That done, he sat down on a log and buried his tear-streaked face in his hands. His quest for glory had ended in grief.

Stoneman's attempt to liberate the prisoners at Macon and Andersonville was ill-executed, ill-fated, and ill-conceived. Given the superior effectiveness of the Confederate cavalry and the distances involved—on a straight line it was about eighty miles from Atlanta to Macon and sixty miles from Macon to Andersonville—a near-miracle would have been needed for it to succeed. Even then the final outcome would have been, in all likelihood, a calamity for the 30,000-some captives at Andersonville. Supposing that their guards had not slaughtered them with cannon fire inside their prison stockade rather than let them escape or be freed—and there is strong evidence that they were prepared to do this—most of the escapees would have been on foot, unarmed, without food, and weak from hunger, disease, and privation. In their attempts to survive while heading north to Union lines, they would have pillaged farms and plantations as they swarmed across the countryside like ravenous locusts. In turn Confederate cavalry and Georgia militia would have hunted them down relentlessly and mercilessly. Few could have made it to Sherman's army, well over a hundred miles distant. Thus it is best that Stoneman's attempt to rescue them failed; success would have produced a far greater disaster than he suffered at Sunshine Church.

Sherman himself recognized, belatedly, that even if Stoneman had freed the Andersonville prisoners the difficulty, he telegraphed Union army chief of staff Major General Henry W. Halleck on August 3, would "then commence for them to reach me." Furthermore, on learning of Stoneman's debacle, he did not criticize as such his disobedience of orders or denounce him for contributing to McCook's defeat. Instead he did something he rarely ever did, to wit, admit that he had committed a military error in sanctioning any attempt at all by Stoneman to liberate the prisoners—an error he explained in an August 11 letter to his father-in-law as the product of "my judgment being warped by our Feelings for 20,000 [*sic*] poor men being penned up like cattle."

After the fall of Atlanta on September 2, 1864, Sherman arranged for Stoneman's release from captivity and then assigned him to a cavalry command in East Tennessee. Stoneman was justified in thinking, as has been surmised, that Sherman would overlook his effort to rescue the Andersonville prisoners even though it was made in violation of orders and resulted in failure. To his credit, Sherman realized that he shared in the responsibility for this failure and so acted accordingly.

During late 1864 and early 1865 Stoneman resumed his search for glory by conducting cavalry raids into the western regions of Virginia and North Carolina. These, though successful, attracted little attention and less acclaim, being merely minor shoves of an already tottering Confederacy toward its grave. After the war he reverted to the rank of colonel in the Regular army and commanded the Department of Arizona until his retirement in 1871. He then moved to California, where he acquired a large ranch and engaged in politics, at which he achieved more success than in war, securing election as governor in 1884. Ten years later, while traveling in western New York, he died suddenly and was buried near his birthplace.

Stoneman did not possess in sufficient quantity those personal qualities usually found in victorious military leaders; most of all, he lacked that attribute which Napoleon deemed more important in a commander than ability—luck. Consequently his main claim to historical fame lies in his futile endeavor to free the Andersonville prisoners and his becoming, ironically, a prisoner himself—the highest-ranking Union general to suffer that fate during the Civil War.

This scarcely constitutes glory.

CHAPTER EIGHT

Theophilus H. Holmes: Pallbearer of the Confederacy

Insofar as I know, this article, which appeared in Civil War Times Illustrated*'s July 1977 issue, was the first historical appraisal of Confederate general Theophilus Hunter Holmes's career to be published, and it so remains. If such is the case, that is understandable. To say the least, Holmes was not a glamorous figure, and although he gave all he had to the Confederate cause, that all was so little that his own soldiers called him "Granny Holmes." Moreover, the military operations with which he was mainly connected took place in the Trans-Mississippi West (Arkansas, Texas, and most of Louisiana), a region whose immense geographical size was in inverse proportion to its limited strategical importance. Even had Holmes been more competent and successful, he would have had minor impact on the course of the Civil War. For this reason it is appropriate that he was dubbed not a gravedigger, but a "pallbearer," of the Confederacy.*

The basic source for this article was my General Sterling Price and the Civil War in the West *(Baton Rouge: Louisiana State University Press, 1968; reprint by same publisher, 1994), which I supplemented with pertinent primary sources. For the Virginia phase of Holmes's wartime career, I relied principally on the relevant portions of volume one of D. S. Freeman's* Lee's Lieutenants *(New York: Charles Scribner's Sons, 1942), a book that I received from my mother and father on my fourteenth birthday.*

SOMETIME DURING THE FINAL DAYS OF THE CIVIL WAR, GENERAL P. G. T. Beauregard wrote in the back of a letter book an "Epitaph of the Confederate States." The Confederacy had been "murdered by Jefferson Davis—aided and abetted" by various members of his government. And at its funeral the pallbearers were "Generals Cooper, Bragg, Kirby Smith, Lt. Generals Hood, Holmes, and Pemberton."

MILLER, ED. *PHOTOGRAPHIC HISTORY.*

Theophilus H. Holmes

A Civil War student can understand why the bitter Beauregard blamed most of those generals for contributing to Southern defeat. The presence of Theophilus Hunter Holmes on the list must occasion some puzzlement, however, for he is one of the least known high-ranking Confederate generals. What did he do—or not do—to draw Beauregard's condemnation? And did he deserve it?

To answer these questions we must first take a quick look at Holmes's antebellum career, for it contains some clues necessary to understanding his wartime role. Born November 13, 1804, near Clinton, North Carolina, he was scion of a wealthy and prominent family, his father having been state governor from 1821 to 1825. On attaining manhood Holmes tried his hand at managing a plantation, but being, in the words of a granddaughter, "indolent," he failed. His father, now a congressman, thereupon secured him an appointment to West Point, where he was in the same class as Robert E. Lee and one year behind Jefferson Davis. After graduating in 1829 he served with the infantry at various frontier posts and in the Seminole War, rising to captain. In 1841 he married Laura Wetmore, also of the North Carolina aristocracy. Their union produced four sons and two daughters.

In the Mexican War Holmes distinguished himself at Monterrey, where he "gallantly led a storming party up a rocky height," seized the enemy position, and won promotion to brevet major. Following that conflict he saw more service in the West, became a full major in 1855, and participated in an expedition against the Navajos. In 1859 the War Department placed him in charge of recruiting, with headquarters on Governor's Island in New York harbor. There his wife died and was buried beneath a tombstone inscribed "She Made Her Husband a Christian."

Early in April 1861 he received orders to join the expedition being fitted out to relieve Fort Sumter. However, he "declined the honor of fighting against his native land," resigned his commission, and headed for home. John B. Jones, a fellow North Carolinian who soon would be the chief clerk of the Confederate War Department, met him aboard a boat traveling from Washington, D.C. "The major," he noted in his diary, "is a little deaf but has an intellectual face, the predominant expression indicating the discretion and prudence necessary for success in a large field of operations."

During the remainder of the spring of 1861 Holmes assisted the governor of North Carolina in organizing troops. In June Jefferson Davis, who as a colonel in the Mexican War had "watched with pride" as his classmate stormed the rocky height at Monterrey, appointed him brigadier general in the Confederate army and assigned him to the Aquia Creek area of Virginia. Then in July, when the Northern army showed signs of advancing, Holmes with two regiments joined Beauregard's forces at Manassas Junction.

Having determined to strike the Federal left with his right, Beauregard early on July 21 drew up a vaguely worded order to Holmes to participate in a movement across Bull Run. For some unknown reason, however, this order never reached Holmes. Furthermore, before Beauregard's advance got underway, the Union army hit his left. Not until midday did Holmes receive instructions to "march to the sound of the firing." He moved fast but when he reached the front the fighting had already ended in Confederate victory.

During the fall and winter Holmes, who was promoted to major general in October, commanded the Fredericksburg District. In March 1862 General Joseph E. Johnston, at the time Confederate commander in Virginia, made a hasty retreat—but neglected to inform Holmes, who consequently was almost left stranded. That same month Davis appointed Holmes head of the

Department of North Carolina where, according to Douglas Southall Freeman, "as far as the records show, he did creditably in reorganizing the defenses of the State, though he may not have been aggressive" in combating Federal amphibious operations along the coast.

On June 21 General Robert E. Lee summoned Holmes and most of his troops to help defend Richmond against McClellan's drive up the Virginia Peninsula. For a while he guarded Drewry's Bluff; then on June 26, at the outset of the Seven Days Battles, Lee ordered him to the north side of the James River. Three days later, after McClellan began retreating to Harrison's Landing on the James, Lee instructed Holmes to advance down the bank of the river as part of a general convergence of forces designed to intercept and crush the enemy.

On the morning of June 30 Holmes marched to New Market Heights and halted to await developments. His force consisted of 6,000 infantry and thirty artillery pieces. At 4:00 P.M. one of Lee's engineer officers informed him that Federal soldiers were fleeing over Malvern Hill two-and-a-half miles to his front. He promptly sent forward six rifled cannons, supported by a regiment, to bombard the hill. Then, fearful that this would be an insufficient force, he advanced his entire division. While doing so he met Lee, who approved his movement. If successful it would block or at least delay McClellan's retreat.

As Holmes's men hurried along the road, they raised a large dust cloud. This attracted the enemy's attention, which took the form of "a perfect shower of shells of tremendous proportion and hideous sound hurled from the heavy naval guns of the Federal fleet on the James River. . . ."

Holmes's raw troops milled about in confusion and some stampeded. According to D. H. Hill, another of Lee's division commanders, Holmes because of his deafness was "totally unaware of the rumpus" until he emerged from a house into which he had gone, whereupon he "put his hand behind his right ear, and said 'I thought I heard firing.'" Hill, however, was not present to witness what he described; he had a strong bias against his fellow North Carolinian, and his account of Holmes's part in the Seven Days Battles is filled with what Freeman terms "inexcusable" errors.

In any event Holmes and his officers soon restored order, and the six rifled cannons opened fire on Malvern Hill. Immediately a storm of shot and shell from overwhelmingly superior Union batteries atop the hill engulfed them. They maintained the unequal duel for an hour, then as darkness fell they withdrew. At the same time Holmes pulled back his division to New

Market Heights, having concluded that an infantry assault on Malvern Hill would be "perfect madness." He was correct. Along with dozens of cannons, 20,000 Federal troops opposed him—not to mention the gunboats.

Receiving no instructions to do otherwise, Holmes did not participate in Lee's mismanaged, bloody, and futile assault on Malvern Hill the following day. In this battle Holmes's oldest son, a lieutenant, was killed.

After a year of war, all that could be said definitely about Holmes was that he had done nothing either outstandingly good or bad. That Davis retained a high opinion of him became evident when in July he appointed him commander of the Trans-Mississippi Department. Moreover, in October he promoted him to lieutenant general, a rank that Holmes initially declined on the honest grounds that he had done nothing to earn it.

Geographically the Trans-Mississippi was the Confederacy's largest military department—Arkansas, western Louisiana, Texas, the Indian Territory, and (in theory) Missouri—but it was also the least important strategically. Its basic role was to support the South's war effort east of the Mississippi River. Thus, early in 1862 Earl Van Dorn's 22,000-man army was transferred (far too late) from Arkansas to aid the counterattack at Shiloh. Arkansans were so outraged by this "abandonment" that their governor threatened to secede from the secession! But by August, when Holmes arrived in Little Rock, Major General Thomas C. Hindman had partially salvaged the military situation in the state by raising a new army of some 30,000 troops—most of whom, however, were poorly trained, ill armed, and reluctant conscripts.

Holmes busied himself with bolstering the defenses of his far-flung department and in preparing an invasion of Missouri to be led by Hindman. Then in November and on into December the War Department repeatedly urged and even ordered him to send 10,000 troops across the Mississippi to Vicksburg, which was threatened by Grant's army advancing overland from Tennessee. Stubbornly Holmes refused to comply. It would take, he argued, anywhere from two weeks to a month for the desired reinforcements to reach Vicksburg, anti-Confederate disaffection would increase in Arkansas, the Federals would overrun the state, and the entire Trans-Mississippi would be lost.

No doubt Holmes, like many another general, was guilty of excessive concern about his own department and the dangers it faced. On the other hand, as he himself pointed out, Richmond greatly exaggerated his strength, crediting him with 50,000 men in Arkansas whereas in fact—and as he had notified the War Department—he had only 22,000 effectives. In any case, his failure to reinforce Vicksburg did no harm, for Grant retreated when Confederate cavalry cut his supply line.

Early in December Union forces smashed Hindman's army at the Battle of Prairie Grove in northwest Arkansas. A month later a Federal expedition captured 5,000 Southern troops at Arkansas Post near the mouth of the Arkansas River. As a result of these disasters Holmes lost the confidence of both civilians and soldiers. The latter dubbed him "Granny Holmes," hundreds of them deserted, and an army surgeon went so far as to suggest that Holmes suffered from "softening of the brain." Another officer characterized Holmes as "weak, vacillating, and totally devoid of energy," and charged that "his entire administration revolved around the axis of a simple love for some wealthy Arkansas widow." For his part Holmes denounced his subordinates as incompetents—"you ought to hear Holmes cuss and roar," wrote a lieutenant who watched him "bawl out" his staff.

President Davis sadly concluded that his old friend was not up to the job. Therefore in February 1863 he informed him that he was being replaced as department commander by General Edmund Kirby Smith but that he would remain in charge of the District of Arkansas. Holmes replied: "I thank you, my dear sir, for sending General Smith to Louisiana and Texas. I was unable to do much there."

In May Grant cut off and besieged Vicksburg. Once again Richmond called on the Trans-Mississippi to provide help. But Kirby Smith, like his predecessor, found it impractical to do anything. Finally, prodded by the War Department, he authorized Holmes (who had asked permission to do so) to attack Union-held Helena, Arkansas, on the Mississippi River.

Holmes assembled 8,000 troops. Since Helena was strongly fortified and garrisoned, his only reasonable hope of taking it was to move with speed and secrecy. Heavy rains, however, had turned the countryside into "one vast lagoon." The Confederate approach march was painfully slow. By the time Holmes reached the vicinity of Helena on July 3, the Federals were ready and waiting.

A reconnaissance showed Helena's fortifications to be much more formidable than expected. Major General Sterling Price, commander of Holmes's main infantry force, advised him to call off the assault. Holmes refused. He was tired of derision and of accusations of being afraid to fight. Once he had gained glory scaling a rocky height in Mexico—now he would regain it on the hills of Arkansas. "General Price," he declared, "I intend to attack Helena immediately, and capture the place, if possible. This is my fight. If I succeed, I want the glory; and if I fail, I am willing to bear the odium."

At midnight the Confederates moved forward. Rugged terrain and vague orders from Holmes to attack at "day-light" produced an uncoordinated assault that soon broke down on the left and right. Only Price's division in the center carried its objective, Graveyard Hill. Holmes then rode to the top of the hill and gave a direct order to one of Price's regiments to storm a Union fort on the outskirts of Helena. Thinking that a general advance was underway, several other regiments followed suit. Crossfire from the untaken Union positions and salvos from a gunboat ripped the Southern ranks. The survivors fled or surrendered.

Holmes galloped about, frantically but vainly trying to rally his troops and mount new attacks. Finally, having lost over 1,600 men, he gave orders to disengage. "It was in this fall back," wrote one of his officers, "that Genl. Holmes exposed himself recklessly and sought death—but it would not come—and half crazy because of his defeat, he commenced the retreat to Little Rock."

The attack on Helena should never have been made. Even had the Confederates taken it, they could not have held it in the face of Union gunboats. Moreover, on the very same day, July 4, that their dead littered the slopes of Graveyard Hill, Vicksburg fell to Grant. Others share with Holmes the responsibility of conceiving this utterly useless operation, but his poor planning and battlefield blunders ruined what little chance it had of succeeding. Literally sickened by his defeat, on July 23 he temporarily relinquished command of the District of Arkansas to Price.

On September 10 a Union advance forced the Confederates to evacuate Little Rock and retreat to Washington, Arkansas. Later that month Holmes resumed command and in October withdrew farther south to Camden, Arkansas, on orders from Kirby Smith. After that he devoted himself to assailing Price and other subordinates, whom he blamed—unfairly—for the Helena fiasco. Meanwhile newspapers, politicians, and army officers clamored for his removal from command. Kirby Smith concurred, but hesitated to act. He considered Price, the only available successor, unqualified, and he feared offending the president, whose friendship for Holmes was well known.

Finally, on January 20, 1864, he wrote Davis recommending that Holmes be replaced with a "younger and more energetic officer." Before

Davis could respond, Holmes learned of what Kirby Smith had done. Angered by this "want of confidence and respect," on February 28 he submitted his resignation. Kirby Smith promptly accepted it. "A succession of circumstances," he explained as tactfully as possible to Holmes, "involving a loss of country, loss of confidence, loss of hope approaching almost to despair, necessitates a change in the administration of the district. . . . I know that the District of Arkansas will never have a purer, more unselfish, and patriotic commander."

Holmes finished out the war as commander of the North Carolina Reserves—boys and old men. Following Appomattox he resided near Fayetteville on a small farm, which, for a while at least, he tilled with his own hands. On June 21, 1880, after a lingering illness, he died. He was buried at his request in a soldier's coffin.

A soldier Holmes was, but not in the full sense of the word a general. As his performance in Arkansas ultimately revealed, he was unfit for a high command involving combat operations. On the other hand Beauregard greatly exaggerated Holmes's contribution to Confederate defeat when he put him in the same category as Bragg, Hood, and Pemberton. What Holmes did and failed to do as commander in Arkansas had, like the Trans-Mississippi Department itself, little impact on the course of the war.

Yet Holmes did play a significant if undistinguished part in the South's struggle for independence. Therefore it is surprising that, so far as can be determined, not so much as a master's thesis has been written about him. Even the North Carolina volume of the *Confederate Military History* contains no mention of him in its 354 pages. He is one Confederate general the South chose to forget.

Part Three

Some Winners Who Became Losers

CHAPTER NINE

Albert Sidney Johnston: The Greatest Might-Have-Been of the Civil War

Of no Civil War general was more expected than Albert Sidney Johnston when he took command of Confederate forces in the West in the fall of 1861. About no Civil War general has there been more controversy than Johnston as to whether he justified that expectation, especially on April 6, 1862, near a little church named Shiloh. This article, which was published under a different title in the March 1997 issue of Civil War Times Illustrated, *evaluates Johnston's career, which first saw him emerge as a winner, then be branded a loser, in the end losing his life while—in the opinion of many then and since—winning a battle that, because of his death, also was lost. In writing it I drew heavily from Wiley Sword,* Shiloh: Bloody April *(New York: St. Martin's Press, 1974); Larry J. Daniel,* Shiloh: The Battle That Changed the Civil War *(New York: Simon & Schuster, 1997); Charles P. Roland,* Albert Sidney Johnston: Soldier of Three Republics *(Austin: University of Texas Press, 1964); and Thomas L. Connelly,* Army of the Heartland: The Army of Tennessee, 1861–1862 *(Baton Rouge: Louisiana State University Press, 1967). Sharp differences of interpretations exist among these books, and my own interpretations neither agree nor disagree entirely with any of them.*

Appended to the article, of which it originally was a part, is a brief essay that also appeared in the March 1997 issue of Civil War Times Illustrated *and bore the title of "Savior of the South?" In it I examine whether Johnston, had he survived Shiloh and remained in command, would have provided the South with what it so fatally lacked—a commander in the West equivalent to Lee in the East.*

THE OPPORTUNITY TO SURPRISE MAJOR GENERAL ULYSSES S. GRANT IN central Tennessee seemed lost. Grant's 40,000 Yankees near Pittsburg Landing would be "entrenched to their eyes," General Pierre G. T. Beauregard advised his superior, General Albert Sidney Johnston, commander of the

40,000-strong Army of the Mississippi. Beauregard urged Johnston to cancel his assault plans.

"We shall attack at daylight tomorrow," Johnston responded after some reflection. Retreat, he realized, would demoralize his raw but eager troops more than defeat. Besides, despite all that had gone wrong, he remained confident of victory. "Tomorrow at twelve o'clock," he told his officers, "we will water our horses in the Tennessee River."

The next morning, April 6, 1862, Johnston ordered his troops to advance. As they began to move, he remarked to a young officer: "My son, we must this day conquer or perish." Though his comment would later seem prophetic, Johnston was simply expressing a common sentiment. "This spirit animated the young men of the South at the time," wrote Colonel George W. Baylor, a Johnston aide. "It was 'death or victory.'" Later on we would have preferred 'badly crippled or victory.'" Johnston would no doubt have agreed.

Johnston had spent most of his adulthood in military service, and now he was the highest-ranking field general in the Confederacy. He stood at the pinnacle of a career he had chosen long ago, when he set aside his father's wishes and a secure livelihood to pursue the promised adventure and glory of soldiering. After a lifetime of learning the poor, dull realities of peacetime army duty he had finally arrived at the adventure and glory. These, however, came with two great risks: Failure and death, both of which lay in wait at every turn that spring day at Pittsburg Landing.

Born on February 2, 1803, in Washington, Kentucky, Johnston was the son of a physician who wanted him to enter the same profession. With that objective in mind, in 1818 he enrolled at Transylvania University in Lexington, Kentucky. There, he became acquainted with a fellow Kentuckian and student, Jefferson Davis, future president of the Confederacy, and formed a relationship that would be the most important one of his career.

Of course, that friendship with Davis might not have gone down in history had Johnston pressed on to become a doctor. Aspirations to a career in medicine fell by the wayside, however, when Johnston obtained an appointment to the U.S. Military Academy from an elder half brother who was a Louisiana congressman. Future Confederate generals Robert E. Lee and Leonidas Polk would enter the academy during Johnston's years there, as would his friend from Transylvania University, Jefferson Davis. Johnston was a member of the West Point class of 1826.

MILLER, ED. *PHOTOGRAPHIC HISTORY.*

Albert Sidney Johnston

A capable but not outstanding student, Johnston graduated eighth in his class. This ranking entitled him to an assignment in the artillery, but he chose the infantry, believing it would provide the best opportunities for distinction and promotion. So strongly did he believe this that he declined an invitation to become an aide-de-camp on the staff of Winfield Scott, the army's most distinguished commander and future general-in-chief.

Johnston was wrong. Commissioned a second lieutenant, he remained at that rank for the next eight years, spending most of his time at Jefferson Barracks near St. Louis, Missouri. His best opportunities during those years were decidedly civilian: He read a great deal, honed his hunting skills, and in 1829 married Henrietta Preston, daughter of a wealthy and well-connected family in Louisville, Kentucky. Apart from a minor expedition to "chastise" some Indians in Wisconsin Territory, Johnston did not participate in a military operation until 1832, when the Black Hawk War broke out in Illinois. Even then, the closest he came to combat was watching militiamen massacre American Indians trying to surrender along the Bad Axe River in the upper Mississippi Valley.

On April 22, 1834, in debt, still a lieutenant with no hope of promotion, and with an ailing wife and three children (including a newborn daughter), Johnston resigned his commission. This proved to be another mistake, at least initially. First his wife, then his daughter died, and a half-hearted attempt to make a living at farming failed miserably. In 1836, at age thirty-three, he was a widower with two small children, little money, and no viable prospects. Out of the army, he was a fish out of water.

Even as Johnston began his slide toward poverty, an opportunity for redemption appeared on an unfamiliar horizon. The simmering animosity between American settlers and the Mexican government was coming to a boil. The Mexican general Santa Anna had signed a treaty recognizing Texas as an independent territory after his defeat and capture at the Battle of San Jacinto on April 21, 1836, but the Mexican government repudiated the pact and proclaimed its intention to reconquer the Lone Star Republic. Johnston saw in this an opportunity to resume his military career. Entrusting his children to their maternal grandmother in Louisville, he journeyed to the republic to offer his services as a private. The Texans welcomed him. In quick succession Johnston became a colonel, adjutant general, acting secretary of war, and on February 4, 1837, "senior brigadier general" in command of the Texas army.

The promotion to senior brigadier general raised Johnston above the army's former ranking officer, Felix Huston. Insisting the appointment was intended to "ruin my reputation," Huston angrily challenged his new superior to a duel. The accusation was utterly absurd, yet Johnston accepted the challenge, knowing that if he did otherwise, his soldiers would think him a coward and reject his authority. Furthermore, although an excellent swordsman, he exercised his right as the challenged party to choose weapons for the duel by choosing pistols, despite Huston's reputation as a crack shot.

At dawn on February 5—the day after Johnston's promotion—Johnston and Huston faced each other at the traditional distance of ten paces, single-shot horse pistols in hand. The ensuing gunfight would have been farcical had it not been potentially homicidal. Four times the duelists exchanged shots with neither being hit. Not until Huston pulled his trigger a fifth time did one of his bullets find its target, passing through Johnston's right hip. Fortunately for the senior brigadier, it broke no bones, and he returned to duty after a month of bed rest.

As army commander, Johnston eagerly hoped for a renewal of war between Texas and Mexico. It was not to be. Internal squabbles in Mexico prevented the country from making good on its threats to invade Texas, and Sam Houston, president of the Lone Star Republic, refused to invade

Mexico because he realized that would damage his relationship with the United States. Houston's successor, Mirabeau Bonaparte Lamar, also refrained from hostilities his bankrupt government could ill afford. Frustrated and disgusted, Johnston returned to private life in May 1840.

Leaving the Texas army proved almost as disastrous for Johnston as his departure from the U.S. Army. Like many others in the West, Johnston had set out to make a fortune in land speculation only to find himself heavily in debt. An attempt to establish a cotton plantation in Texas with borrowed money failed because he did not set aside enough money to buy slaves, without whom massive agriculture was impossible. The only bright spot in this gloomy period of his life was twenty-three-year-old Eliza Griffin, whom he met during his frequent trips to visit his children in Louisville. He wooed Griffin, a cousin of his first wife, and married her in October 1843.

For the next two years Johnston and his bride divided their time between Texas and Kentucky while he tried in vain to sell the plantation. Finally, in 1845 he decided to cultivate it himself, a decision possibly prompted by the birth of Albert Sidney Jr. that April. This second attempt at farming was no more successful than the first, and he sank into poverty, albeit of a genteel sort.

As he had before, Johnston escaped a desperate personal situation by heading to a place where war—and thus financial opportunity for a soldier—seemed imminent. This time a conflict was taking shape between the United States, which had annexed the Lone Star Republic, and Mexico, which continued to claim Texas and attacked American troops north of the Rio Grande in April 1846. Failing to obtain a commission in the Regular U.S. Army, Johnston secured election as colonel of the 1st Texas Infantry, which marched into northern Mexico with the army of future U.S. president Zachary Taylor. Unfortunately, Johnston's troops had enlisted for only six months, and when Taylor told them he did not care whether or not they went home, they did so, leaving their colonel without a command. Taylor, however, saved Johnston by making him a staff officer in one of his divisions. Johnston served with conspicuous valor in the storming of the Mexican stronghold of Monterrey (September 20–25, 1846), during which his quick thinking saved his life and that of Jefferson Davis, then the colonel of a Mississippi regiment.

Johnston's own term of service expired soon after the fall of Monterrey. Still without a command, he left Mexico and returned to his plantation and his futile struggle against poverty. In the fall of 1849 he sold his holdings for a mere $2,000. He was now approaching fifty, and his attempts to acquire wealth had failed.

Again Zachary Taylor, whose victories in Mexico had won him the presidency in 1848, came to his aid. Learning of Johnston's plight from friends, he appointed his erstwhile staffer as army paymaster for western Texas, with the rank of major. It was a grueling job—every two months Johnston had to travel 720 miles through rugged and sometimes dangerous country—but it provided Johnston financial security and, more important, put him in position to benefit unexpectedly from his longtime friendship with Jefferson Davis.

In 1854 Davis, now secretary of war in President Franklin Pierce's cabinet, made Johnston a colonel and gave him command of the newly authorized 2nd Cavalry Regiment, an elite outfit with Robert E. Lee as lieutenant colonel, George H. Thomas and William J. Hardee as majors, and numerous other officers destined to become prominent generals during the Civil War.

For the next four years, Johnston served in Texas, for a while acting as department commander. Then, in 1858, the War Department placed him in charge of a 2,000-troop expedition across the Great Plains and the Rocky Mountains to Utah to establish government authority over recalcitrant Mormon settlers. It was an impossible mission—the Mormon Church held the real power in the territory and nothing short of total military rule could have changed that fact—yet Johnston displayed such resourcefulness, tact, and good judgment that he greatly enhanced his reputation and was appointed brevet brigadier general.

In late 1860, after returning from Utah and enjoying a much-deserved leave of absence, Johnston received his next assignment: Command of the Department of the Pacific, which comprised California and Oregon. Accompanied by his family, he traveled via steamship to San Francisco, arriving in January 1861. If all went well, there was a good chance that his next post would be in Washington, D.C. Winfield Scott soon would be seventy-five years old and was in failing health; some were saying he had recommended Johnston as the officer best qualified to succeed him as the army's commanding general.

But all did not go well. In the election of 1860, the almost solid electoral vote of the North elected Republican Abraham Lincoln president on a platform that called for the eventual extinction of slavery by prohibiting its expansion. In response, seven states of the lower South—Johnston's self-professed home state of Texas among them—seceded from the Union and established the Confederate States of America. Johnston knew immediately what he would do. Believing in the right to own slaves and in the right of secession, he resigned from the U.S. Army on April 9, 1861.

Two months and one week later, Johnston set out with a party of like-minded Southerners from Los Angeles across the deserts of California, Arizona, and New Mexico for Texas, leaving his family to follow by ship as soon as his pregnant wife could travel. Despite hostile Indians and efforts by Federal troops to intercept the party, Johnston and his companions made the 800-mile journey without mishap, reaching the Rio Grande on July 27. From Texas he journeyed by stagecoach and train to Richmond, Virginia, the Confederacy's capital. He arrived in early September and at once visited the Confederate White House, where his old friend Jefferson Davis, now the president of the Confederacy, had taken up residence. "That is Sidney Johnston's step!" exclaimed Davis, rising from an upstairs bed in which he had been lying ill. "Bring him up!"

Davis had already named Johnston a full general with a commission dated so he ranked first among all Confederate field commanders. "I hoped and expected that I had others who would prove to be generals," Davis had explained, "but I knew I had one, and that was Sidney Johnston." When Johnston left Richmond several days later, he held the largest and in many respects the most important command in the Confederacy: "Department No. 2," which comprised Tennessee, northern Alabama, Mississippi, Louisiana, all of the Indian Territory and, as soon as they seceded or could be occupied, Missouri and Kentucky.

Johnston assumed his command on September 14 in Nashville, where he told a cheering crowd that this was a people's war and could be sustained only by the people. The crowd cheered all the more, impressed by Johnston's words and by his powerful appearance. Standing six feet one inch tall, weighing a well-proportioned 200 pounds, and with dark hair and mustache that belied his fifty-nine years, no one, not even Robert E. Lee, appeared more appropriately cast in the role of military leader It was now up to Johnston to demonstrate the substance beneath his exterior.

Johnston faced two interrelated missions: to defend the western Confederacy's northern frontier against invasion, and to secure control of neutral Kentucky and Missouri. If Johnston could achieve this last goal, the South would not only be safe from invasion but also be in a position to invade the North, if the Union were to persist in what would then be an unwinnable war against the South.

Three major obstacles stood between Johnston and his goals. First, the vast majority of Kentuckians and Missourians, including many slave owners, either remained loyal to the Union or refrained from actively supporting the Confederacy. Second, the Federal forces in Kentucky and Missouri had an ever-increasing manpower advantage and the naval capability to penetrate the Southern heartland via the Mississippi, Tennessee, and Cumberland Rivers. Third, Johnston had only about 40,000 poorly equipped and ill-trained troops spread along a 500-mile front, with little hope of substantial reinforcement in the near future. Davis had given him high rank and great responsibility, but not the appropriate military strength, which the president reserved for territories he deemed more critical to Confederate survival.

Johnston did what he could with what he had. Being too weak to take the offensive, he established a defensive cordon, posting a small army near Cumberland Gap and a larger one at Bowling Green, Kentucky, and manning forts along the Cumberland, Tennessee, and Mississippi Rivers. These armies and forts covered the only practical Federal invasion routes between the Appalachian Mountains and the Mississippi. As for the west side of the Mississippi, all Johnston could do was hope that Missouri's Confederates would hold their positions until reinforcements arrived from Arkansas under Major General Earl Van Dorn, who went to the state with instructions to help liberate Missouri from Unionist domination.

Throughout the remainder of 1861, Johnston's line held, mainly because the Federals believed they were outnumbered. Then, early in 1862, the line crumbled. Union brigadier general George H. Thomas routed the Confederates defending Cumberland Gap at the Battle of Mill Springs, Kentucky, on January 19. Next, on February 6, Union gunboats bombarded Fort Henry on the Tennessee into submission, enabling General Grant's army to occupy it without firing a shot. Finally–and this was the crowning calamity—ten days later, Grant took Fort Donelson on the Cumberland and with it 12,000 prisoners.

These defeats left Johnston no choice but to salvage what was left of his army by withdrawing from Kentucky and relinquishing middle Tennessee. The Federals now could, and did, advance south via the Tennessee River toward northern Mississippi, and southeast via the Cumberland River to Nashville, which they occupied on February 25. Grant was not the only Northerner who thought the whole Confederacy would soon collapse and the war would soon end.

Many Southerners angrily denounced Johnston as incompetent and clamored for his removal. Their reaction is understandable, but, on the whole, unjustified. Johnston simply lacked the means to maintain his defensive line once the Federals mustered the will and the power to break it. To complicate his already difficult situation, he was ill-served by subordinates who were the wrong men in the wrong place at the wrong time. The generals charged with guarding Cumberland Gap, the half-blind brigadier general Felix Zollicoffer and the often blind-drunk major general George Crittenden, had ignored Johnston's warning to stay south of the Cumberland, thereby enabling Thomas to smash their forces north of the river at Mill Springs. Likewise, Johnston's chief of engineers, Lieutenant Colonel Jeremy Gilmer, who had orders to construct a bastion on the Tennessee that would be stronger and better located than Fort Henry, decided on his own that there was no danger of the Yankees advancing before spring, so he did nothing. Last and worst, the commander at Fort Donelson, Brigadier General John B. Floyd, who had instructions to save his garrison if he could not hold the fort, did neither and lost both.

Johnston had made his own mistakes. He should have given Crittenden and Zollicoffer orders, not merely advice, and he should have checked to ensure Gilmer was following orders. He devoted too much of his attention and limited resources to defending the Mississippi and central Kentucky rather than the actual keys to the integrity of his line: the Tennessee and Cumberland Rivers. Finally, once Fort Henry fell he should have evacuated Fort Donelson as no longer tenable; if he decided to take a stand there to delay the Federal advance on Nashville, he should have taken charge of the fort's defense personally instead of entrusting it to a general already renowned for poltroonery. Nevertheless, Johnston should not be blamed too much for failing to do what would have been difficult under the best circumstances and, under the actual circumstances, was nearly impossible.

Johnston himself offered no excuses. He accepted full responsibility for what had happened. "The test of merit in my profession with the people is success," he wrote to a friend. "It is a hard rule but I think it right." Thus the only way to redeem failure was with success, and this he resolved to do. So, too, did Davis, who rebuffed assertions that Johnston was "no general" and should be dismissed. If Johnston was not a general, Davis retorted, "we had better give up the war, for we have no generals."

In late March 1862, Johnston concentrated his remaining forces at Corinth, Mississippi, where heavy reinforcements sent by Davis from Louisiana and Florida joined him. He also ordered Van Dorn's army of some 15,000 men from Arkansas, where its attempt to invade Missouri had ended in defeat at the Battle of Pea Ridge on March 6 and 7. Davis sanctioned this move even though it meant abandoning the upper portion of the Confederate Trans-Mississippi region to Federal control.

By April 1, Johnston had assembled almost 40,000 troops at Corinth. Organized in three corps, they were under the command of Major Generals Leonidas Polk, Braxton Bragg, and William J. Hardee. There was also a reserve corps under Brigadier General John C. Breckinridge. Although Van Dorn was still in transit–delayed by inadequate transport–Johnston decided to launch an immediate counteroffensive with the goal of demolishing Grant's 40,000-strong army near Pittsburg Landing, Tennessee, on the Tennessee River. Johnston wanted to crush Grant's force before it could be bolstered by Major General Don Carlos Buell's 35,000 Federals, who were moving down from Nashville. Accordingly, on the night of April 2, he ordered his army to set out at daylight for Pittsburg Landing, where it was to attack Grant by surprise on the morning of April 4.

Plotted on a map, these movements seemed easy enough. Only twenty miles separated Corinth from Pittsburg Landing, and two roads connected them. Yet at this stage of the war, armies were so inexperienced at marching that the Confederates did not arrive within striking distance of Grant until the evening of April 5. Worse, some advance elements clashed with outlying Federal units, and after a heavy rain, many of the Rebel soldiers fired their muskets, against orders, to test whether they still worked.

Johnston gathered his commanders for a council of war late in the afternoon of April 5. Considering the delays in reaching Pittsburg Landing and the inadvertent announcement, by gunfire, of their arrival, it seemed unlikely the Rebels still had the element of surprise. Johnston's second in command, General Beauregard, urged him to cancel the attack and return to Corinth. Johnston, however, was ready for battle. "I would fight them if they were a million," he told a staff officer.

At daybreak on Sunday, April 6, the Confederates began advancing. They did so in three waves: Hardee's corps first, then Bragg's, and then Polk's and Breckinridge's. The deployment, Beauregard's idea, weakened the corps' offensive power, narrowing the attack's fronts and ultimately mixing the units into a confused hodgepodge. Johnston probably approved the plan just to avoid further delays.

By all normal criteria, Beauregard should have been right: The Federals should have been waiting for the Rebels, ready to fight. But they were not. Grant was so preoccupied with combining Buell's army with his own and advancing to Corinth to crush Johnston that it never occurred to him Johnston might advance from Corinth to crush *him*. As for Brigadier General William T. Sherman, who commanded the division in the front of Grant's force when he was Union commander in Kentucky in the fall of 1861, he was so sure that Johnston was about to descend on him with overwhelming force that he suffered a nervous breakdown and was relieved from command. Now, eager to redeem himself, he went to the opposite extreme, dismissing out of hand all reports from his troops that they had seen and even engaged large bodies of aggressive Rebels near their camps.

Thanks to Grant and Sherman, Johnston's assault managed to come as a surprise. Moreover, the Federals were far from being "entrenched to their eyes," as Beauregard had put it. In fact, they had no fortifications of any kind or, for that matter, any coherent front. They could be and were assailed in the open and in detail. It was little wonder that thousands of them fled in panic and that those who kept fighting found it necessary to continue falling back before what seemed to be enormous enemy hordes. Grant thought the Confederates numbered 100,000.

Johnston, astride a magnificent horse named Fire-eater, followed close behind his battle line. Riding through a Union camp, he came upon some stragglers searching the area for loot and shamed them back into the fight by picking up a tin cup and remarking, "Let this be my share of the spoils today." Normally, an army commander would have remained toward the rear, in a position to direct the movements of his forces as a whole. But Johnston had Beauregard to maneuver units, and so he probably believed that he could best contribute to victory by being up front with his soldiers, most of whom were fighting in their first battle. Perhaps, too, he remembered the recent failures of his subordinates to execute orders and thought his presence might correct the problem.

By midday the Confederates had driven to within a few hundred yards of Pittsburg Landing, and it seemed that Johnston and his staff indeed would be able to water their horses in the Tennessee River. The largest obstacle in their path came in the form of three badly battered, but still fighting, divisions on the Union left. Perceiving this, Johnston ordered Breckinridge's reserves to attack the Yankees in front, and Bragg to strike their flank. Charge followed charge, only to be repulsed each time by so devastating a fire that Confederates dubbed this Federal stronghold the "Hornets' Nest." Breckinridge noticed a Tennessee regiment holding back while he prepared another assault and called its conduct to Johnston's attention. Johnston replied that he would send Tennessee governor Isham B. Harris, who was serving as one of his aides, to rally the regiment. Breckinridge said he doubted that would suffice. "Then," said Johnston, "I will help you."

Riding to the front of the unit, he urged the troops to use their bayonets, shouting, "I will lead you!" So inspired, the Rebels rushed forward and won their objective. Johnston turned about and headed rearward, his horse bearing the marks of two bullets and the sole of his left boot having been ripped by another. "Governor," he said to Harris, pointing to the boot, "they came very near putting me *hors de combat* in that charge."

Hardly had Johnston spoken these words when an enemy battery opened a galling enfilade. At once he sent Harris to order a regiment to charge the battery. On returning from his mission, Harris saw Johnston sway in his saddle.

"General are you wounded?" he cried. "Yes, and I fear seriously." Harris placed an arm around Johnston and escorted him to a sheltering ravine, where he and another staff officer lifted the general from his horse and laid him on the ground. Although he noticed blood staining the right knee of Johnston's trousers, Harris assumed the general had been struck in the body, so he frantically examined Johnston's torso, but found no serious injury.

He then gave Johnston a swallow of brandy, but to no avail. Johnston soon lost consciousness. When another staff officer tried to revive him by pouring whiskey down his throat, the liquid merely trickled down his chin. The officer placed a hand on Johnston's chest. The heart beat no longer.

On learning of Johnston's death, Beauregard took command and the fighting continued. Late in the afternoon the Confederates finally overpowered the "Hornets' Nest," taking a large number of prisoners. Even so, Grant held on at Pittsburg Landing until night, when one of his divisions that had been stationed downriver joined him with 5,000 men, and Buell arrived with 20,000 reinforcements.

In the morning Grant took the offensive, slowly but surely pushing back the now heavily outnumbered Confederates. At 2:00 P.M., reluctantly realizing that his army was in danger of destruction, Beauregard ordered it to disengage and march back to Corinth. Thus ended what most historians name the Battle of Shiloh. With it ended Johnston's attempt to regain middle Tennessee and issue a fresh challenge to Union control of Kentucky.

An autopsy revealed Johnston had bled to death. While leading the Tennesseeans' charge, a .577-caliber minié ball fired from a British-made Enfield rifle had struck the back of his right calf just below the knee and punctured an artery. Given the angle of entry it is conceivable that it was fired by one of Johnston's own men, some of whom were deployed behind him, to his right. Many of them carried Enfields, which were rare among the Federals at this point in the war, especially in the Western Theater.

If Johnston had realized the nature of his wound, he easily could have stopped the bleeding with the tourniquet he carried in his pocket. And had he not left his personal physician behind to tend to Union casualties, he would have been attended by a doctor, who would have found the wound and stopped the bleeding. In short, Johnston should not have died, yet he did, becoming the highest-ranking general killed during the entire Civil War. Only later would the South realize that any chance of Confederate victory in the West had died with him.

The thought of General Albert Sidney Johnston lying dead on the ground at Pittsburg Landing, Tennessee, with a wound no worse than a bullet hole in his leg, raises an immediate question: Shouldn't Johnston have survived the Battle of Shiloh? Considering that he was not alone and was carrying a tourniquet in his pocket, the simple answer is yes.

So much for the apparently simple. Johnston's death also raises some more complex questions. First, if Johnston had remained in command at Shiloh instead of dying as the fighting approached its climax, would he have won the battle and altered the course of the Civil War in the Western Theater? Second, regardless of the battle's outcome, had he lived, could he have given the Confederate forces in the West what they lacked for the rest of the war—a great commander, the equivalent of General Robert E. Lee in the East? None of Johnston's successors—Pierre G. T. Beauregard, Braxton Bragg, Joseph E. Johnston, or John Bell Hood—proved capable of what Lee so brilliantly did: Hold, and often more than hold, against the Yankee invaders.

Most historians agree that the South lost the war, and the North won it, in the West. So, essentially our two questions about Johnston boil down to one big one: Might the South have won the war if Albert Sidney Johnston had lived?

Fact and logic suggest the answer to the first question is no. By the evening of April 6, 1862, after the first of the battle's two days, the Confederate army had lost nearly a quarter of its men. At least another quarter had dropped from the ranks out of exhaustion or demoralization, or to plunder the captured Yankee camps. Most of the remaining units were too weak, weary, disorganized, and scattered to continue fighting effectively, if at all. In short, Johnston's Rebels were physically incapable of destroying or defeating Major General Ulysses S. Grant's Federal force.

This was demonstrated by the assaults General P. G. T. Beauregard mounted after he took over Johnston's command. After an initial success in capturing the "Hornets' Nest," Beauregard could muster only a few feeble and fragmented attacks. Those efforts were easily repulsed by Federals gathered in a compact defense line around Pittsburg Landing and supported by gunboats and a massive artillery concentration. When darkness came, Beauregard correctly decided he had achieved everything possible that day and suspended further offensive action until morning.

By pausing for the night, Beauregard believed he was merely postponing Confederate victory. During the afternoon of April 6, two contradictory reports had arrived regarding Major General Don Carlos Buell's 35,000 Federals, who were on the way from Nashville to reinforce Grant. One report had them bound for Decatur, Alabama, not Pittsburg Landing. The other stated they were marching toward the landing but would not reach it until April 8. Either way, it seemed to Beauregard and the other ranking Confederate generals that Grant would be finished off on April 7, long before Buell's arrival. The Confederate generals were so confident in their assessment that they laughed at statements from Federal prisoners (among them a division commander) that Buell would join Grant during the night.

Conceivably, had Johnston remained in command—something he could not have done even if he had survived the wound that killed him—he might have provided the will and found the means to defeat the Union forces on April 6. In all likelihood, however, he would have done essentially the same as Beauregard did, for the same reasons, and with the same outcome. To contend otherwise, as some of his advocates do, is to credit him with powers of leadership bordering on the incredible and to claim he would have achieved what no other commander, Union or Confederate, achieved during the whole Civil War: Total battlefield victory over a major, still potent enemy army.

Last, but perhaps most important of all, even if Johnston had managed to smash Grant's army before Buell's arrival, his own army would have been too depleted, exhausted, and disorganized to follow up its triumph by defeating Buell. The effects of battle would have made Johnston's force numerically inferior to Buell's fresh 35,000-man force, which could easily have grown to twice that size by adding Union reinforcements from western Tennessee and along the Mississippi River. Johnston could not have resumed offensive operations before uniting with Major General Earl Van Dorn's army of some 15,000 men, and that could not have happened until the end of April. By then the odds against Johnston's success would have been nearly insurmountable. Probably the most a Confederate victory at Shiloh would have accomplished was to put the Federals on the defensive, boost Southern morale, and terminate Grant's military career—which might have been accomplishment enough.

The answer to the second question raised by Johnston's death—whether Johnston could have been for the Confederate West what Lee was in the East—is more promising than the first. Johnston possessed many of the same attributes that made Lee a great commander: Aggressiveness, willingness to take great risks, resolution and persistence in overcoming obstacles, composure and decisiveness when faced with a crisis, and an intellect and personal character that inspired trust, even devotion, in others. Given the opportunity to gain more battlefield experience—something that all the top Civil War generals, Lee included, required before they mastered their trade—Johnston might very well have developed into a military leader superior to any of his successors in the West. He also held an important personal advantage over two of those generals, Beauregard and Joseph Johnston: the confidence of Confederate president Jefferson Davis.

But whether Albert Sidney Johnston could have equaled Lee's performance is another matter. Johnston had a much larger and more vulnerable area to defend than did Lee, and he had fewer men and resources. His opponents would have been the likes of Grant, George H. Thomas, William S. Rosecrans, and William T. Sherman. Lee, on the other hand, until 1864 when he took on Grant, had the good fortune to oppose the likes of George B. McClellan, John Pope, Ambrose Burnside, Joseph Hooker, and George Meade (an excellent defensive fighter, as he proved at Gettysburg, but incapable of defeating Lee offensively, as he demonstrated after Gettysburg).

Finally, unlike Lee, Johnston lacked the support of outstanding lieutenants such as Thomas J. "Stonewall" Jackson, James Longstreet, and J. E. B. Stuart. Instead, his chief subordinates were the solid but uninspired William J. Hardee, the brave but bumbling Leonidas Polk, and the militarily able but personally despicable Braxton Bragg.

Johnston could, conceivably, have prevailed in spite of these handicaps, but probably the most he could have done was prolong effective Confederate resistance in the West by avoiding the blunders and consequent disasters of his successors. This may not seem like much, but it might have been enough. After all, in 1864 the South, despite its defeats in the West, came close to winning the war by causing the North to lose the will to continue fighting. It is possible, therefore, that the South, with fewer and less devastating defeats in the West, might have won the war.

Of course, we cannot know, but only speculate about, what the story of the Civil War would have been had Albert Sidney Johnston not bled to death in a ravine near the Tennessee River. For that reason, he will forever remain the Confederacy's "General Who Might Have Been."

CHAPTER TEN

Death Comes to the Bishop: When Luck Ran Out for Leonidas Polk

Judged by objective standards, Confederate general Leonidas Polk was a loser. With one exception, every major battle in which he participated—all of them as a corps commander in the Confederate Army of Tennessee—ended in defeat or retreat, and in most of these encounters he contributed significantly if not decisively to these negative outcomes. And in the exception, the Battle of Chickamauga (September 19–20, 1863), the Army of Tennessee won in spite of his actions rather than because of them, which as usual was not what he had been ordered to do. Small wonder that during the Atlanta Campaign, a Rebel officer, on learning that Polk was in a precarious position, commented that "some people are always having trouble."

But by a subjective criterion—his own—Polk was a winner during the first three years of the Civil War. When that conflict began he was an Episcopal bishop and had not seen any military service since resigning from the U.S. Army not long after graduating from West Point in 1827. Nevertheless, his West Point friend, Confederate president Jefferson Davis, appointed him a major general in June 1861 and promoted him to lieutenant general a year later, despite Polk's record of egregious blunders that would have resulted in anyone else being permanently shelved for incorrigible incompetence. Not until Polk's dismal nonperformance at Chickamauga did Davis, most reluctantly, agree to transfer the "bishop-general" out of the Army of Tennessee. Even then his luck held. Placed in charge of the Department of Mississippi, he thus avoided involvement in the Confederate fiasco at the Battle of Chattanooga (November 23–25, 1863), and in May 1864 he returned to the Army of Tennessee as again a corps commander.

Then, though, his luck ran out—and in a very drastic fashion. How that happened is the story told in the ensuing article, which appeared in the Summer 1998 issue of Columbiad: A Quarterly Review of the War between the States *under the title of "Who Killed the Bishop?" The cessation of publication of this scholarly journal in early 2000 left its loyal readers wondering "Who killed* Columbiad?*"*

CONFEDERATE GENERALS SUFFERED FROM A SERIOUS, ONE MIGHT SAY fatal, fault—they tended to get killed. It is not necessary to list the seventy-three brigadier and major generals who died as a result of combat or the two who were slain in duels and the one who was killed by an outraged husband. It will suffice to consider only those who held loftier ranks. At the highest level of command, one full general and three lieutenant generals of the Confederacy left this world because they happened to be at the wrong place at the wrong time.

The full general, of course, was Albert Sidney Johnston. He bled to death at Shiloh on April 6, 1862, after a bullet, possibly fired by one of his own soldiers, severed an artery in his right leg. Johnston died before he or his aides realized that he had suffered a serious wound. Then and since, some have believed that had he remained in command, the Confederates might have achieved victory at Shiloh and won the war.

The most famous general to die from a battlefield wound was Lieutenant General Thomas J. "Stonewall" Jackson. In his case there is no doubt that he fell victim to bullets fired by his own troops who, in the night-gloom of the forests around Chancellorsville, mistook him and his staff for enemy cavalry. Even more ironically, although his left arm had to be amputated, it seemed he would live to attain still more victories and still greater glory; instead, pneumonia assailed his weakened body and he died. With his death Confederate general Robert E. Lee lost his right arm, and the South, so it has been argued, lost the war.

Chronologically, the last Confederate lieutenant general to fall in battle was Ambrose Powell Hill, shot as he tried to rally his beleaguered corps outside of Petersburg, Virginia, on April 2, 1865. His death made no difference to the outcome of the war. Long before it occurred, the South was defeated and Hill knew it. So, like the other soldiers of the Army of Northern Virginia, he fought on not in the hope of victory but out of a desire to preserve honor in defeat. This he achieved, as did they.

At Chancellorsville, the star of the Confederacy glowed its brightest. At Petersburg it no longer shined. On the morning of June 14, 1864, when Lieutenant General Leonidas Polk rode up to the top of Pine Mountain near Marietta, Georgia, that star still flickered. Polk accompanied General Joseph E. Johnston, commander of the Confederate Army of Tennessee opposing Union major general William Tecumseh Sherman's legions as they pushed toward Atlanta, and Lieutenant General William J. Hardee, like Polk a corps commander. One of Hardee's divisions defended Pine Mountain, and Johnston wished to determine whether or not it should remain or withdraw. If the latter, Polk needed to know ahead of time, for his corps held the sector to the right of Hardee's.

In a pocket of his uniform coat Polk carried something not usually found on generals of whatever rank: four copies of a religious tract. The tract, *Balm for the Weary and Wounded,* was written by Father John T. Quintard, rector of St. Luke's Episcopal Church in Atlanta and chaplain-at-large to the Army of Tennessee. Polk carried the copies because in addition to being a general, he was the missionary bishop of the Episcopal Diocese of the Southwest. Like Johnston and Hardee, Polk was a graduate of West Point (class of 1827). Unlike them, he had resigned his commission shortly after receiving it to become a priest. Thanks to influential family connections, an imposing physical presence, and high administrative abilities, he rose rapidly to bishop. Bishop Polk planted thriving Episcopal churches in a region hitherto virtually monopolized by Catholics and Calvinists, and took the lead in establishing the University of the South at Sewanee, in his home state of Tennessee.

But before the university could open its doors, secession and war came. Polk offered his services to Confederate president Jefferson Davis, whom he had known at West Point. When Davis asked him to come to Richmond, he went, and returned to Tennessee as a major general in command of the Mississippi Valley. Until his good friend General Albert Sidney Johnston could arrive from California, where he had been stationed at the outbreak of the war, Davis wanted someone to take charge of Confederate forces in the West and Polk was his choice. What the bishop lacked in practical military experience he would make up for in zeal and character.

Polk possessed ample zeal. Unfortunately, he was deficient in qualities of greater importance to a general. Accustomed as a bishop to giving orders, he disliked taking them, and consequently he would alter or ignore them if he believed he knew better. He was popular with his troops, who always fought well, but he often managed them poorly on the battlefield. His strategic judgment was no better than his tactical ability; while in command of the Mississippi Valley he committed blunders that cost the Confederacy dearly. Later, as a corps commander under Albert Sidney Johnston and General Braxton Bragg, he ruined several critical opportunities for victory by attacking when he should have defended and by moving too late, or to the wrong place, or not at all.

His character, although admirable in many respects, likewise suffered from some serious flaws, the prime ones being an inability to admit his own

John B. Lindsey, ed. *The Military Annals of Tennessee*. Nashville, 1886.

Leonidas Polk

mistakes and a knack for shifting blame for his failures to others. Thanks to that knack and to Davis's steadfast friendship, in the fall of 1862 he obtained promotion to lieutenant general despite what at best was a lackluster record. With skills honed in church politics, the bishop may have surpassed every other general in the Confederate army as a politician.

Because of Bragg's criticism of Polk's performance in the Kentucky Campaign (September–October 1862) and at the Battle of Murfreesboro (December 31, 1862–January 2, 1863), the main target of the bishop's blame-shifting during most of 1862 and 1863 was Braxton Bragg. Bragg was then the Army of Tennessee's commander and Polk's commanding officer. Polk bitterly resented Bragg's critical appraisal of his performance, and he countered it by charging Bragg with incompetence and seeking both within the army and outside of it to secure Bragg's removal from command. He was by no means alone in his low opinion of Bragg, and to a high degree it was justified. Nevertheless, his intrigues against Bragg fostered dissension and distrust in the Army of Tennessee's high command, thereby making a bad situation far worse.

Bragg, understandably, would have liked to rid himself of the bishop but was not in a position to do so until after the Battle of Chickamauga

(September 19–20, 1863). Declaring, with considerable accuracy, that Polk's failure to attack when ordered had cost the Confederates a complete victory, Bragg relieved him while at the same time offering to resign. In effect, he forced President Davis to choose between Polk and himself. Reluctantly, Davis transferred Polk to General Joseph B. Johnston's army in Alabama and Mississippi. Since that region was of little strategic importance after the fall of Vicksburg, except as a source of supplies, it seemed that the bishop had been placed on the military shelf.

Instead, his new post proved to be a blessing in disguise. Bragg's devastating defeat in November at Missionary Ridge compelled him to step down as commander of the Army of Tennessee. To replace him, Davis—with many misgivings—named Joseph Johnston. This left Polk in command of the Army of Mississippi. Then in May 1864 Sherman launched his invasion of Georgia, whereupon Davis instructed Polk to reinforce Johnston, an order that he obeyed, for a change, with exemplary promptitude. Eight months after leaving, Polk was back with the Army of Tennessee as its senior lieutenant general.

Polk's main contribution to the Confederate military effort in Georgia was the nearly 20,000 troops he brought with him from Alabama and Mississippi. Without them Johnston would have been so heavily outnumbered he would have retreated faster than he did and Sherman would have taken Atlanta much sooner. Otherwise, during the 1864 campaign, Polk did nothing particularly good or especially bad. As a rule, Johnston placed his corps in the center while assigning Hardee's and Lieutenant General John Bell Hood's corps to the more vulnerable flanks. Obviously, Johnston did not have a high opinion of Polk as a general.

Johnston did, however, respect him as a bishop. On the evening of May 17, 1864, at Polk's behest, supported with a letter from Johnston's wife asking Polk to "lead my soldier nearer to God," Johnston asked for and received baptism from the bishop, who six nights previously had performed the same rite for Hood. Polk perceived no contradiction and experienced no conflict between serving Mars and being a man of God. On the contrary, he combined the two roles, both symbolically and literally, by wearing his clerical regalia over his army uniform to preach to his troops on Sundays and by mingling discussions of strategy with discussions on theology when conversing with his staff and fellow generals.

That is why he carried the four copies of Quintard's tract when he rode up to the top of Pine Mountain with Johnston and Hardee. Once the military problem of whether to stay at Pine Mountain or retreat had been settled, Polk intended to present his fellow generals with an inscribed copy of the tract. Of the remaining two copies, one was for Hood and the other he would keep for himself.

Upon reaching the crest of Pine Mountain, which is only 300 feet high, the three generals dismounted and entered a log and dirt bastion containing the South Carolina battery of Lieutenant René T. Beauregard, son of Confederate general Pierre Gustave Toutant Beauregard. Standing atop the parapet, Colonel William S. Dilworth, acting commander of Findley's Florida Brigade, pointed out to Johnston, Hardee, and Polk the Federal works and batteries in the valley below. Then, noticing that the generals' staffs also had collected in the bastion, Dilworth asked them to retire to the rear. Such "a large crowd," he explained, was "sure to attract the fire of the enemy"—the previous day a cannon shot had barely missed Major General Patrick Cleburne while he was visiting the mountain. The staff officers thereupon moved back, but Johnston, Hardee, and Polk remained.

Dilworth again turned his gaze toward the Union lines. As he did so, he saw a puff of white smoke billow forth from a cannon to the north of the mountain. At once he jumped down from the parapet, and a moment later a solid shot shrieked overhead. The Yankees, obviously, had noticed the gathering on the mountain. This was no place for Johnston and two of his top lieutenants. They must, Dilworth told them, take cover on the reverse side of the mountain.

None of them moved. For Civil War generals, Northern and Southern alike, it was more than a point of honor, it was a matter of necessity never to show fear under fire. By doing so they would lose the respect of their soldiers and with it their ability to lead them in battle with maximum effectiveness.

Now frantic, Dilworth insisted that the generals at least separate. This they did. Johnston strolled off to the left and Hardee to the right, accompanied by Dilworth at his side and Polk behind him. Then a second projectile came screaming in, quickly followed by a third. Dilworth stopped, looked back, but could not see Polk. Suddenly a yell went up from the men in the bastion: "General Polk is killed!"

Hardee and Johnston started back to where Polk had been standing. Dilworth grabbed Hardee by the arm and pleaded with both generals not to further expose themselves to the Yankee shells, which now began falling in salvos. Besides, they could do nothing to help Polk. Finally Dilworth prevailed, and Johnston and Hardee went to Dilworth's tent on the back side of the mountain, where they waited for the arrival of Polk's body.

After a while litter bearers brought the corpse to the tent. All present gasped with horror on beholding it. A 3-inch solid shot, probably the second fired by the Federals, had struck Polk in the left side and passed through his chest, mangling both arms and ripping away his lungs and heart. So died—instantly and mercifully—the bishop.

Union sources assert that Polk was killed by a fragment of an exploding shell, but for obvious reasons this can be only an assumption. Dilworth, who was in the best position to know the facts, stated in an account of Polk's death published soon afterward in an Atlanta newspaper that the fatal projectile was a solid shot—a statement that would seem to be confirmed by the nature of Polk's injuries and also by General Johnston, who in a postwar conversation with Sherman said that the bishop was struck by an "unexploded shell," which would be the equivalent of a solid shot. No one, evidently, witnessed Polk's death, hence it is impossible to give a definite reason why he was hit in the left side while presumably walking with his right side exposed to enemy fire. There are several possible explanations, however, the most likely one being that Polk had turned, or was in the act of turning, to his left to take a look back when the fatal shot ripped into his chest.

Who killed him? Who issued the order that caused some Union gun crew to fire a missile that tore apart an Episcopal bishop and Confederate general named Leonidas Polk?

One answer appears in Lloyd Lewis's 1932 biography, *Sherman: Fighting Prophet*. Lewis asserts that the fatal projectile came from a battery commanded by Captain Hubert Dilger, a former Prussian artillery officer whom Union troops called "Leatherbreeches" because he wore doeskin pants. None of the sources cited in Lewis's sketchy notes, however, actually supports this assertion with eyewitness testimony. And even if one or more accounts did purport that one of Dilger's guns fired the deadly shot, Lewis's account would have to be rejected for two conclusive reasons. First, it is contradicted, as we shall see, by other much more authoritative accounts; and second, Dilger's battery belonged to the 1st Division of the Union XIV Corps, which on June 14 operated to the northeast of Pine Mountain and was not in position to fire the shot that killed Polk. Eyewitness Confederate testimony states that the shot that killed Polk came from a Federal battery located due north of the mountain.

If one were to believe Brigadier General Walter Gresham, commander of a division in the Union XVII Corps, the actual slayer of Polk was another Northern artillery officer, Captain Edward Spear Jr. In a letter to his wife on June 21, 1864, Gresham wrote: "Others claim the honor but there is no doubt about Spear's guns doing the work [;] for prisoners that we captured the day of the charge pointed out to me just where Polk was killed which [was] immediately in my old front—Genl [James B.] McPherson & Genl Sherman both say my Dro [Detachment of Regulars] has the honor of killing the rebel Bishop & General."

Gresham, however, was badly misinformed and perhaps also deliberately lying in order to impress his wife and the people back home. This was not an uncommon practice among politically ambitious Civil War generals such as Gresham, who ultimately became postmaster general, secretary of state, and an unsuccessful presidential aspirant. On June 14, Gresham's division occupied the extreme left of the Union line, which meant that it was to the northeast of Brush Mountain, the position held by Polk's troops. The distance from the peak of Brush Mountain to the crest of Pine Mountain is about four miles, and in 1864 the intervening countryside was densely wooded. In all likelihood Captain Spear could not have seen any Confederates atop Pine Mountain. Even if he could, he would not have fired so much as a single shot at them, because none of the cannons in Sherman's army possessed a range longer than 1,900 yards (slightly more than a mile). This included the pieces in Spear's batteries, all of which were considered light artillery. Had Spear tried to bombard Pine Mountain, his projectiles would have fallen nearly three miles short of their intended target.

It should also be noted that Gresham's official report on the Atlanta Campaign makes no reference to Spear's guns killing Polk. It merely states that his division skirmished with the Confederates on Brush Mountain until the Rebels evacuated it on June 19, whereupon the Federal troops occupied the position.

Another Federal general who claimed the dubious distinction of killing the bishop was Brigadier General John W. Geary, a division commander in the XX Corps. Describing operations on June 14, when his division was posted to the northwest of Pine Mountain, Geary asserted: "I noticed a group of rebel officers collected near some tents near the summit; calling Captain [James D.] McGill's attention to it, I directed him to bring his battery on the spot. The shells struck in the midst and around the group, causing evident consternation among them and their immediate retreat. Prisoners afterward taken pointed out that as the spot where Lieutenant-General Polk was killed."

Several reasons could be given for rejecting Geary's statement as false, but two will suffice. Like Gresham, Geary was an ambitious political general whose extraordinarily long and elaborate report is filled with exaggerations, prevarication, and self-glorification. His account of how Polk was killed offers a prime example of all three, for it is clear from Confederate testimony that Polk died before any shells began exploding on Pine Mountain.

In subsequent years a soldier in Geary's division, Edmund R. Brown, became so disgusted with various and numerous attempts to garner the credit for having caused Polk's death that he wrote the following in his *The Twenty-Seventh Indiana Volunteer Infantry in the War of the Rebellion,* published in 1899:

> At least a dozen batteries, and more than a hundred gunners, claim the distinction of firing the fatal shot. Infantry regiments innumerable claim it was fired by the battery they were supporting, and probably half the soldiers in Sherman's army claim that they saw it fired. The latter claim would be hard to disprove, as the shot was fired in open day light and the mountain was visible to a large part of the army. The fact, as Sherman states it, is that this shot was one of a hundred or more, fired by several batteries in volleys. So it would be impossible, or almost so, to tell by what battery the shot was fired, much less who sighted the gun.

Brown's indignation is understandable and one can sympathize with it. Nevertheless, his statement is no more accurate than the assertions of Gresham and Geary. As we have seen, the shot that killed Polk was not "one of a hundred or more, fired by several batteries in volleys," and Sherman never said that it was—indeed, quite the contrary. Furthermore, it is not only possible but also easy to discover "by what battery the shot was fired" and even to ascertain the name of the person who "sighted the gun."

One need only consult the readily available memoirs—those of Sherman, Major General Oliver Otis Howard, and Major General David S. Stanley, plus another book that will be named in due course.

On the morning of June 14, Sherman rode to his positions opposite Pine Mountain to determine a way to dislodge the Confederates without directly assaulting that height. First he conferred with Major General George H. Thomas, commander of the Army of the Cumberland, which consisted of the IV, XIV, and XX Corps. Thomas informed him that portions of the IV and XIV Corps had worked their way around to the east side of Pine Mountain. Sherman thereupon directed Thomas to push both corps between that height and Kennesaw Mountain to the south, thus forcing the Confederates to evacuate the former so as to avoid being cut off. This was precisely the move Johnston feared and why he went with Hardee and Polk to examine the situation at Pine Mountain.

Next, Sherman visited the command post of General Howard, most of whose IV Corps faced Pine Mountain from the north. There Sherman noticed a group of Confederates near a battery on the crest of the mountain, only about 600 yards distant, peering at the Union lines through field glasses. "How saucy they are!" he exclaimed. Then, pointing to the group, he told Howard to make them take cover with some cannon shots. Howard answered that he would have done this already, but Thomas had instructed him to employ his artillery only when absolutely necessary so as to conserve ammunition. This, responded Sherman, was good policy as a rule, but "we must keep up the morale of the bold offensive," and hence Howard was to order one of his batteries to fire three volleys at the Confederates on the mountain.

Howard passed the order on to the chief of artillery of Stanley's division, Captain Peter Simonson, who in turn directed the 5th Indiana Battery to fire several shots to establish the range, after which its six cannons would deliver the three volleys.

As previously described, the first shot went high. The second, most likely, struck Polk, and the third evidently slammed into the log and dirt bastion where Johnston, Hardee, and Polk had been standing, for immediately thereafter Simonson's guns began firing shell salvos, as did two other batteries of Stanley's division. McGill's battery of Geary's division also joined in the bombardment, as stated in Geary's report, but contrary to that report it did not do so until after Sherman (according to his memoirs) personally ordered Geary to open fire on the mountain.

So we have the answer to the question, "Who killed the bishop?" In a literal sense, it was the crew of the cannon that fired the fatal missile, which came, according to David D. Holm's *History of the Fifth Indiana Battery* (a book based on the diary of one of the battery's officers), from a 3-inch caliber Rodman rifled cannon sighted by Corporal Frank McCollum.

But the person truly responsible for Polk's death was Sherman. Had Sherman not showed up at Howard's command post at the same time (about 11:00 A.M.) that Johnston, Hardee, Polk, and their staffs arrived on the crest of Pine Mountain, and had Sherman not been so annoyed by the sight of Confederates impudently studying his lines through field glasses without bothering to take cover that he ordered Howard to drive them away, Polk would have lived to die some other day and in some other way.

Sherman was too far away to recognize any of the Confederates on Pine Mountain, and in his memoirs he claims that he did not even know that they were officers. Not until evening, after Union signal corpsmen deciphered Confederate wigwag messages from the mountain asking that an ambulance be sent "for General Polk's body," did Sherman have reason to suspect that the bombardment he had ordered had slain the bishop, a surmise soon confirmed by some captured Confederates.

On the morning of June 15, Stanley's troops occupied Pine Mountain following its evacuation by the Confederates during the night. Near the log and dirt bastion they found a stake to which was attached a note that read, "You damned Yankee sons of bitches has killed our old Gen. Polk." Then, beside a large pool of clotted blood, they beheld a tree on which had been carved, "Gen. Polk killed June 14, 1864." Some of them dipped their handkerchiefs into the blood and also picked up pieces of rib and arm bones as souvenirs.

Today Polk's remains lie, along with those of his wife, beneath the altar floor of Christ Church Cathedral in New Orleans. This is the appropriate place. Bishop, not general, was his true vocation, and his becoming the latter cost him his life. Yet his death was simply a case of bad luck. Had he taken one step less or one stride more when walking away from the bastion atop Pine Mountain, he would have lived.

On the other hand he was fortunate in the timing of his death. It occurred when it still was possible for him to believe that with God's help the South would achieve victory. His death spared him the bitter experience of ultimate Southern defeat and the acrimonious postwar controversies surrounding his role in that defeat. In these ways, at least, Sherman did him a favor when he ordered Howard to have cannon volleys fired at the "saucy" Confederates atop Pine Mountain.

CHAPTER ELEVEN

Jim Lane of Kansas: "King of the Jayhawkers"

James H. Lane, to the extent that he is remembered at all, is known almost only among Civil War historians and by people with an interest in what took place in Kansas and Missouri between 1855 and 1865. In his own day, though, Lane possessed a national fame for his prominent role in the "Bleeding Kansas" troubles of the 1850s and his spectacular activities as "King of the Jayhawkers" during the Civil War. Again and again, thanks to his mastery of the arts of demagoguery, he triumphed over his rivals, even when defeat seemed inevitable. But faced with the prospect of political ruin as a consequence of his personal failings, he literally destroyed himself, thereby rendering, as one contemporary put it, "his own verdict on his life and actions."

This article appeared in the April 1973 issue of Civil War Times Illustrated *and was mainly derived from my* Frontier State at War: Kansas 1861–1865, *first published in 1958 by the Cornell University Press in Ithaca, New York, then in several reprints, with the latest being a paperback containing some revisions and bearing the title of* Civil War Kansas: Reaping the Whirlwind *(Lawrence: University Press of Kansas, 1998).*

LATE ON THE NIGHT OF APRIL 18, 1861, ABRAHAM LINCOLN STOOD AT the entrance to the East Room of the White House and gazed at several score men sprawled on the velvet carpet, stacked rifles nearby. He was glad that they were there, these men. Across the Potomac Rebel flags flaunted defiantly and rumors circulated through Washington that the Virginians were going to attack. If they did, the corporal's guard of Regular troops garrisoning the capital would be overwhelmed—and the North might lose the war before it really began.

So when some fifty Kansans—mostly politicians who had come to Washington office-seeking—volunteered to help defend the city, Lincoln happily accepted their services and posted them in the White House itself.

KANSAS STATE HISTORICAL SOCIETY

James H. Lane

In particular he was grateful to the organizer of these "Frontier Guards," Senator James Henry Lane of Kansas. Henceforth Lane stood high in the president's favor, a circumstance the senator did not hesitate to exploit.

In an era of opportunism, Jim Lane was a supreme opportunist. Among the demagogues of his time—and few periods had more—he was preeminent in energy, persistence, and sheer gall. Moreover, until the very end, and despite occasional setbacks, few were more successful. To describe his stormy career is to offer a study in demagoguery, American Civil War style.

But first the man himself. He looked, said a fellow Kansan, "like nobody else." Lean, almost emaciated in body, he had a narrow, hollow-cheeked face, the "sad, dim eyes of a harlot," tumultuous black hair, and thin lips which could curl in "a Mephistophlean [*sic*] leer." When out in the hustings in Kansas he wore denim overalls, a calfskin vest, and a moth-eaten bearskin overcoat. No one seeing him once was likely to forget him ever—an asset to a politician.

Despite, or perhaps because of, his grotesque appearance, he exercised tremendous personal magnetism. Even enemies—and he had bitter ones—admitted that he had an intriguing personality, "wonderful tact," and a keen mind. Men who knew his faults overlooked them and gave him their support, for as he himself once said, "They have called your humble servant all the hard names they could think of, but a fool—they have never yet called Jim Lane a fool." His quips and catchphrases were repeated throughout Kansas, and countless anecdotes were told about him—many of them unfit for mixed company, by Victorian standards. In his own lifetime he was a folk figure, regarded by Kansas with a certain pride as "one of our things."

Life began for him on June 22, 1814 in Lawrenceburg, Indiana. His father was a Democratic congressman and, although his mother wanted him to be a preacher, he chose to follow the paternal example rather than the maternal wish. By the time he was thirty-two he had sufficient standing to become colonel of a regiment of Indiana volunteers in the Mexican War, during which he performed capably at the Battle of Buena Vista and "captured" Santa Anna's wooden leg. Using his martial exploits as a political springboard, he first won election as lieutenant governor of Indiana, then followed his father to the House of Representatives in Washington.

The Senate seemed next in line. But then he committed a terrible blunder: Along with numerous other midwestern Democrats he voted in 1854 for Stephen A. Douglas's Kansas-Nebraska Bill. In so doing he ignored the fact that it threw open to slavery territory guaranteed to freedom by the Missouri Compromise of 1820. But his constituents, who were fiercely opposed to the spread of the "peculiar institution," did not ignore that fact. So loud and long were their howls of outrage that he did not even try for reelection. Instead he left Indiana and set forth to recoup his political fortune in the very land that caused him to lose it—the Territory of Kansas.

Aboard a ramshackle buggy pulled by an equally decrepit moccasin-colored horse, he showed up at Lawrence, Kansas, on April 22, 1855. The next day he opened a law office, then surveyed the political landscape. The big issue, obviously, was slavery. On one side stood the Proslavery party, on the other the Freestaters. The first was made up mainly of Missourians who wanted to make Kansas a slave state controlled politically and economically by themselves. The latter consisted predominantly of Northerners who opposed slavery in Kansas either because they regarded it as evil or else simply because they did not care to live around or compete with blacks, be they slave or free.

Like most Northerners at the time Lane had no moral qualms about slavery as such. "I would," he declared soon after arriving in Kansas, "as leave sell a negro as a mule." But he had been made painfully aware of the strong Northern sentiment against the spread of slavery. Therefore, after a false start in which he tried vainly to organize a pro-Douglas Democratic party, he cast his lot with the Freestaters—a decision that some of his enemies alleged was prompted partly by the refusal of the proslavery territorial legislature to grant him a divorce from his wife, who had gone back to Indiana in anger over his flagrant philandering.

In any case he soon became one of the leaders of the Freestate party. At Big Springs he wrote its official platform, then presided over the Topeka Convention, which drew up a state constitution barring free blacks as well as slaves from Kansas. Next, following the bloodless "Wakarusa War" of December 1855, during which his main contribution was to urge a suicidal attack on an army of Missouri "Border Ruffians" besieging Lawrence, he went to Washington, where he attempted to secure Kansas's admission to the Union under the Topeka Constitution. The Senate, however, led by Douglas, scorned both him and the constitution, a shabby-looking document of twenty-four pages covered with smudges, erasures, and cross-outs. Enraged, he challenged Douglas to a duel, only to be laughed at once again.

While he was thus engaged, a new army of Border Ruffians invaded Kansas and on May 21, 1856, "sacked" Lawrence—that is, they burned the hotel, demolished two printing presses, and looted houses and stores. Soon afterward John Brown and four associates retaliated by hacking into pieces with broadswords five "proslavery" settlers on Pottawatomie Creek, an atrocity that led in turn to more Border Ruffian incursions and an escalating round of raids, skirmishes, and murders.

When he learned of events in "Bleeding Kansas," Lane embarked on a whirlwind speaking tour of the North to raise men and money for the beleaguered Freestaters. Successful, in June he headed west through Iowa with a party of several hundred immigrants popularly known as "Lane's Army of the North." But just before reaching Nebraska he received a message from some of the leading citizens of Lawrence asking him to stay out of Kansas: His presence would only make matters worse by provoking the territorial authorities, who had issued a warrant for his arrest on charges of treason.

"If the people of Kansas don't want me," he wailed, tears flowing from what an acquaintance termed his "easy lachrymals," "I'll blow my brains out!" Sam Walker, the man who had delivered the message, assured him that the people did want him. At once he stopped crying, and a short time later was galloping toward Kansas followed by thirty armed men, among them John Brown.

He rode over 125 miles in forty hours. Every one of his companions dropped by the way, exhausted, and he arrived in Lawrence alone. After only a few hours' sleep, he mobilized the local forces and led them on a sweep against three proslavery "forts" (log cabins with loopholes) in the vicinity. A wagonload of burning hay produced the fall of one fort, and the defenders of the second fled at the approach of the Freestaters, whose number Lane augmented by placing straw dummies in wagons. Before the third and strongest fort could be attacked, however, Lane suddenly and without explanation headed back into Nebraska, taking half of the troops with him. Even so, the remainder, under Sam Walker, went on to take this last fort in the only real fighting of the campaign.

When Lane returned two weeks later, Kansas was swarming with Border Ruffians hell-bent on vengeance for the capture of the forts. Once again hastily raising an "army," he skirmished with a force of 1,000 Missourians at Bull Creek, causing them to retreat. Next he led 400 men to the territorial capital at Lecompton, where a number of Freestaters were being held captive. Only the timely intervention of 600 United States dragoons backed by six cannons forestalled a pitched battle between the pro- and antislavery forces. After being assured that the prisoners would be released, Lane's followers dispersed, with Lane himself avoiding arrest by masquerading as a private. The Federal troops likewise confronted the invading Border Ruffians, who forthwith went back home. Barely—just barely—an all-out civil war had been prevented in Kansas, a conflict that might have spread to the rest of the nation as well.

"I saved Kansas!" boasted Lane. But in fact his military activities, although dramatic, merely provoked another Missouri invasion and nearly led to a clash with United States troops that would have been disastrous for the Freestate cause. What actually decided the outcome of the Kansas struggle was the steady, unspectacular flow into the territory of Northern immigrants, who by 1856 heavily outnumbered the proslavery settlers. Nevertheless many Kansans gave Lane the credit, as have some historians. Furthermore, he acquired along both sides of the border a reputation as a "powerful fighter"—all on the strength of capturing two log cabins.

During the next several years the Kansas cauldron bubbled but did not again boil over into the anarchy of 1855–56. Ever eager to keep his name before the public, Lane resorted to a variety of attention-getting devices. Thus on one occasion he proposed that he and Senator David Rice Atchison of Missouri decide the question of slavery in Kansas by waging single combat before a jury of two dozen Congressmen. Later he challenged Territorial Governor James W. Denver to a duel, only to suffer the humiliation of having Denver, a crack shot with several successful "affairs of honor" to his credit, ignore him.

Another man who refused to take Lane seriously was his Lawrence neighbor, Gaius W. Jenkins. He accused Lane of jumping his claim and on June 3, 1858, backed by two men, began chopping down a fence separating the two holdings. Lane emerged from his house, shotgun in hand, and twice warned Jenkins to stop. But Jenkins, who had a Sharps carbine with him, finished destroying the fence and advanced into Lane's yard. Lane thereupon fired, killing him. In turn one of Jenkins's friends shot Lane in the leg.

A court acquitted Lane, but public opinion condemned him. During the weeks that followed he limped the streets of Lawrence, "care-worn, haggard, reduced almost to a skeleton, the picture of despair." At night he suffered from visions of Jenkins's body. "the 98 buckshot wounds in bold relief." His law practice did so poorly that at times his family (his wife had returned) lacked food, and once he walked forty miles to collect a twenty dollar fee.

Not once, however, did he lose sight of the fixed goal of his ambition, the United States Senate. In 1859, with statehood for Kansas in prospect, he launched a comeback. First he joined, with much fanfare and a mighty show of repentance, the politically influential Methodist Church. Next he began travelling, "with dilapidated garb and equipage, across the trackless prairies." Wherever he stopped, crowds gathered to listen. No one in Kansas, and few outside, could compete with him on the stump. Pacing up and down the platform, waving his skinny arms and doffing surplus clothing, he spoke in a voice that ranged from deep gutturals to high-pitched screeches, blackguarding his enemies, defending his own character, and promising everything and anything calculated to gain supporters. And every so often, at climactic moments, in a manner said to be "weirdly electrifying," he would stop, point a long, bony finger at the enrapt audience, and suddenly shriek, "GREAT GOD!"

By the time Kansas entered the Union, early in 1861, Lane had regained the popularity lost in the Jenkins affair and stood as the acknowledged leader of the Radical wing of the dominant Republican party—a motley combination of the "Fifty-Sixers," as the early settlers were called (the roughly dressed, hard-drinking, gun-toting "b'hoys" so common in this raw frontier state) and the extreme abolitionists. Lane appealed to this latter group, small in number but big in influence, by advocating "direct action" against slavery—that is, raids such as those conducted into Missouri by John Brown, James Montgomery, and other "jayhawkers" for the purpose of "liberating" slaves. As one shrewd Kansas critic noted, Lane's "invariable tactic" was to claim that he embodied "some great principle," thereby making the "sincere, the honest, and the earnest his enthusiastic supporters." With him now this "great principle" was abolitionism. "I once favored slavery," he explained, "but then I went to a Southern planter with a young carpenter who was seeking work. After learning the object of our visit, the planter laid himself back with his thumbs in the armholes of his vest and replied, 'I bought two carpenters yesterday.' GREAT GOD! If such men are buying carpenters, machinists, and engineers, how soon will they sell you and me in their marts of human merchandise?"

On April 4, 1861, the Kansas legislature, meeting in the straggling little town of Topeka, elected him senator. When he heard the good news, tears of joy filled his eyes, he pulled out a pistol and announced that if he had lost he would have blown out his brains on the spot. Four days later he left for Washington. "Now," he declared, "we will see what a *live* man can do!"

A great deal, it turned out. The key to political power in Kansas at this time was Federal patronage. To quote a contemporary observer, practically "every third man" in the state was "either a military character or politician, and most of these office-seekers." Furthermore, a prolonged drought and depression had made getting a government job almost a life or death necessity for numerous Kansans. Consequently the leader who could deliver the patronage would be able to dominate Kansas politics.

Thanks to Lincoln's gratitude for the Frontier Guards, Lane became that leader. In the words of one disappointed Kansas office-seeker, "Lane gets anything of the President that he asks for while others go begging." When the senator returned from Washington in May he could say truthfully, "Doesn't Jim Lane look after his friends?"

That summer the war spread to the frontier as Unionists and Secessionists battled to control Missouri. Fearful of attack by the Confederate Missourians, Kansas raised several regiments, which were stationed at Fort Scott near the border. Lane, with the acquiescence of Lincoln, took command of this "Kansas Brigade," determined, as he put it, "to bet high on small cards." Not only would a successful military campaign enhance his popularity in Kansas, it would add to his growing national fame.

Early in September a large Confederate army under Sterling Price moved northward through western Missouri. Hearing that the area was "infested by the marauding and murdering bands" of Lane, Price detoured to attack Fort Scott. The Kansas Brigade skirmished with Price's advance guard, then retreated, abandoning the fort. Price, content with thus "chastising" the Kansans, resumed his northward march. Lane waited until he was sure Price was safely distant, then entered Missouri at the head of a "smart little army" of 1,500.

The moment they crossed the border the "Jayhawkers" began to loot, burn, and—by some reports—murder and rape. "Everything disloyal," cried Lane, "from a Durham cow to a Shanghai chicken must be cleaned out!" At Osceola they robbed the bank, pillaged stores and houses, and set fire to the courthouse. Many of them became so drunk that they could not march and had to ride in wagons piled high with plunder, which included as Lane's personal share a piano and a quantity of silk dresses, which he subsequently distributed to "female admirers." And as the column lurched along, scores of blacks joined it, a few even serving as soldiers. Thus Lane provided proof of the prediction he had made in the Senate in July: "Slavery cannot survive the march of the Union armies."

The expedition infuriated the people of west Missouri and fanned the flames of guerrilla war in that region. Most Kansans, on the other hand, applauded Lane. Not only had he once more saved them from invasion, he had evened some old scores with the Missourians. Moreover, his "liberation" of slaves harmonized with the growing feeling in Kansas that salvation of the Union required the destruction of slavery.

Following the Missouri campaign, Lane opened a vicious assault on his longtime rival, New England–born, Puritan-minded Charles Robinson, who as governor threatened the senator's patronage monopoly by virtue of his authority to commission officers in the Kansas regiments. First, in a sensational speech at Leavenworth, he accused Robinson (who had been the head of the Freestate party in the 1850s) of being a "traitor" because he had criticized the conduct of the Kansas Brigade. Next he tried to deprive

Robinson of his office on a legal technicality, but the state supreme court refused to go along. Finally he engineered Robinson's impeachment on charges of defrauding the state in a bond transaction. Although acquitted, Robinson was so besmirched in reputation that he retired from public life. His successor, Leavenworth merchant Thomas Carney, was a "Lane man."

At the same time, Lane succeeded in having another crony, Brigadier General James G. Blunt, appointed commander of the Kansas military department. Blunt, according to one Kansas soldier, had "a worse reputation than even Lane himself." Under his auspices each of the numerous forts in Kansas became "a sort of mint" for contractors whose gratitude took the form of political support and financial kickbacks for the general's senatorial patron.

By the summer of 1862 Lane was the recognized "King" of Kansas politics. His ambition fed by his power, he even dreamed of riding the abolitionist horse into the White House. To that end he proposed a great "Southern Expedition" to liberate the slaves of Texas. Frustrated in that scheme, he succeeded (with Lincoln's secret backing) in recruiting two black regiments in Kansas. Among the first to be raised in the Civil War, they won him the praise of abolitionists who believed that the spectacle of black men in blue uniforms would hasten the defeat of the Confederacy.

Beginning in 1863, however, he experienced a succession of setbacks. First a reshuffling of the Union high command in the West resulted in Blunt being replaced by Brigadier General Thomas Ewing Jr., who promptly denounced those who were "stealing themselves rich in the name of liberty." Next Governor Carney rebelled against the "King" and began using his patronage power and large private fortune in a campaign to supplant Lane, who was up for reelection in 1864. And as if this were not bad enough, on August 21, 400 Missouri bushwhackers under the dread William Clarke Quantrill slammed into Lawrence. Declaring that they had come to avenge the destruction of Osceola and other Kansas outrages, they engaged in a four-hour orgy of looting, arson, and murder that left the town in ruins and 180 of its male inhabitants dead.

Lane escaped being one of that number by fleeing in his nightshirt into a cornfield, where he huddled with a drawn penknife in hand, resolved if discovered by the raiders to kill himself by plunging the blade into his brain through an eye—the method his oldest brother had used to commit suicide in 1836. Quantrill's men, however, informed that Lane was out of town, made little effort to locate him but contented themselves with setting fire to his expensive new brick house, which they reported finding crammed with plunder from Missouri. Had they captured him, they would have taken him to Missouri and burned him at the stake.

Lane tried to turn the Lawrence disaster to his own political advantage by charging that bungling by Carney and Ewing enabled Quantrill to enter and then depart Kansas unscathed. He also called on the men of Kansas to assemble at Paola for a retaliatory invasion of Missouri, but Major General John M. Schofield, top Union commander in the West, warned that he would use troops to halt any such expedition. Hence on the appointed day only a few hundred men showed up at Paola, where they stood in the rain listening to a speech by Lane, then went back home.

Affairs continued to go badly on into 1864 for the embattled "Grim Chieftain," as Lane sometimes was called. Old allies, resenting his dictatorial ways, joined with old opponents to form a separate party committed to the election of Carney as senator. Businessmen dissatisfied with Lane's handling of army contracts and railroad matters likewise rallied behind the Carney candidacy. And many ordinary Kansans were disgusted by the odor of corruption surrounding Lane, and by such incidents as the one in which a young woman horsewhipped him on a Washington street for having made an "insulting proposition." To be sure, he fought back hard, stumping the state and cracking the patronage whip. Nevertheless he grew so discouraged over his reelection prospects that a friend found him alone in a Leavenworth hotel room, lying in bed even though it was daytime, and suffering from "appalling melancholy," even "aberration of mind."

But then, in October, on the very eve of the election, fortuitous events and the folly of his enemies saved the day. In a last desperate challenge to Union control, Sterling Price's army again swept through Missouri, threatened St. Louis, then turned westward. As he had so often before, Lane proclaimed that Kansas was in danger and urged that the state militia be sent into Missouri to forestall invasion. But Carney and his henchmen, suspecting another of Lane's notorious tricks, declared that Price would not attack Kansas and that Lane merely wanted to get the militiamen out of the state so that they could not vote against him. Thus they were most embarrassed when Price approached Kansas City, to be driven back only after a series of hard-fought battles in which Lane and Blunt played conspicuous parts. Once more Lane was Kansas's hero; his opponents became the objects of derision. Lane's ticket won the election, and early in 1865 the legislature returned him to Washington. As one Kansas editor put it, "If the people of Kansas cannot have an honest man in the Senate they prefer that the *rascal* who represents them, should be a man of brains."

All seemed well again for Lane. Then John Wilkes Booth's bullet ended his special relationship with Lincoln. Obsessed with the need to keep control of Federal patronage, he sought to establish the same sort of relationship with the new president and so voted early in 1866 to uphold Andrew Johnson's vetoes of the Freedmen's Bureau Bill and the Civil Rights Bill, both measures sponsored by the Radical Republicans. But by so doing he repeated his 1854 blunder with the Kansas-Nebraska Bill. Kansans overwhelmingly backed the Radicals, and as a Kansas newspaper observed, "Lane is nothing, if not radical, and when he ceases to act with the radicals, he will play out and disappear from the political stage forever." The state's press, pulpit, and platform branded him a "Republican Judas," and legislators called for his resignation. Simultaneously, stories appeared in Eastern newspapers accusing him of graft in connection with Indian supply contracts.

For some time he had manifested increasingly serious signs of mental disorder. Now, faced with total disaster, he began to talk of suicide, and even attempted to leap from a St. Louis hotel window. A doctor took him to a farm near Leavenworth, where friends and relatives kept a close watch on him. Somehow he managed to obtain a derringer, which he hid in his coat. On Sunday, July 1, 1866, he went on a wagon ride with several companions. When the wagon stopped for a gate, he leaped out, shouted "Goodbye, gentlemen!" placed the barrel of the pistol in his mouth and pulled the trigger. Horribly mutilated, he lingered in agony ten days before "the scheming brain worked and suffered no more."

He was buried in Oak Hill Cemetery, Lawrence. His old enemy Charles Robinson would have inscribed on his gravestone, "His suicide was his own verdict on his life and actions." But perhaps a more charitable, yet just, epitaph was the comment of another Kansas politician who knew him well: "Lane could have been a great leader had he possessed a rudimentary perception of the value of personal character as an element of success in public affairs." As it was, he was a man who sometimes served good causes, but on the whole badly and almost always for dubious reasons.

CHAPTER TWELVE

William Clarke Quantrill

Quantrill's name resonates throughout the annals of the Civil War with an eerie quality unmatched by any other, so much so that his fame is surpassed only by that of the top military and civilian leaders of that war. Thus there now exists for him what exists for none of those leaders, a fan club called the William Clarke Quantrill Society, which publishes a newsletter, "The No Quarterly," and holds annual meetings, usually in some place associated with its hero. (To be fair, not all members deem him to be such, at least in the normal sense of the word.) More movies about him or in which he is depicted have been made than of any other Civil War personage except Lincoln. Unfortunately, the most-often-shown one, Dark Command, *which came out in 1940 and still can be seen on television, is far more farcical than historical; and the most recent one,* Ride with the Devil, *went to the devil insofar as box-office receipts were concerned, for it ceased to be distributed soon after its release in the fall of 1999.*

Perhaps the makers of this movie, which was produced at great expense by a major studio, floundered because they failed to overcome the obstacle that historians face in dealing with Quantrill and the guerrilla war along the Kansas-Missouri border: Distinguishing between fiction and fact, myth and truth. This article, which appeared in the January/February 1992 issue of Civil War History: The Magazine of the Civil War Society, *endeavors to do this, as does the book from which it was derived, my* William Clarke Quantrill: His Life and Times *(New York: Frederick Fell, 1962; hardback reprint, Columbus, Ohio: General's Books, 1992; paperback reprint, Norman: University of Oklahoma Press, 1999). The sole change in the article is an updating of the strange story of Quantrill's bones—a story that supplies further proof of the fascination he continues to exercise. Although ultimately a "loser" in life, Quantrill remains a "winner" in death.*

"I DON'T EXPECT TO SEE ANY OF YOU ALIVE AGAIN." SO SAID ELI SNYDER to three young abolitionists setting out from Osawatomie, Kansas, on a cold

December morning in 1860. The three men were off to free the slaves of Morgan Walker, a well-to-do farmer in Jackson County, Missouri. Within days, Snyder's expectation was fulfilled, and the three would-be liberators were dead—a consequence of trusting William Clarke Quantrill.

In 1860, Quantrill was calling himself Charley Hart. He met the three ill-fated abolitionists in Lawrence, Kansas, and gained their trust by saying he was one of them. He spoke of raiding Walker's farm, and they agreed to join him. But Quantrill instead warned the Walkers, and arranged a trap.

As they neared Walker's in descending December darkness, Morgan Walker's son Andrew and four neighbors waited tensely, concealed on either side of the front porch of the Walker's two-story stone house, double-barreled shotguns in hand. About 7:00 P.M., three men came onto the porch and pounded on the door. When Morgan Walker answered, they rushed inside with drawn pistols and announced that they had come to take his slaves. "Go ahead," he replied.

Quantrill thereupon instructed the others to go after the slaves while he remained in the house. They turned and stepped out onto the porch. The shotguns roared. One raider fell dead, and the other two somehow escaped, though one was grievously wounded. Two days later, a posse led by the Walkers found them, thanks, ironically, to a tip from a slave, and killed them. According to one account Quantrill himself finished off the wounded man—Chalkey T. Lispey—by putting the muzzle of a revolver into his mouth and pulling the trigger.

So ended a small episode in Quantrill's long and bloody career of treachery, terror, and murder. The Walkers were curious about why he had betrayed the three men. Revenge, said Quantrill. In 1856, he said, he and his older brother had set out for California. While they were passing through Kansas a band of jayhawkers—abolitionist bandits—attacked them, killed his brother and left Quantrill for dead. He survived, however, and later infiltrated the jayhawkers. He proceeded to kill every member of the band responsible for the murder of his brother except two. With the Morgan Walker ambush, he had at last completed his vengeance. This was the story he told the Walkers.

Looking at Quantrill, the Missourians saw a lean, stalwart young man with blonde hair and gray-blue eyes. "He seemed to be a very pleasant fellow," one of them later commented, "his appearance was any other than that of a killer." But William Quantrill was a killer, and a liar as well. His story was almost entirely false. He was born in Canal Dover (now Dover),

Ohio, on July 31, 1837, the first child (he had no older brother) of Thomas and Caroline Clarke Quantrill. Following the death in 1854 of his father, a tinsmith and schoolteacher, Quantrill taught in various schools in Ohio, Indiana, and Illinois before going in 1857 to Kansas with a group of settlers from the Canal Dover region. He promised his mother, who had been obliged to take in boarders to support herself and her other children, that he would establish a farm to which the family could move and start life afresh. Instead, he was expelled from the Kansas settlement for stealing. He then went to Utah as an army teamster and prospected unsuccessfully for gold in Colorado before returning to Kansas and teaching.

As he admitted in a letter to his mother, he was merely "roving around," and "such a course must end in nothing." Yet convinced that there was "something else for me to do," that he was destined for greater things, he went to Lawrence, Kansas, in the spring of 1860. There, under the name of Charley Hart, he became a jayhawker of sorts. During the summer and fall, he along with others of his kind made several raids into Missouri to free slaves—but then sent them back to slavery on receiving ransom from their owners. He also kidnapped free blacks to sell into slavery, stole horses, rustled cattle, and committed sundry other crimes. In November, the Lawrence authorities issued an order for his arrest and although he eluded apprehension it was clear that he had no future in Kansas other than prison or the hangman's noose.

And so Quantrill fled to the safe haven of Missouri and began honing his hatred for his new enemy: Kansas, and in particular, Lawrence. Despite his Ohio background and having been raised, according to his mother's subsequent testimony, as an "abolitionist," he had come to hate the free state of Kansas. "The devil has got unlimited sway in this territory," he said. He believed Kansas and Lawrence deserved to be punished and perhaps with the Missourians he would have a chance to do so.

That chance came with the Civil War. In Missouri, the conflict was not only between Northerner and Southerner but also of pro-Unionists versus pro-Confederates and, along the western border, of Kansans against Missourians as the former took advantage of the turmoil to pay off old scores dating back to the territorial struggle of the 1850s. Starting in the fall of 1861, gangs and even whole armies of jayhawkers roamed through western Missouri, plundering, burning, and sometimes killing. To defend and retaliate against these incursions, and also to ward off Federal troops and Unionist militias, some Missourians formed guerrilla or "bushwhacker" bands.

AUTHOR'S COLLECTION

William Clarke Quantrill

Andrew Walker, son of Morgan Walker, headed such a band in Jackson County, but because he was unable to devote full time to it, he resigned, and by unanimous consent of the other members William Quantrill took command. It was a natural choice. He was a good shot, a fine horseman, and—most important—was brave, enterprising, and cool-headed when in a tight spot. In fact he seemed to revel in such pressure-filled situations: He had a peculiar way of smiling, even giggling, during fights.

For a while Quantrill's little band confined itself to harrying local Unionists, ambushing Federal patrols, and conducting other routine guerrilla operations. Then, on March 7, 1862, they raided the village of Aubry, Kansas. This was not the first attack on a Kansas settlement by Missouri guerrillas but it was by far the most ferocious. Not only did the raiders pillage houses and stores, but they shot down five unarmed civilians. It was Quantrill's first taste of revenge against Kansas, and it whetted his appetite for more.

Following the Aubry raid, hundreds of Union troops, many of them Kansans, scoured Jackson County, bent on destroying Quantrill's gang. They almost succeeded. Three times they surprised and trapped the gang in houses where the raiders were spending the night, and only Quantrill's quick thinking and daring enabled them to escape. At least once, Quantrill's men had to fight their way out of an ambush with pistol and shotgun. As a rule, though, Quantrill and his men were more than a match for the Federals, especially as they became more experienced. The Confederates were better armed (each carried at least four Colt Navy revolvers), better mounted, and knew the countryside intimately. If pursued by a force too strong to fight, they found refuge in numerous secure hiding places, and friendly neighbors kept them well-supplied with food, clothing, horses, and information about Federal movements. More men came to join them, among them big Cole Younger, later renowned as a bank robber. By the summer of 1862, Quantrill headed the largest, most formidable, and most feared bushwhacker gang in western Missouri.

On August 11, Quantrill played a key role in helping a regular Confederate force capture Independence, Missouri, and its entire garrison. His reward, bestowed by a grateful Confederate commander, was a captain's commission as a partisan ranger. Pleased by this official recognition, Quantrill celebrated it in the way he enjoyed most—by raiding Kansas. At Olathe on September 6 and 7, his bushwhackers, 150 strong, murdered a dozen men, "shooting them down," to quote a witness, "like so many dogs." On October 17 at Shawneetown they killed 7 defenseless soldiers and 15 civilians. All along the eastern border of Kansas the name of Quantrill became known—and dreaded.

With the advent of cold weather, which stripped the leaves from the underbrush that gave bushwhacking its name, he took his men to Arkansas, where they attached themselves to Brigadier General Jo Shelby's Missouri cavalry. In December, Quantrill journeyed to Richmond, Virginia, where he sought a colonel's commission in the partisan ranger service. Although he subsequently claimed to have received it, evidence indicates that he did not. Nevertheless his ambitions and aspirations were soaring as 1862 gave way to 1863.

In May he returned to what now was being called "Quantrill country." As before the Federals endeavored to wipe out his gang, but as before, they failed. Indeed, soon they, not the bushwhackers, were on the defensive. Near Independence, Quantrill ambushed and killed 9 Missouri militiamen, and at Westport, on the outskirts of Kansas City, his men attacked 150 Kansas cavalry killing 20 without suffering a single casualty. Yet, spectacular as they were, these exploits were mere prelude to the raid Quantrill was secretly planning. On August 10, at a meeting of western Missouri guerrilla chiefs he had summoned, he declared: "Let's go to Lawrence!" The other men reacted with shock and alarm. From the beginning of the war the bushwhackers had talked of "cleaning out" Lawrence. It was the citadel of Kansas abolitionism, the headquarters of the Red Legs, as the jayhawkers now styled themselves, and embodied all that the guerrillas hated in Kansas. But it also was forty miles from the border, contained 3,000 people, and had a strong home guard unit. Even if they safely eluded Federal patrols and reached Lawrence, they would not be able to take it, and before they could make it back to Missouri they would be cut off and overwhelmed.

Point by point Quantrill answered these objections, all of which he had foreseen. He at last persuaded his listeners that it could be done, his most convincing argument being that precisely because it was such a hazardous enterprise, the Kansans would not expect it and so would be caught off guard. Any lingering reluctance to make the raid disappeared several days later when news arrived that a building in Kansas City, where female relatives of the guerrillas were imprisoned, had collapsed, killing and maiming a half-dozen of the women. The bushwhackers believed that the Yankees had staged the disaster.

At midafternoon on August 20, 1863, Quantrill crossed into Kansas five miles south of Aubry. He rode at the head of approximately 450 men—the largest guerrilla force assembled under one command during the Civil War. The Union commander at Aubry learned of the incursion but merely passed word of it to army headquarters in Kansas City and made no effort to alert Federal troops in the interior of the state. Throughout the rest of the day and night the bushwhacker column snaked ever closer to Lawrence. At dawn on August 21, Quantrill and his men reached a hill overlooking the town from the east. Some of the guerrillas lost their nerve: "Let's give it up—it's too much!" Snarling, "You can do as you please—I am going into Lawrence!" Quantrill charged forward at full gallop, followed by a horde of longhaired, wild-looking young men, blazing revolvers in hand.

The raiders achieved total surprise—Lawrence was completely at their mercy, and they showed none, except to women and children. Shouting "Osceola!"—the name of a Missouri town devastated early in the war by Kansans—they proceeded to loot, burn, and murder. While they did so, Quantrill drove about the streets in a buggy, then went to the top of Mount Oread, a steep height on the western outskirts. He looked down on the scene below and liked what he saw. Here, truly, was revenge.

Four hours later the bushwhackers departed, leaving heaps of rubble and ashes where the business district had stood, scores of ransacked and flaming houses, and the bullet-riddled corpses of nearly 200 men. No guerrilla raid, or cavalry raid, for that matter, of the entire war could compare in destructiveness and horror.

The Union pursuit was too late and too weak to prevent the raiders from returning safely to Missouri, where they scattered to their hideouts. On August 25, Brigadier General Thomas Ewing Jr., commander of the District of the Border (and William T. Sherman's brother-in-law), issued—as he had been planning to do even before the Lawrence massacre—"General Orders No. 11" expelling most of the population of Jackson and two adjoining counties. (Among those forced to leave was eleven-year-old Martha Young, who would one day give birth to future president Harry S. Truman.) Ewing's object was to deprive the bushwhackers of their civilian support, thereby forcing them away from the border. But the order had little effect on the guerrillas. Quantrill's foraging parties had no trouble finding plenty to eat, and when, early in October, he set out for Texas with 400 followers, it was for the same reason he had headed south the year before—the leaves were beginning to fall.

On October 6, 1863, near Baxter Springs, Kansas, Quantrill unexpectedly came upon a column of Union cavalry and wagons. It was the personal escort and train of Major General James G. Blunt, commander of the District of the Frontier. Blunt, seeing the guerrillas, at first thought they were troops from a nearby Federal fort—an understandable error since many of Quantrill's men wore Federal uniforms. By the time Blunt realized his mistake it was too late. Two hundred screaming bushwhackers charged, firing as they came. It was all over in a few minutes. Eighty-nine of the 100 men in Blunt's party lay dead and, in most instances, were stripped naked and mutilated. Blunt himself escaped only because his superb horse outdistanced the three guerrillas who chased him.

Quantrill was exultant. First Lawrence—now Baxter Springs! He was in a mood to celebrate, and for the first time his men saw him drunk as he revelled with captured Yankee whiskey. Less than three years ago he was just another outlaw, an outcast, now he was the king of the bushwhackers, the terror of the border. But as Baxter Springs marked the zenith of Quantrill's career, it was also the beginning of its decline—a decline that was even more rapid than the rise.

Once in Texas, Quantrill heard from Thomas C. Reynolds, the Missouri Confederate governor-in-exile, who urged Quantrill to join the regular service and at the same time warned him: "All authority over undisciplined bands is short-lived. The history of every guerrilla chief has been the same. He either becomes the slave of his men, or if he attempts to control them, some officer or private rises up, disputes his authority, gains the men, and puts him down. My opinion of you is that you deserve a better fate. . . . "

Already, Quantrill could see evidence of decay in his command. Many of his men, especially the older ones, had left him, some because they were appalled by what had happened at Lawrence and Baxter Springs, others out of resentment over what they deemed to be an unfair division of loot. Moreover, far from hailing and rewarding his exploits, the Confederate authorities disavowed what one of them called his "savage, inhuman" mode of warfare "in which men are to be shot down like dogs, after throwing down their arms and holding up their hands supplicating for mercy." When some of the guerrillas robbed and murdered civilians in Texas, the local Confederate commander attempted to arrest Quantrill, but the elusive raider and his remaining followers fled to the Indian Territory.

The final phase of his plunge from power came in April 1864 shortly after he returned to Missouri. For sometime his chief lieutenant, the fearless and utterly ruthless George Todd, had been in charge of the band's actual operations while Quantrill occupied the ambiguous position of "colonel" in command of all western Missouri guerrillas. One night, while playing cards with Quantrill, Todd decided to become in name what he already was in fact—the leader. Deliberately and flagrantly, he cheated. Quantrill protested. Todd threatened him. Quantrill said he was afraid of no man. Immediately Todd whipped out a revolver and shoved it into Quantrill's face.

"You are afraid of me, aren't you, Bill?"

"Yes, I'm afraid of you," Quantrill admitted.

Todd lowered the pistol and the change of command was complete. Governor Reynolds had been proved a prophet. Silently Quantrill mounted his horse and rode away. Picking up his teenage mistress, Kate King, along the way, he went to a hideout in northern Missouri, where he remained all through the spring and summer.

While Quantrill lay low, the war in Missouri attained new heights of blood-soaked ferocity.

The climax came in late September, when Major General Sterling Price's army invaded Missouri in a last desperate effort to gain it for the Confederacy. Price's army was badly defeated at the Battle of Westport, October 23, 1864, and among the dead in the campaign was George Todd. As the Confederate army fled southward, some of the guerrillas followed it;

others remained behind, not knowing what to do. Clearly the Confederate cause in Missouri was "played out," and with it guerrilla warfare.

But Quantrill, who probably had been expecting such an outcome, chose this time to stage a comeback. Gathering fifty-some veteran guerrillas, including Frank James, brother of Jesse James—he led them through Arkansas and Tennessee into Kentucky. Here he resumed his old ways but without his former success, and both he and his men became, if not already so, nothing more than bandits who robbed and killed indiscriminately. Determined to suppress all such marauders, the Union commander in the state sent a special force of "Federal guerrillas" under Captain Edwin Terrill, once a Confederate soldier, to track down "Captain Clarke," as Quantrill now styled himself.

On the morning of May 10, 1865, Terrill caught the Missourians off guard in a barn near Bloomfield, Kentucky. Quantrill, unable to mount his frightened and rearing horse, fled on foot and was brought down by a bullet that lodged against his spine, paralyzing his lower body. Two days later Terrill, having learned his true identity, had him taken to Louisville where, on June 6,1865, he died in a prison hospital. He was buried in Louisville's Catholic cemetery.

But not forever. In 1887 his mother and William W. Scott, a boyhood friend and now a newspaper editor, retrieved the skeleton and reinterred it, again without a tombstone, in the Quantrill family plot in what had become simply Dover, Ohio. Or so Mrs. Quantrill thought. Scott, hoping to make some money out of them, secretly retained the skull and several arm and leg bones, with the eventual result that the former came into the possession of a local social fraternity and the latter part of the collections of the Kansas State Historical Society, Topeka. There they remained until the autumn of 1992, when the skull was buried in the Dover cemetery near the largest portion of whatever is left of Quantrill's skeleton and the other bones placed beneath a marker in the Confederate cemetery at Higginsville, Missouri. Even in death Quantrill continued, in the words of the letter he wrote his mother in 1860, his "roving around."

Such, then, is the story of William Clarke Quantrill. He was brave, and skillful as a leader, and in his defense it can be said that he lived in a time and place where terrible things were done by men on both sides, Kansan and Missourian, Union and Confederate. Nevertheless there can be no excusing what he did—lie, betray, steal, destroy, murder, and massacre.

Part Four

And Two Losers Who Became Winners

CHAPTER THIRTEEN

Sam Houston's Last Stand

For understandable reasons history and biography have focused on Sam Houston's preeminent role in the Texas War of Independence in 1835–36 and given comparatively scant attention to his attempt a quarter of a century later to prevent Texas from joining the Confederacy by restoring the Lone Star Republic. He failed, yet had he lived a little longer he might—underscore this word—have succeeded, making him once again what he almost always had been: a winner.

This is the oldest of the mostly old articles that this book comprises, in the sense that it was first written in the spring of 1952 as a paper for Professor Avery Craven's seminar at the University of Chicago, where I then was a graduate student, on the coming of the Civil War. I rewrote the paper during the winter of 1964–65, and it was published by American Heritage *in its December 1965 issue. I think that Craven gave the paper an "A" but am not certain.*

THE PEOPLE GATHERED ON THE GALVESTON WHARF BROKE INTO CHEERS as soon as they saw him. There was no mistaking the tall, white-haired man in the Mexican sombrero and serape descending the gangplank of the packet that had just docked. It was the old hero, Sam Houston, returning to Texas from Washington, where just a short time before he had completed his final term in the Senate. In cheering him that spring day in 1859, Texans felt that they were cheering Texas itself, so closely was he identified with the state, so great had been his part in its origin and development. More than that, they were honoring a man who could look back upon a career that extended over more than half the nation's history—that, indeed, had contributed mightily to the shaping of that history.

Born in the Shenandoah Valley of Virginia in 1793, Houston travelled at the age of fourteen in a covered wagon with his widowed mother to the wilds of Tennessee. There he lived much of the time among the Cherokee

Indians, who adopted him into their tribe and gave him the name of Co-lon-neh, "The Raven." Ever afterward he found the company of Indians as congenial as that of whites (and sometimes more so). From an early age his strongest interest was the military life. When the War of 1812 began, he joined the army and became an officer; at the Battle of Horseshoe Bend in eastern Alabama—where on March 27, 1814, Andrew Jackson and his Cherokee allies all but annihilated a stubborn band of Creeks—young Ensign Houston displayed outstanding gallantry, suffering terrible wounds and gaining the personal notice and favor of General Jackson.

After the war Houston entered politics and with Jackson's backing became first a member of Congress, then governor of Tennessee. Some of his friends were beginning to speak of the White House when suddenly, without a word of explanation, he resigned the governorship, left his beautiful young wife of only a few weeks, and fled to the land of the Cherokees in what is now Oklahoma. All that is known with any certainty is that he had discovered that his wife loved another man, and that rather than hold her in a meaningless marriage, he sacrificed his political prospects and took himself out of her life.

For the next several years he was a broken man. The Indians with whom he lived conferred upon him a new name—Oo-tse-tee Ar-dee-tah-skee, "Big Drunk." But eventually he pulled himself together and in 1833 headed for Texas to realize the "great destiny" that he had always believed awaited him in the West. He quickly rose to prominence in Texas affairs, and when in 1835 the Americans there rebelled against the rule of the Mexican dictator Santa Anna, Houston became commander of the Texas army. Cleverly avoiding battle while his own forces grew stronger and the enemy's weaker, he surprised and defeated Santa Anna at San Jacinto on April 21, 1836, thereby securing for Texas its independence.

Houston served two terms as president of the new Lone Star Republic, and by skillful diplomacy helped bring about its annexation to the United States in 1845. During the years that ensued, he served as a senator in Washington, where he joined Clay and Webster in trying to maintain peace between North and South. Meanwhile, his first marriage having been dissolved, he married Margaret Lea—a union that was to prove as happy as the first had been tragic.

Upon returning to Texas from Washington in the spring of 1859, Houston was sixty-six, but although the wounds of Horseshoe Bend and San Jacinto ached painfully on rainy days, and although his once-thick

Miller, ed. *Photographic History.*

Sam Houston

chestnut hair was thin and white, his massive six-foot-two-inch frame was straight and vigorous, and his blue eyes remained clear and commanding. Above all, he retained his sense of destiny, and with it a young man's ability to dream. His present dream was nothing less than becoming president of the United States and saving the nation from the civil war that threatened it.

It was only natural that Houston would want to culminate his career with the highest office and greatest honor of all. To understand his desire to save the Union—at a time when many of his friends would willingly have seen it dissolved—one must realize that Houston was a loyal disciple of Andrew Jackson.

Back in 1830, when South Carolina had first threatened secession, Old Hickory had declared, "Our Union: it must be preserved!" In the mounting crisis of the 1850s, Houston made this his guiding principle. Like Jackson, he believed that slavery was an artificial issue, concocted and exploited for partisan purposes by unscrupulous demagogues on both sides of the Mason-Dixon line. But he feared that unless something was done to reduce sectional hostility, the inevitable result would be the breakup of the Union.

What was needed, he decided, was some great new issue or cause that would distract the public mind from the slavery controversy and restore national unity. After trying and discarding various other devices, he finally took up the gaudy banner of Manifest Destiny: He would unite the American people by appealing to their powerful lust for territorial expansion.

To the south lay Mexico—enticingly rich, invitingly weak. Houston envisioned himself as taking the lead in establishing an American "protectorate" there. Not only would the North and South forget their differences to join in this glorious enterprise, but a grateful and admiring nation would reward him with the White House. As president, Houston would act in the tradition of Jackson, harmonizing the interests of all sections and discrediting all those fanatics and demagogues who would destroy the Union. Such, at any rate, was Houston's reasoning. It was indeed, as Walter Prescott Webb called it, a "grand plan," characteristic in its magnitude of the man who conceived it. And, so far as a Mexican conquest was concerned, it was not nearly as fantastic as it may appear in retrospect.

To begin with, American conquest of Mexico was not a new idea. In 1805, Aaron Burr had plotted to seat himself on the throne of the Montezumas. In 1848, there had been a strong movement to keep the United States flag flying permanently over Mexico City, where Winfield Scott's victorious troops had planted it. And only recently President James Buchanan had openly advocated annexing the upper portion of Mexico. Moreover, filibustering was in the air in the 1850s. In 1851 a band of Americans had invaded Cuba, and in 1856 a pint-sized bravo named William Walker had made himself—for a brief time—master of Nicaragua. Houston simply proposed to conduct a filibuster on a giant scale.

Moreover, the chronic political chaos in Mexico provided both an excuse and an occasion for intervention. In his last speech before the Senate, Houston had argued that most Mexicans would welcome an American protectorate as an escape from anarchy; from a strictly military standpoint, therefore, conquest would be easy.

But before he could conquer Mexico, Houston had first to reconquer Texas. In 1854 he and John Bell of Tennessee had been the only two Southern senators to vote against Stephen A. Douglas's Kansas-Nebraska Bill, the controversial measure that repealed the Missouri Compromise of 1820, which had barred slavery in that portion of the Louisiana Purchase that lay north of latitude thirty-six degrees thirty minutes. Since most Texans believed that the Kansas-Nebraska Bill favored the South, Senator Houston's opposition to it lost him much of his support. In 1857, when he ran for governor, he suffered a resounding defeat—the first time Texans had ever rejected his leadership. He was returning home in 1859 determined to avenge this loss and regain his customary hold over their minds, hearts, and votes. Once in the governor's chair at Austin he would, God willing, carry out his Mexican plans.

The prospects were most propitious. The settlers in the southern and western counties blamed Governor Hardin Runnels, the man who had defeated Houston in 1857, for failing to protect them against Indian raids and the depredations of Mexican guerrillas under red-bearded Juan Cortinas. In addition, Texans everywhere in the state had now begun to realize that the Kansas-Nebraska Act had merely led to trouble for the South; in 1859 they were prepared to vote for Houston for the very same reason they had voted against him in 1857—his staunch opposition to the act.

Houston ran simply as "Old Sam Jacinto, the People's Candidate." So confident was he of victory that he made only one speech during the campaign, whereas in 1857 he had made dozens. In that speech, delivered at Nacogdoches, he denounced his opponents as secessionists motivated by an unholy desire for office and power. The South, he declared, was in no real or immediate danger from the North; but if it were, it would find safety under the Constitution and within the Union.

When the votes were tallied, the old hero had 36,257 to 27,500 for Runnels. The defeat of 1857 was avenged.

Houston took office in December and immediately began laying the groundwork for his invasion project. Since he had no legal authority for engaging in such an enterprise, he had to proceed covertly and indirectly. But to a man some called the Great Designer, this was no particular embarrassment.

His first move was to increase the strength of the Texas Rangers to nearly 1,000 men. The purpose of this buildup, he announced, was to drive back the Indians and to subdue Cortinas. In actuality, he saw the Rangers as the spearhead of the southward thrust across the Rio Grande. At the same time he endeavored to obtain weapons for an even larger army. Early in March he asked the War Department to send 2,000 percussion rifles, 1,000 Sharps carbines, and 3,000 Colt revolvers to Texas—to help it protect itself, he explained, against the Mexicans and Indians.

Here Houston met his first check. The authorities in Washington were aware of his Mexican interests and easily saw through his subterfuge. Moreover, although the Buchanan administration itself favored a Mexican protectorate, it did not care to have Houston establish one, especially in view of his presidential aspirations, which were also well known in Washington. Secretary of War John Floyd politely but firmly declined the request for additional arms.

Houston was disappointed but not discouraged. He had beaten the Mexicans in one war without aid from the Federal government, and he could do it again. Besides, if Washington refused to furnish the necessary means, perhaps London would.

British bankers held several million dollars' worth of Mexican bonds. The Mexican government (if such it could be called) had repudiated its debts, and the bankers faced a total loss on their investment. Houston believed they might be willing to finance his Mexican filibuster in return for a guarantee that their bonds would be redeemed once the protectorate was a reality. He arranged a meeting in New York between representatives of the British bondholders and three of his own agents. "All the talk about raising funds in the United States is gammon," he wrote to one of his men. "If the Bond Holders cannot be approached, it would take years to raise a reliable force to achieve any glorious result. . . . As to the plan of operation, that is a small matter; and if we have the sinews . . . it will be an easy matter to give motion to the achievement in the right direction."

While the negotiations were pending in New York, Houston was casting about for a man to command his Mexican invasion. Had he been twenty or even ten years younger, of course, he would not have looked for another. But as things were, he needed a champion to wield the sword for him.

During the recent war with Mexico, one young officer had stood out above all the others for courage, skill, and endurance. By a fortunate coincidence this officer arrived in Texas early in 1860 to take command of the operations against Cortinas. He was from Virginia, he held the rank of lieutenant colonel in the United States Army, and his name was Robert E. Lee.

Houston contacted Lee through A. M. Lea, a close friend who previously had recommended the tall Virginian as an ideal leader for the Mexican expedition. Lea reported on Lee to Houston late in February: "You will find that I have not painted an imaginary character. If you invite him to a conference about the defense of the frontier, you will find true all I have said of his manners and ability. As he is a 'Preux chevalier, sans peur et sans reproche,' he is very careful to do nothing that may cast a slur upon his name. He would not touch anything that he would consider vulgar filibustering; but he is not without ambition, and, *under the sanction of Govt.* might be more than willing to aid you to pacificate Mexico; and if the people of the U. States should recall you from the 'Halls of Montezumas' to the 'White House' at Washington, you would find him well fitted to carry out your great idea of a Protectorate. He is well informed in matters of state, honest, modest, brave and skillful. . . ."

Houston must have been impressed by this praise (which indicates, incidentally, how highly Lee was regarded even before he became a great general), for he instructed Lea to offer the Virginian command of the supposed invasion. On March 1 the colonel replied: "I am very much obliged to you for your friendly letters of the 24th, 25th and 26th ult. which arrived together in the last mail. I feel that I owe to your kindness rather than to my merit your recommendations to Govr. Houston. I am aware of his ability, and first became acquainted with him upon my entrance into the Military Academy. He was President of the Board of Visitors that year and the impression he made has never been effaced. I have followed with interest his career since, and have admired his manly qualities and conservative principles. His last position in favor of the Constitution and Union elicits my cordial approbation. Should military force be required to quiet our Mexican frontier, I have no doubt that arrangements will be made to maintain the rights and peace of Texas, and, I hope, in conformity to the Constitution and laws of the country. It will give me great pleasure to do all in my power to support both."

One has to read between the lines to perceive Lee's full meaning. In effect he was saying that if a military expedition against Mexico received the sanction of the Federal government, he would be pleased to lead it. Otherwise, he could be no party to it; if need be he would even act against it with his troops.

In declining Houston's offer, Lee was doubtless guided both by his high standard of duty and by a realistic appraisal of the nature of the governor's scheme. Nevertheless, one cannot help but speculate that, if only for a moment, he knew temptation. He had been in the army for thirty years, yet despite his many services and unequalled record, he was still only a lieutenant colonel. Men inferior to him in performance and ability, but superior in the art of Washington wire-pulling, had been promoted over him. In 1860, the prospect of his ever becoming a general must have seemed exceedingly dim.

The failure to enlist Lee's services caused Houston to turn to his old friend and fellow Texan, Ben McCulloch. Not only was McCulloch privy to Houston's plans, but he was renowned as the dashing and highly successful commander of the Texas Rangers in the Mexican War. "Ben will do for a very 'Big Captain' as my Red Brothers say," Houston remarked.

By August the governor had done everything within his power to raise and equip an army capable of conquering Mexico. The rest depended on the British bondholders. If they decided to back the expedition, then perhaps before the year was out, 10,000 Texas cavalry headed by McCulloch would be crossing the Rio Grande on their way to the Halls of Montezuma. Houston, as governor, would order the invasion on the grounds of defending his state against Mexican depredations. Then, at the opportune moment, he would resign the governorship and proclaim himself "protector" of Mexico, justifying this action with the assertion that he would be bringing law, peace, and order to the anarchic Mexicans, and promoting the cause of democracy and civilization in the Western Hemisphere. And the name of Houston would lead all others as the popular choice for president—if not in 1860, then surely in 1864.

But it was not to be. The British bondholders turned down Houston's proposal. As he had feared, they were not prepared to trust someone so far from London in so risky an enterprise. And without money nothing could be done.

At least for the time being. Before abandoning the idea completely Houston made one last effort. The secession crisis of 1861 provided the opportunity.

Public sentiment in Texas following Abraham Lincoln's election overwhelmingly favored emulating South Carolina and the other Southern states that were pulling out of the Union. Houston knew that the secession of Texas was sooner or later inevitable.

But was it inevitable that Texas join the new "confederacy" being set up at Montgomery, Alabama? Was there any reason why the old Lone Star Republic could not be reestablished? And, as an independent nation, why could not Texas take over Mexico?

Houston gave public expression to these thoughts early in January 1861, in a reply to J. M. Calhoun, "Commissioner from Alabama," who had come to Austin to invite Texas to join in forming a confederacy:

"Should Alabama, without waiting for the action of Texas, withdraw from the Union, and Texas by the force of circumstances, be compelled at a future period, to provide for her own safety, the course of Alabama, South Carolina, and such other States as may follow their lead, will but strengthen the conviction, already strong among our people, that their interest will lead them to avoid entangling alliances, and enter once again upon a national career. . . . Texas has views of expansion not common to many of her sister States. Although an empire within herself, she feels that there is an empire beyond, essential to her security. She will not be content to have the path of her destiny clogged. The same spirit of enterprise that founded a Republic here, will carry her institutions Southward and Westward."

Unfortunately, Houston's go-it-alone policy went counter to the desire and expectations of most Texans. Only some of the old settlers, with nostalgic memories of the Republic, supported him. When he spoke in Waco in favor of a "separate Republic of the Lone Star," the crowd responded with three cheers for South Carolina, and newspapers throughout the state denounced him as a "submissionist" and a "traitor to the South." Never before—not even in 1857—had Houston's popularity sunk so low.

He believed, however, that "given time, I can, in any situation, bring Texas to my bidding." He had done so on numerous occasions in the past, and he now sought to do so again by employing delaying tactics designed to prevent the state from seceding until he could bring about a change in public sentiment.

But the secessionists, who readily guessed Houston's intention, were too powerful and determined to be denied. Over his strenuous objections they had the legislature call into being a state convention, which on February 1, 1861, voted 167 to 8 in favor of secession as the first step in joining the Confederacy.

Houston's opposition, however, forced the convention to submit its action to a popular referendum—the only one held in any of the first seven Southern states that left the Union. The referendum, he hoped, would serve to postpone secession while he took his case for a new Lone Star Republic directly to the people.

During the early part of February he set out to stump the state. At Galveston, where hotheads had threatened to kill him if he spoke, he declared to a large and hostile audience: "Some of you laugh to scorn the idea of bloodshed as the result of secession. But let me tell you what is coming. . . .

Your fathers and husbands, your sons and brothers, will be herded at the point of the bayonet. . . . You may, after the sacrifice of countless millions of treasure and hundreds of thousands of lives, as a bare possibility, win Southern independence. . . . but I doubt it."

It was a magnificent performance, but all quite futile. Pro-Confederate mobs and night riders terrorized many Unionists into voting for secession or at least staying away from the polls. Many other Texans were simply indifferent to the outcome, or else felt that the result was foreordained. Altogether, fewer than half the eligible voters went to the polls, and those who did voted three to one in favor of secession. Accordingly, on March 2, the convention proclaimed Texas out of the Union. Ironically, it was both the twenty-fifth anniversary of Texas's independence and the sixty-eighth birthday of Sam Houston.

Next the convention took steps to remove the governor from office, or at least force him to abandon his opposition to the secessionist program. After ratifying the Confederate constitution, the convention passed a law requiring all state officials to take an oath of allegiance to the Confederacy. It then notified the governor that he was to appear before it on the morning of March 16, at its meeting hall in the cream-colored limestone capitol, to take the oath.

Houston debated about whether or not to obey the summons. From the first he had refused to recognize that the convention had any legal existence. If he took the oath, he would not only be humbling himself before his triumphant enemies but would also be sanctioning what he deemed usurpation. On the other hand, if he refused, then he would be deposed as governor and lose all chance of realizing his Mexican ambitions or of controlling the course of affairs in Texas.

On the night of March 15 he went to his room on the second floor of the rather ramshackle frame house that served as the "temporary" executive mansion of Texas. Taking off his coat, vest, and shoes, he began pondering what his decision should be. All through the night his wife and children could hear him pacing back and forth in his bedroom and in the upper hall, "wrestling with his spirit," one of his daughters later said, "as Jacob wrestled with the angel. . . ."

By morning he had made up his mind. Coming down the stairs, still in his shirt sleeves and stocking feet, he entered the kitchen where his wife was preparing breakfast and announced in a quiet voice: "Margaret, I will never do it."

Later in the morning the convention assembled according to schedule, the members filled with a sense of impending drama. At the appointed time the president of the convention stepped up to the rostrum and called: "Sam Houston!"

There was no reply.

"Sam Houston!"

Again there was silence.

For the third and final time he repeated: "Sam Houston!"

No answer. The governor sat alone in his office in the basement of the capitol, whittling on a pine stick.

Upon Houston's failure to appear, the convention declared the post of governor vacant and appointed Lieutenant Governor Edward Clark to fill it. The Southern nationalists were the masters of Texas. Its flag was to be not the Lone Star but the Stars and Bars.

Houston denounced the convention for usurpation and declared that he remained the rightful governor. But he knew he was beaten. "It is, perhaps, meet that my career should close thus," he stated in a letter to the people of Texas. "I have seen patriots and statesmen of my youth one by one gathered to their fathers, and the government which they have reared rent in twain. . . . I stand the last almost of my race. . . ." Beyond written protest, however, Houston would not go. Twice armed support was offered him, and twice he refused it.

On the night of March 19, as he was packing to leave the governor's mansion, a group of friends visited him. They were prepared, they announced, to fight to keep him in power. Although deeply moved by their loyalty, Houston told them to abandon such thoughts: "It would be criminal to deluge the capital of Texas with blood of Texans, merely to keep one poor old man in a position a few days longer."

A second offer of help came from a much higher source: President Abraham Lincoln. It was not Lincoln's first approach. Sometime in February, while still president-elect, he had sent a letter to Houston by means of an agent named George D. Giddings in which he proposed, as soon as he should be inaugurated, to send an army to help Houston keep Texas in the Union.

The governor showed the letter to four close friends and asked their advice. Only one favored accepting Lincoln's proposal. Houston thereupon burned the letter, saying as he did so: "Gentlemen, I have asked your advice and will take it, but if I were twenty years younger I would accept Mr. Lincoln's proposition. . . ." He then told Giddings to inform Lincoln that he did not desire his assistance, and that instead of more Federal troops in Texas, those already there should be withdrawn in order to avoid civil war.

Lincoln, misled by inaccurate newspaper accounts of Houston's fight against secession, apparently thought that Giddings, a Democrat, had failed to report the governor's views correctly. In any case, late in March, following his inauguration, he sent Colonel Frederick W. Lander to Texas with a confidential message for Houston. At the same time, the War Department ordered Colonel Carlos A. Waite, commander of the Federal garrison in Texas, to establish an entrenched camp for the purpose of giving "aid and comfort to General Houston."

Lander arrived in Austin about March 29—two weeks after the convention had deposed Houston—and communicated to him the plan to support him with Waite's army. Once again the Texan thrust aside Lincoln's assistance; he even wrote to Waite, protesting against "the concentration of troops in fortifications in Texas." He loved the Union but he loved Texas as much, if not more. He would not plunge his state into civil war in order to keep it in the Union against its manifest wish, tragically mistaken though he thought that wish to be.

Back in 1854 he had predicted that secession would lead to war, and that war would result in the South's going down "in unequal contest, in a sea of blood and smoking ruin." Now, making his way homeward from Austin, he stopped at Brenham and made a speech in which he repeated this warning. His listeners merely laughed; the local secessionists threatened to kill him if he did not stop making such "treasonable statements."

So Houston's dream came to an end. He had waited too long to achieve it. Had he been younger, and had the Civil War been averted or postponed, he might have succeeded. As it was, his scheme was doomed to failure from the start. He had hoped to heal the division of the country through expansion; but the division, culminating in secession and war, made expansion impossible. (Even if Houston's plan had succeeded, a Texas-initiated protectorate over Mexico might have precipitated the very conflict he sought to prevent, for the North undoubtedly would have regarded it as a Southern plot to extend the sway of slavery.) Yet in waging his fight to keep Texas in the Union, or at least out of the Confederacy, he had displayed magnificent courage and prophetic foresight. There are those who would contend that this last battle, though it ended in defeat, was his greatest one.

After the outbreak of the war that he had feared and predicted, Houston loyally supported the Confederacy—in public. In private, he continued to speculate on the possibility of reviving the Lone Star Republic, and even dabbled in some intrigues to that purpose.

Houston lived long enough to see his warning—that secession would lead to disaster for the South—begin to come true. Moreover, he had the satisfaction of knowing that he had regained much of his old popularity, as more and more Texans came to regret that they had not listened to him. By the summer of 1863 Texas newspapers were mentioning Houston as a likely candidate for governor, and most of them conceded that if he ran he would win.

So old Sam had been right after all: Given time, he *could* always get Texans to come around to his way of thinking. Only now there was no more time. On July 26, 1863, after a short illness, he died at his ranch near Huntsville—truly the last of his race.

CHAPTER FOURTEEN

The Fall and Rise of William Tecumseh Sherman

This three-part article appeared in the July, August, and October 1979 issues of Civil War Times Illustrated *under the title (not mine) of "The Life of a Rising Son" and was fortunate enough to garner an award for being, according to a poll of subscribers, the best article published in that magazine in 1979. Parts one and two are presented here with only a few minor changes. Part three, on the other hand, contains some major factual and analytical revisions, although not as many as I had anticipated. These revisions stem from my becoming better acquainted with the Atlanta Campaign and Sherman's performance during it, while writing* Decision in the West: The Atlanta Campaign of 1864 *(Lawrence: University Press of Kansas, 1992). As a result, I came to an unconventional view of Sherman as a general, one that shocked and even offended some. I shall not defend it here, beyond stating that it is based on what I perceive to be facts, not preconceived prejudice.*

THE FAILURE

Among Union generals, Sherman is ranked second only to Grant. Most of his contemporaries so regarded him and few historians have challenged their judgment. Furthermore, everyone has always recognized that he possessed a brilliant if somewhat eccentric intellect, that he was a man of unique and fascinating personality, and that he embodied traits that made him "peculiarly American." From the outset of the Civil War down to the present, however, there have been widely divergent opinions concerning his talents and methods as a military commander.

Some have portrayed him as a ruthless bully on horseback, violating the laws of war, terrifying "almost helpless" Southern civilians into submission; or as a bungler who never fought or won a full-scale battle and owed success to luck, skillful lieutenants, and the mistakes of a weak enemy. Still others go to the opposite extreme, claiming that Sherman was one of the great captains of all time, the progenitor of modern warfare.

If we look for the real Sherman in histories and biographies, we will find scores of bright books on the man, but none that provides a scholarly, thorough, and systematic study of him as a commander. All one will find is unanimous, and sometimes violent, disagreement. But as Sherman once said about making war, so it can be said about writing history: It is not popularity seeking.

Sherman's military career began in 1836 at the age of sixteen when his foster father, Senator Thomas Ewing Sr. appointed him to West Point. There is no indication that Sherman (his first name was originally Tecumseh in honor of that famous warrior) desired such a career and much evidence that he embarked on it simply out of a sense of obligation to Ewing, who had taken him into his own home in Lancaster, Ohio, following the 1829 death of Sherman's father, a state judge. At the military academy he was a good student but a sloppy soldier: He accumulated so many demerits for discipline and infractions of the dress code that he finished sixth in a class of forty-three rather than fourth as entitled by his academic record. Nevertheless he became, and thereafter basically remained, a member of America's small, semi-isolated guild of professional soldiers, firmly convinced that only West Pointers were qualified for high command.

Graduation in 1840 was followed by army service that took him from New York to San Francisco and from Pittsburgh to New Orleans, but brought him no combat experience other than a few skirmishes with the Seminoles in Florida. During the Mexican War, when so many fellow West Pointers were winning fame and promotion on the battlefield, he spent most of his time on recruiting duty in Pennsylvania and occupation duty in California. By 1853 he was merely a captain in the Commissary Department, with no prospect of being anything else in the foreseeable future. Meanwhile he had acquired a wife—Ewing's pious daughter Ellen—and two children. This marriage strengthened his ties to the Ewing family and intensified the pressure on him to prove himself worthy of such an alliance. As it was, he could not support Ellen and the children in appropriate style on his army salary alone and was dependent to a degree on Ewing's financial assistance.

He asked his friend, Henry S. Turner, a former army officer who was then a partner in a St. Louis banking firm, for a job. Turner, who believed that Sherman was wasting his "intellectual energy" in the peacetime service, offered to appoint him manager of a branch bank in San Francisco. Sherman accepted, took a six-month leave, went to San Francisco, concluded he

MILLER, ED. *PHOTOGRAPHIC HISTORY.*

William T. Sherman

could make a fortune in banking and real estate, and so resigned his commission. For a while affairs went well and he built a fine house for his family. Then a business panic struck California. Sherman's bank survived but made little or no profit. The home office closed it—and then closed itself. As a consequence, in the summer of 1857 Sherman found himself "used up financially." Without cause he blamed himself for this dismal outcome. "What I failed to do," he wrote his father-in-law, "and the bad debts that now stare me in the face, must stand forever as a monument to my want of . . . sagacity."

He paid most of his debts by selling all of his property, but was unable to secure a satisfactory business position and was unwilling to reenter the army except at a higher rank than he left it. Late in 1858 he returned to Lancaster to take charge of Ewing's saltworks. Ellen was delighted to be back home. Sherman felt humiliated. As he frankly told Ewing, "I have been Captain so long that subordination will come a little hard. . . ." Deepening his sense of failure was the fact that his younger brother John was rising rapidly in politics, having just been elected to a second term in the Federal House of Representatives.

Before he had to descend into the saltworks, however, Ewing's oldest son, Thomas Jr., asked Sherman to join his law firm in Leavenworth, Kansas Territory. Sherman at once hastened to "Bleeding Kansas," where he was admitted to the bar "on the ground of general intelligence and reputation." But clients were few, he lost his only case, and a corn speculation scheme, in which Ewing Sr. and Ellen invested large sums at his urging, failed. In the summer of 1859 he again returned to Lancaster in defeat. "I look upon myself," he wrote Ellen before leaving Leavenworth, "as a dead cock in the pit. . . ."

But if unfortunate in business he was lucky in his friends. One of them, Major Don Carlos Buell, notified him that the position of superintendent of the newly established Louisiana Seminary of Learning and Military Academy (present-day Louisiana State University) was available. Sherman promptly applied, and thanks in part to the recommendations of P. G. T. Beauregard, Braxton Bragg, and Richard Taylor he received the appointment. During the ensuing months he proved to be a capable administrator and a popular teacher. Ellen, however, refused to join him in Louisiana and badgered him to return to Ohio. Her attitude annoyed Sherman, who believed that he had found his proper niche in life, at least for the time being. "As to my coming to Lancaster, and laying around doing nothing, I say without fear of being adjudged blasphemous I would rather be where your damn sinners [are]."

Ellen finally agreed to come to Louisiana where the house the academy had promised Sherman had been built. But scarcely had it been completed when early in 1861 Louisiana followed the rest of the Deep South out of the Union. Sherman, who had expected and dreaded this, immediately resigned as superintendent. Although he sympathized with the South and considered slavery the natural status for blacks, he was passionately devoted to the Union and regarded secession as synonymous with revolution and anarchy.

So Ellen had her way after all and Sherman once more was, as he put it, a "vagabond." On returning North he went to Washington where, accompanied by his brother, now a Republican senator, he offered his services to the recently inaugurated President Lincoln. Lincoln, however, told him that military men were not needed—compromise would restore the Union peacefully. Such wishful thinking disgusted Sherman. A long, hard war, he predicted, would be needed to subdue the Southern rebellion.

He decided to bide his time until the government realized the seriousness of the crisis. Meanwhile, since he now had five children to support, he took a job from his old associate Turner as president of a streetcar company in St. Louis. He was in that city when the Confederates fired on Fort Sumter. Shortly thereafter the Lincoln administration, which now needed military men very much, proposed making him a major general of volunteers, quartermaster general of the army, even assistant secretary of war. He rejected all of those posts. "The first movements of our Government will fail," he wrote brother John, "and the leaders will be cast aside. A second or third set will rise, and amongst them I may be, but at present I will not volunteer as a soldier or anything else."

Early in June, the War Department at his and John's behest offered him a commission as colonel in the Regular army. This he accepted. In common with other West Pointers he distrusted volunteers—only trained and disciplined Regulars, he declared, could put down the Rebels, whom he described as being far more realistic and purposeful than the people of the North. He believed that the politicians would make scapegoats of those generals who, even through no fault of their own, failed. For politicians as a class he had utter contempt. Indeed, he despised democracy itself, equating it with mob rule, and he frankly avowed a preference for monarchy or dictatorship. Ideologically, Sherman "the American" had more in common with European aristocrats than he did with his countrymen.

Sherman reported to the army (to use the term loosely) to find that Brigadier General Irvin McDowell was assembling troops at Washington for the purpose (most Northerners were confident) of crushing the rebellion and winning the war. But instead of the regiment of Regulars he desired and expected, he was assigned command of a brigade of volunteers. He took a dim view of these raw troops, many of whom were ninety-day enlistees clamoring to go home. "With regulars," he wrote Ellen, "I would have no doubt, but these volunteers are subject to stampedes."

On July 21, at Bull Run, Sherman's fears came true. The Federal soldiers, after initially driving back the outflanked enemy, broke into a retreat that turned into a panic-stricken rout when they themselves were unexpectedly assailed on the flank. Sherman was disgusted not only with their conduct on the battlefield but also with the way they acted on the march to it. "No curse could be greater," he declared, "than invasion by a volunteer army. No Goths or Vandals ever had less respect for the lives and property of friends and foes. . . ."

Yet he himself performed well at Bull Run, especially in view of the fact that it was the first battle in which he had ever participated, much less commanded troops. Assigned the mission of pinning down the Confederates by feinting an attack on their front, he promptly and intelligently executed orders to make a real attack, which contributed substantially to the early Northern success. Then, following the Union collapse, he kept his brigade in reasonably good order while it abandoned the battlefield. Finally, on reaching Washington, he took charge of rallying and reorganizing troops to defend the capital in case the Rebels attempted to follow up their victory. In sum he displayed coolness, courage, initiative, and good judgment. The only serious weakness he revealed was in engaging his brigade regiment by regiment instead of as a whole. This was a fault common to all Northern commanders at Bull Run, however, and probably inevitable given their inexperience in handling large bodies of troops. It speaks well for Sherman that after the battle he obtained the latest manuals on tactics and used them to retrain himself so that he could better train his men.

Late in August the War Department promoted Sherman to brigadier general and ordered him to Kentucky. The promotion somewhat surprised him—he considered himself "disgraced" by his involvement in the Bull Run fiasco and told Ellen that "I suppose soon I can sneak into some quiet corner." On the other hand, the transfer to Kentucky delighted him. For he believed, presciently as it turned out, that in the West the war would be won and the great military reputations made. For the time being, however, as he notified Lincoln, he preferred "to serve in a subordinate capacity, and in no event to be left in a superior command." He still feared that the unreliability of the volunteers and the unrealistic attitude of the government would inevitably result in disaster for Northern commanders. "Not till I see daylight ahead," he confided to Ellen, "do I want to lead."

Lincoln responded to Sherman's unique diffidence by posting him as second in command to Brigadier General Robert A. Anderson, who was in charge of the Department of the Cumberland and who had requested Sherman's services. Anderson, the "Hero of Fort Sumter, was endeavoring to organize Union forces in Kentucky, his native state. But, as Sherman discovered on arriving at Louisville, he had succeeded in raising only a few troops and most of them were poorly armed and trained. Worse, after about a month Anderson fell ill and asked to be relieved. As a result Sherman was thrust into exactly the sort of position he had wanted to avoid—top command in a vital theater of war.

His reaction was one of semi-hysteria. He believed that General Albert Sidney Johnston's Confederate army, which had moved up from Tennessee into Kentucky, possessed overwhelming numbers and intended to seize Louisville and invade Ohio and Indiana. Actually Johnston had fewer men than Sherman, and far from planning an offensive, he feared that Sherman would attack him. But Sherman, lacking an intelligence service and prey to an overactive imagination, had no doubt that he again faced defeat and disgrace. He bombarded the War Department with frantic pleas for large quantities of additional troops and equipment, warning that unless he got them "I will not be responsible for events. . . ."

Instead of reinforcements, however, Washington sent messages urging him to "liberate" East Tennessee, where most of the inhabitants remained loyal to the Union. This response persuaded him that he was being deliberately "sacrificed" by the politicians. "To advance," he wrote Ellen, "would be madness and to stand still folly. . . . The idea of going down in History with a fame such as threatens me nearly makes me crazy, indeed I may be so now."

Some people who observed him in his quarters on the ground floor of a Louisville hotel concluded that there could be no doubt about it—he was demented. Tall and thin, always looking like he needed a shave and his red hair never combed, he spent hours pacing back and forth, incessantly smoking cigars, head bent forward, hands behind his back, eyes darting about but seeing nothing. Other times he sprawled in a chair, thumbs in his vest, and spoke to whoever was present in a rapid, staccato fashion, jumping from subject to subject and expressing himself in language that was both vivid and vehement. When or if he ate and slept, no one could tell. He seemed to live on nervous energy and to be consumed by it at the same time.

On October 16, Secretary of War Simon Cameron arrived in Louisville on a tour of inspection. Sherman went to confer with him. In the room were several reporters—a breed Sherman deemed little better than spies. Cameron, lying on a bed with a whiskey bottle nearby, said, "Now General Sherman tell us your troubles." Sherman demanded that the reporters leave—they should not be present at such a discussion. But Cameron overruled him—"We are all friends, here." Sherman then proceeded to declare that he needed 60,000 men just to defend Kentucky, 200,000 to carry out an offensive. Astounded, Cameron quite correctly replied that such numbers simply were unavailable and that Sherman must be overestimating the Rebel strength. Later Sherman and his apologists claimed that in referring to 200,000 troops he had in mind a campaign to open up the entire Mississippi Valley, and that since it ultimately took that many (and more) he was not guilty of exaggeration but rather showed realistic foresight. The subject of Sherman's interview with Cameron, however, was not long-range strategy but the immediate situation in Kentucky. Additionally, various documents, including some of Sherman's own dispatches, make it evident that he was thinking of the proposed invasion of East Tennessee and not of a march on New Orleans.

Cameron promised to order reinforcements to Kentucky—which he did. On the other hand, soon after leaving Louisville he told one of the reporters who had been present during his meeting with Sherman that the general was "unbalanced and that it would not be [wise] to leave him in command." This reporter in turn published a story, which was widely reprinted, deriding Sherman's "insane request" for 200,000 troops and implying that Sherman was mentally deranged. Worse, the official account of the Sherman-Cameron interview, which appeared early in November, spoke of Sherman's "gloomy . . . overestimate" of the enemy's strength. Angered and upset, Sherman on November 6 asked Major General George B. McClellan, the recently installed supreme commander of the Union army, to replace him with someone of more "sanguine mind." McClellan, who had just received a report from one of his top aides stating that Sherman was not "sufficiently master of his judgment to warrant the intrusting to him of an important military command," promptly sent Sherman's old friend Don Carlos Buell, now a brigadier general, to take charge in Kentucky.

The prospect of relief from the tribulations of command did not relieve Sherman's apprehensions, however. On November 11 he instructed his West Point classmate, Brigadier General George H. Thomas, commanding in eastern Kentucky, to make ready to retreat at once—Johnston was about to advance on Louisville with 45,000 men. Thomas answered that he would do so, although he doubted that the Confederates were that strong or intended to attack. In this he was absolutely right: Johnston had only 12,500 troops, many of them unarmed, whereas Union forces in Kentucky now numbered over 40,000. Sherman's belief, or rather delusion, that Johnston planned to strike at Louisville derived (as he himself admitted to

Thomas) from the boasts of Confederate sympathizers in that city, not from reliable intelligence.

Sherman also remained despondent; in fact, he became more so. To brother John he declared, "If anybody can do better than I can for God's sake let him. I prefer to follow not to lead, as I confess I have not the confidence of a Leader in this war, and would be happy to slide into obscurity." And to Ellen he wrote, "I am almost crazy."

Alarmed by his condition, one of his staff officers urged Ellen to come to Louisville. She did so, bringing two of the children. At her behest John soon followed. Together they tried to restore Sherman's spirits and confidence but achieved little if any improvement. As John told his brother, "You have been so harassed with the magnitude of your labors and have allowed yourself so little rest . . . that your mind casts a sombre shadow upon everything."

On November 15 Buell arrived and took command in Louisville. Six days later Sherman, predicting that "some terrible disaster is inevitable" in Kentucky, left for St. Louis. There he reported for duty to Major General Henry Wager Halleck, commander of the Department of Missouri. Halleck was a friend of Sherman's from California days and had a high opinion of his ability. He ignored the stories about Sherman's instability and sent him to inspect Union forces in central Missouri, with authority to take command of them if he saw fit.

Within a week Sherman was sending Halleck frantic dispatches to the effect that a huge Confederate army was about to descend on Jefferson City and St. Louis. Unable to believe, but unwilling to reject these assertions out of hand, Halleck instructed Brigadier John Pope to check on them. Pope reported with complete accuracy that the enemy were too weak to pose a serious threat. At the same time new stories appeared in the papers depicting Sherman as going about with a "half-wild expression" and quoting him as having said that "the rebels could never be whipped."

Halleck immediately ordered Sherman back to St. Louis. To McClellan he wrote: "I am satisfied that General Sherman's physical and mental system is so completely broken by labor and care as to render him for the present entirely unfit for duty." Judging that Sherman needed rest, he gave him twenty days' leave. Accompanied by Ellen, who had rushed to St. Louis on hearing that her husband once more was in trouble, Sherman returned to Lancaster.

Soon the *Cincinnati Commercial* published, under the headline, "General William T. Sherman Insane," an article asserting that Sherman was "stark mad" while commanding in Kentucky, that in Missouri "the shocking fact that he was a madman was developed by orders that his subordinates knew to be preposterous and refused to obey," and that he had now been "relieved altogether from command." Numerous other newspapers reprinted the story.

Through his brother-in-law Phil Ewing, Sherman published a rebuttal to the *Commercial's* article, which he charged had been written by a reporter whom he had arrested in Kentucky for defying military regulations. Nevertheless, he felt totally crushed. Again he had failed, again he had disgraced himself, again he had brought shame on his family. Efforts by Ellen, John, and Thomas Ewing Sr. to cheer him up proved unavailing, as did assurances from Halleck that he had not lost confidence in him. After returning to St. Louis, where Halleck assigned him to drilling recruits, he wrote John: "I am so sensible now of my disgrace from having exaggerated the force of our enemy in Kentucky that I do think I should have committed suicide were it not for my children. I do not think I can again be entrusted with a command. . . ."

Perhaps no general subsequently considered great performed more miserably when first given command responsibility than did Sherman in Kentucky and Missouri. There were three reasons why this was so. One is obvious and simple: inexperience. The Confederate general Richard S. Ewell remarked that as a result of his prewar military career he learned everything there was to know about commanding a troop of cavalry but forgot everything else. Sherman did not have the opportunity to learn even that much, and not until Bull Run did he as much as witness a battle. Hence he was right in not seeking a top command at the outset of the war, and it was unfortunate for him that he was thrust into one nevertheless.

The second reason likewise is quite apparent: Sherman lacked mental balance. Although it was made by a man who disliked him, there was considerable truth in the comment that Sherman's "brain is like a splendid piece of machinery with all of the screws a little loose." In Kentucky and Missouri those screws threatened to pop out altogether. Furthermore, he possessed too much imagination—a serious defect in a military man. Sherman once described himself as being "somewhat blind to what occurs near me," but as having a "clear perception of things and events remote." The trouble was that the "things and events," which he saw so clearly at a distance, often were not actually there.

The third reason is more basic and also more complex. Sherman was gifted with an exceptional intelligence, enormous energy, and an impressive personality. Naturally he was aware of his superiority and just as naturally aspired to, even anticipated, a high degree of success in life. Further stimulating his ambition was a desire to prove himself worthy of the charity and support of his foster father and of the hopes and confidence of his wife and the rest of the Ewing-Sherman clan. But instead of rising spectacularly to the top, he spent his years from twenty to forty bobbing up and down, going nowhere in particular. Meanwhile his younger brother John was achieving the distinction that the family had predicted for him. By 1861 Sherman was a classic example of a not uncommon type: A man who believes that because of his own qualities he deserves success but who, because of his past experience, doubts he ever will attain it; bad luck and the shortcomings of others will always deny it to him.

This seemingly paradoxical mixture of ambition and pessimism explains, even more than his realization that he lacked combat experience, why Sherman sought a subordinate post when the Civil War started. It also explains his conduct when placed in command in Kentucky and after being given a quasi-independent assignment in Missouri. By exaggerating the strength and aggressiveness of the enemy, by declaring his own forces hopelessly inadequate, and by denouncing the politicians in Washington for ignoring the dangers facing him, he prepared in advance alibis for the inevitable disaster to come. By constantly castigating himself and by expressing the wish to retire into some "quiet corner"—even commit suicide—he made it impossible for his family to reproach him for failing to succeed: Nothing they could say in criticism of him could match his own self-condemnation.

Sherman at the beginning of the Civil War possessed the physical courage and mental quickness to perform well in the heat of combat, as he demonstrated at Bull Run, but he lacked the strength of mind and character to exercise successfully a highly responsible independent command. What he needed was someone to guide and steady him, and to bear the burden of responsibility while he became better acquainted with war, developed the ability to view affairs more realistically, and—most important of all—learned to trust himself.

Early in 1862, while Sherman drilled troops in St. Louis, another native of Ohio was commanding them farther down the Mississippi River at Cairo, Illinois. He was slightly younger and much shorter than Sherman, but like him had graduated from West Point, resigned from the army, and experienced a rather dismal time of it as a civilian. In the summer of 1861, while commanding a regiment of volunteers in northeast Missouri, he had set out to attack a camp of Confederate guerrillas. It was the first time ever he had been in sole charge of a military operation and as he approached the camp, he later wrote, "my heart kept getting higher and higher until it felt to me as though it was in my throat." But on coming into sight of the camp he found that the Confederates had fled. "My heart resumed its place." Also, it occurred to him that the enemy had been as much afraid of him as he had been of the enemy. "This was a view of the question I had never taken before but it was one I never forgot afterwards. From that event to the close of the war, I never experienced trepidation upon confronting any enemy, though I always felt more or less anxiety. I never forgot that he had as much reason to fear my forces as I had his. The lesson was valuable."

The name of the man who learned this valuable lesson was Ulysses S. Grant. Sherman had known him slightly at West Point and had exchanged a few words with him in 1857, when he met him peddling firewood on the streets of St. Louis. Starting with 1862 a very special relationship would develop between these two men, one that was useful to Grant but absolutely essential to Sherman.

THE SUBORDINATE

The most important decision Major General Henry Wager Halleck made during the Civil War came when, as commander of Union forces in Missouri and western Kentucky, he permitted Brigadier General U. S. Grant to attack and capture Forts Henry and Donelson in February 1862. This broke open the Confederates' front in the West and caused them to retreat from Kentucky and middle Tennessee. Following in their wake, the Federal army of Major General Don Carlos Buell occupied Nashville on the Cumberland River, and Grant moved south along the Tennessee River.

As this took place, Halleck made what possibly was his second most important decision: He gave Sherman, who had been relegated to drilling recruits in St. Louis after his failures in Kentucky and Missouri, another chance. According to Sherman's highly sympathetic biographer, Lloyd

Lewis, he did so out of a self-interested desire to ingratiate himself with the politically influential Ewing-Sherman clan. Conceivably this was at least a minor consideration, but the weight of evidence and logic supports the conclusion that Halleck was motivated mainly by friendship and a belief that Sherman was capable of rendering, as he assured him, "important service" once his "nervous system so shattered by hard labor, anxiety & exposure" had been restored.

On February 13, after Grant launched his campaign against Forts Henry and Donelson, Halleck posted Sherman to Paducah, Kentucky, with instructions to forward troops and supplies to Grant. He performed this task with commendable efficiency. Also, he gained Grant's attention and thanks by writing him notes of encouragement and offering to serve under him at the front despite being senior in rank.

Following the capture of the forts, Halleck placed Sherman in command of a newly organized division and assigned him to Grant, who, meanwhile, had been promoted to major general. Sherman loaded his troops (who regarded him with a certain apprehension because of the newspaper stories about his being crazy) aboard steamboats and proceeded up the Tennessee River with orders to cut the strategic Memphis and Charleston Railroad, which ran near the Tennessee-Mississippi line. Unable to do so because heavy rains had turned the roads into quagmires, he turned back and joined other Union forces that had disembarked at Pittsburg Landing. This area, he reported, would be the best place from which to attack the Confederates, who were concentrating at Corinth, Mississippi, some twenty miles to the southwest. Grant agreed, and during the latter part of March assembled 33,000 troops at Pittsburg Landing plus 5,000 more at Crump's Landing five miles to the north.

Halleck instructed Grant not to advance until reinforced by Buell's 35,000-man army, which was moving overland from Nashville. While awaiting Buell, Grant decided to use this lull in operations to better train his own forces, most of whom were raw recruits. Accordingly he deployed the five divisions he had at Pittsburg Landing with an eye to convenience in drilling them rather than fighting a battle. For the same reason he dismissed as impractical and unnecessary the fortifying of their position. Sherman fully concurred. Like Grant, like nearly all professional military men at this stage of the war, he believed that entrenchments merely made soldiers timid. Furthermore, both he and Grant were confident that the Confederates, who by all accounts were badly demoralized by their recent setbacks, would not be so foolhardy as to leave their base to assault the Federal army at its base: this would have been contrary to the principles of sound strategy.

Both Grant and Sherman were mistaken—almost fatally so. Confederate commander General Albert Sidney Johnston was desperate to reverse the tide of war in the West and to redeem his own woefully impaired military reputation. Therefore he decided to destroy Grant before Buell arrived. On April 3 his army, 40,000 strong, marched northward from Corinth. Bad roads, ineptitude, and inexperience delayed its progress, but during the night of April 5 it reached the vicinity of Pittsburg Landing. The next morning it struck—and struck hard.

The British military historian B. H. Liddell Hart, who rarely finds fault with Grant and Sherman, states that they were victims of a "strategical" surprise but denies that they experienced a "tactical" surprise. Undoubtedly he is right about the first. When the Confederates attacked, Grant was, as he had been for most of the past several days, seven miles away at Savannah, Tennessee, the east side of the Tennessee River, waiting for Buell. As always during his absences Sherman acted as his de facto deputy at Pittsburg Landing. On April 4 Rebel cavalry appeared near the Federal camp, and on the next day several clashes occurred between patrols from both armies. Furthermore, many Southern soldiers as they approached the Union lines fired their muskets in order to reload them with fresh charges. General P. G. T. Beauregard, Johnston's second in command, was so convinced that the Yankees could not help being alerted that he proposed calling off the attack and returning to Corinth.

He need not have worried. Grant and Sherman no more anticipated a Confederate offensive than did American commanders the World II Japanese air raid on Pearl Harbor. Sherman, who probably feared making the same mistake he had in Kentucky and Missouri of exaggerating the enemy threat, scoffed at reports of large Rebel forces being nearby and at those who delivered the reports. On the afternoon of April 5 he telegraphed Grant, "I do not apprehend anything like an attack upon our position." Grant in turn sent a dispatch to Halleck in St. Louis declaring, "I have scarcely the faintest idea of an attack (general one) being made upon us. . . ."

As for Liddell Hart's claim that there was no "tactical" surprise, he supports this (as did Grant and Sherman themselves) by pointing out that most of the Northern troops were able to form in line of battle before the Confederates charged. This is a pointless argument, however. No army as large and undisciplined as Johnston's could possibly have approached its objective without being detected. Indeed, on the morning of April 6 a Union patrol, sent out on the initiative of a Northern major, actually attacked the advancing Southerners before they made their assault. Furthermore, the Confederates were formed in such a fashion, the terrain of such a nature, and the Union camps so scattered that only small portions of both armies were engaged at first, which meant that most of the Federal units had ample time in which to deploy. In brief, only if the Yankees had been deaf, blind, and drunk could Johnston have achieved "tactical" surprise in the sense of catching them totally unprepared.

Sherman's division held the extreme Union right and was the second to be assailed, the first being Brigadier General Benjamin Prentiss's division, which was posted to the southwest of Sherman's in the direct line of the Confederate advance. Many of Sherman's inexperienced men fled from the shock of unexpected battle, but most of them remained in their hastily formed lines. Sherman helped keep them there by his own calmness, even cheerfulness, under fire. In the words of a newspaper correspondent, his "usually hot nerves" seemed to be soothed by combat.

For several hours his division checked fierce Rebel charges, inflicting and suffering heavy losses in the process. Then, along with the rest of Grant's army, it fell back slowly until by late afternoon it was close to the Tennessee River. During the evening and night 5,000 reinforcements belatedly arrived from Crump's Landing and 20,000 more from Buell's army. In the morning Grant counterattacked, and the Confederates, with Johnston dead and their strength reduced to no more than 20,000, began retreating back to Corinth.

Grant in his report on the battle singled out Sherman for "special mention" for having "displayed great judgment and skill in the management of his men." Halleck, on arriving at Pittsburg Landing to take personal charge of Grant's and Buell's armies, went further, informing the War Department that "It was the unanimous opinion here that Brig. Gen. W.T. Sherman saved the fortune of the day of the 6th and contributed largely to the glorious victory of the 7th." And Lloyd Lewis in his *Sherman, Fighting Prophet* contends that "So stoutly did Sherman hold the Union right that Johnston failed in his scheme for rolling up the Federal line like a sheet of paper," an opinion echoed by Liddell Hart, who states Sherman's resistance on the right flank "formed an invaluable brake on the Confederate advance during its original impulse."

There can be no doubt that Sherman and his troops did preserve the Union right. This achievement, however, needs to be placed in a more realistic perspective than it appears in the above quotations. First of all, Johnston did not plan to "roll up" Grant's line from the right. On the contrary, he intended to deliver his main thrust against the Federal left with the object either of cutting off Grant from the Tennessee or else forcing him back to that river. That he first struck the Union center (Prentiss) and then the right (Sherman) was the product of circumstances rather than design.

Secondly, Sherman's division enjoyed an extremely strong position even without fortifications. Its right was protected by Owl Creek, its front by Shiloh Creek. Furthermore, unlike Prentiss's division, it benefited from having Brigadier General John McClernand's division within close supporting distance. As a consequence it was nearly impregnable against frontal assault, as witness the fact that Brigadier General Patrick Cleburne's Confederate brigade, which spearheaded that assault, lost almost one-half its men. Not until Prentiss, who bore the brunt of Johnston's initial attack, retreated were the Rebels able to dislodge Sherman's and McClernand's intermingled forces by hitting their now exposed left flank.

Thirdly, and finally, after Sherman's withdrawal the Confederates made no further serious attacks on him; they lacked the strength and were concentrating on the Union left. This was fortunate for him, for as Liddell Hart points out, by then his division was "only a remnant," which "really formed an appendix to the line of McClernand's division." Most of its men were dead, wounded, or missing, many of them being fugitives. It played only a minor role in the subsequent fighting on April 6, and contributed little to Grant's attack the following day.

To sum up, Sherman performed well in the Battle of Shiloh, but no better than several other division commanders, notably Prentiss, whose stubborn stand in the "Hornet's Nest" gave Grant the time he needed to form a defensive perimeter on the banks of the Tennessee from which he was able to fend off the last feeble Confederate assault and then launch his counterattack. Furthermore, his failure (of which Prentiss also was guilty) to heed the signs and reports of a major enemy offensive was a major reason why Johnston's desperate gamble came so close to success. To his credit, he made no claim to exceptional accomplishment at Shiloh. When, following the battle, he was promoted on Halleck's recommendation to major general, he informed his wife Ellen, "I received today the commission of Major

General, but, I know not why, it gives me far less emotion than my old commission as 1st Lieutenant of Artillery. The latter, I knew, I merited; this I doubt. . . ."

Even so, the promotion, the commendations from Halleck and Grant, and the praise bestowed on him by a number of newspapers restored Sherman's reputation and bolstered his self-confidence. "I have worked hard to keep down," he wrote Ellen with obvious glee, "but somehow I am forced into prominence and might as well submit." To his father-in-law he declared proudly, "I know I can take what position I choose among my peers." Shiloh, for Sherman, was the turning point.

It also strengthened his ties to Grant. He realized that he shared with him much of the responsibility for the Confederates' near victory, which, had it been fully achieved, would almost surely have ended both their military careers in disgrace. When several newspapers denounced Grant as a bloody bungler for allowing himself to be surprised in an unfortified position, Sherman defended him in a public letter while privately vowing "to get even with the miserable class of corrupt editors." More important, on learning that Grant planned to leave the army out of resentment over being relegated by Halleck to the meaningless post of second in command, he persuaded him to reconsider and remain—which, in a sense, was possibly Sherman's greatest contribution to the Northern cause. Grant had good reasons in being grateful to Sherman, who for his part regarded Grant as a man in whom one could place "absolute faith."

He doubted, however, that Grant possessed the intellect to be a great "strategist." Instead he considered "Old Brains" Halleck the North's only "Great Man thus far." He credited him with conceiving the plan by which the Confederate front in the West had been broken, was "astonished" by the "sagacity" he showed in his ponderous march on Corinth, and hailed his occupation of that town on May 30 as "a victory as brilliant and important as any recorded in history." When Halleck was summoned to Washington to serve as commander of all Union forces, he declared that there was no other general in the West who could replace him. Even allowing for Sherman's quite justified feeling of gratitude to Halleck for rescuing him from the military scrap heap, these extravagant words of praise for that timid general and his clumsy operations indicate that Sherman himself was still far from ready for high command.

Following the capture of Corinth the Union army spread out to occupy western Tennessee and northern Mississippi. Sherman took command of the

Memphis area. For the first time he had to deal with a large hostile population. At the beginning of the war he had spoken of reconciling Southerners to the Union. Now he believed that it was impossible to "change the hearts of the people of the South," from which he drew the conclusion that if the Southerners "cannot be made to love us, they can be made to fear us" by making "war so terrible that they will realize the fact that, however brave and gallant and devoted to their country, still they are mortal. . . ."

In September, following a series of guerrilla attacks on unarmed Union supply ships along the Mississippi, Sherman had his soldiers burn the river village of Randolph, Tennessee, in retaliation and announced that henceforth ten families would be expelled from Memphis every time a boat was fired on. He did not carry out the latter threat, but in October he sent troops over to Arkansas, where they destroyed a number of dwellings of persons suspected of aiding guerrillas. These measures, it should be noted, were no more harsh than those that other Northern commanders adopted in attempting to combat partisan warfare. Indeed they were mild in comparison with what his own brother-in-law, Brigadier General Thomas Ewing Jr., did in Missouri in 1863. He depopulated four counties in an effort to suppress Quantrill's bushwhackers. The principal difference between Sherman and other Union officers who struggled against guerrillas lies not in practice but in the frankness and vehemence with which he justified reprisals against the civilians who in fact did aid the guerrillas. Moreover, he remained sufficiently objective to realize that the conduct of the Federal troops often was of such a nature as to arouse legitimate wrath among Southerners. In an order to his division he declared that "This demoralizing and disgraceful practice of pillage must cease, else the country will rise on us and justly shoot us down like dogs and wild beasts."

In December 1862 Grant made his first attempt to take Vicksburg, employing a plan worked out in collaboration with Sherman. Not only did the two friends hope to eliminate the last major Confederate stronghold on the Mississippi River, but they wanted to anticipate Major General John McClernand, a highly ambitious and influential Illinois politician to whom Lincoln had given command of an expedition against Vicksburg in return for raising troops in the Midwest. Both Sherman and Grant considered McClernand vain, incompetent, nonprofessional, and a dangerous rival to their own military position and prospects.

Grant moved overland with 40,000 soldiers and threatened Lieutenant General John C. Pemberton's 24,000-man Confederate army at Grenada, Mississippi, with the object of preventing Pemberton from reinforcing Vicksburg, which was held by a garrison of only 6,000. At the same time Sherman at Memphis hastily loaded 30,000 troops (most of whom had been recruited by McClernand) aboard transports and headed down the Mississippi, escorted by Rear Admiral David D. Porter's gunboat flotilla. On December 26 he landed just north of Vicksburg on the east bank of the Yazoo River. The next day he received word that McClernand was on his way to take command of the expedition. On the other hand, there was no news from Grant and there were signs that Vicksburg was being reinforced. Fearful that delay would ruin any chance of victory he assaulted the Rebel defense line, which consisted of forts and trenches atop steep bluffs overlooking Chickasaw Bayou.

The attack was a total failure. Sherman lost 1,776 men, the Confederates only 187. Publicly Sherman took full responsibility for the defeat, privately he blamed poor leadership by Brigadier General George W. Morgan, whose division spearheaded the assault. Neither diagnosis, however, was correct. Unknown to Sherman, Grant had retreated northward from Grenada, thereby enabling Pemberton to reinforce Vicksburg so heavily with first-rate troops that it would have required a miracle for Sherman to break through the defenses on the Chickasaw Bluffs.

Grant's official reason for retreating was the destruction of his main supply base at Holly Springs, Mississippi, by Rebel cavalry on December 20. No doubt this was an important factor, but as Liddell Hart notes, Grant himself admitted that he could have lived off the countryside for another two months. Quite likely the news that McClernand was en route to Memphis had an even greater impact on Grant, for as soon as he received it he decided to go to Memphis and assume personal charge of the Vicksburg expedition. To be sure, he sent Sherman word of his withdrawal but this could not reach Sherman in time to prevent what was now a pointless assault on Chickasaw Bluffs. In effect Grant left Sherman in the lurch. But if Sherman resented Grant's conduct, he never mentioned it. In his memoirs he merely stated that "Grant sent me word" of his withdrawal but "it did not reach me in time."

On January 2 McClernand arrived on the Yazoo River and superseded Sherman, who was relegated to command of a corps. Realizing that it would be futile to renew the attempt to take Vicksburg, McClernand adopted a suggestion from Sherman and moved against the Confederate fort at Arkansas Post on the Arkansas River. A land assault directed by Sherman got nowhere, but fire from Porter's gunboats scared some of the 5,000 defenders into making an unauthorized surrender, thereby enabling the Federals to seize the fort on January 11. Amusingly, when Grant first heard of McClernand's expedition to Arkansas Post he denounced it as a "wild goose chase," but on learning that it had succeeded and that Sherman had originated it he promptly dubbed it a "very important" victory.

McClernand claimed and obtained credit for the conquest of Arkansas Post, whereas several newspapers condemned Sherman for the repulse at Chickasaw Bluffs. Once more his spirits drooped; again he talked of resigning. In particular he resented serving under McClernand: "Mr. Lincoln intended to insult me and the military profession by putting McClernand over me," he complained to his brother, Senator John Sherman. He felt better, however, after Grant, with Halleck's backing and Lincoln's acquiescence, assumed command of all forces operating along the Mississippi. The result was that McClernand became, like himself, just a corps commander. Also, his gratitude to Grant increased when Grant supported him in expelling a hostile reporter from his camp.

Late in April Grant began the brilliant campaign of maneuver, battle, and siege that culminated on July 4 with the capture of Vicksburg and Pemberton's army. At the outset Sherman was pessimistic—he feared that Grant was taking excessive risks. But when it ended he frankly acknowledged to Grant that he had been right and Sherman wrong. In a moment of perceptive analysis of both himself and Grant he told a confidant, "I am a much brighter man than Grant; I can see things quicker than he can, and know more about books than he does, but I'll tell you where he beats me, and where he beats the world: he don't care a cent for what he can't see the enemy doing, but it scares me like hell!"

Despite his initial misgivings about Grant's strategy, Sherman executed his assignments in the Vicksburg operations with exemplary efficiency. First his corps, the XV, kept Pemberton off balance by bluffing another attack on Vicksburg from the north while Grant with his other two corps, McClernand's XIII and Major General James B. McPherson's XVII, marched down the west bank of the Mississippi River and crossed by boats to the east bank below the fortress city. Then he marched quickly to reinforce Grant, bringing badly needed supplies and transport. Next he participated in the sweep eastward to Jackson, Mississippi, where he destroyed that town's rail connections while Grant turned west, routed Pemberton at Champion Hill, and drove him back into Vicksburg. Up to this point Sherman's corps had done little fighting but now it joined in Grant's two futile attempts to storm Vicksburg. In large part, during the second attempt it suffered severe casualties because a report by McClernand, that he was on the verge of a breakthrough, caused him to prolong the assault. This incident and a brazen attempt by McClernand to grab the credit for defeating Pemberton provided Grant with a most welcome excuse for relieving that politician-general from command. For both him and Sherman this was a victory that in its way was as satisfying as the capture of Vicksburg.

As soon as Pemberton surrendered, Grant sent Sherman with seven divisions to drive away the small Confederate army that General Joseph E. Johnston had assembled east of Vicksburg. Johnston made a brief stand at Jackson, then retreated to Meridian, Mississippi. Sherman did not pursue. Instead he completed the job of destroying Jackson, which he had started earlier. "Jackson will no longer be a point of danger," he informed Grant. "The inhabitants are subjugated. They cry aloud for mercy. The land is devastated for 30 miles around."

It is clear Sherman had a penchant for raids. Soon after Shiloh he had led a task force deep into Mississippi to burn a railroad bridge, and during the Yazoo River Expedition he had detached a division to wreck a railroad line in Arkansas (a pointless venture, which conceivably cost him what chance he had of success at Chickasaw Bluffs by delaying his attack there). By the summer of 1863 he conceived of large-scale sweeps through the country as a good, perhaps the best, means to break Confederate resistance by literally bringing home to Southerners the folly of their wickedness in trying to destroy the Union.

He evidently came to consider it futile to make a serious effort to prevent his troops from pillaging, vandalizing, and destroying private property—the sort of conduct that he had angrily denounced during the first year of the war. The Vicksburg campaign revealed to him the ease with which even a big army could live off the land—provided it kept moving.

Grant highly praised Sherman's performance in the Vicksburg operations and so did Sherman. To his brother John he wrote: "The share I have personally borne in all these events is one in which you may take pride for me. You know how I have avoided notoriety; and the press . . . may strip me of all popular applause, but not a soldier in the Army of the Tennessee but knows the part I have borne in this great drama. . . . In the events resulting thus, the guiding minds and hands were Grant's, Sherman's, and McPherson's. . . . " This was boasting—but it was true.

In October Grant became overall commander in the West, with the special assignment of redeeming the situation at Chattanooga, where the Union Army of the Cumberland, after being defeated at Chickamauga, was hard-pressed by General Braxton Bragg's Confederates. As a consequence Sherman succeeded Grant as head of the Army of the Tennessee. He would have preferred, he told John, to have remained a corps commander, "But with Grant I will undertake anything within reason."

Grant transferred the Army of the Tennessee to the Chattanooga area. On November 24 he mounted an offensive designed to dislodge Bragg from Missionary Ridge, the heights overlooking Chattanooga from the east. A corps under Major General Joseph Hooker seized Lookout Mountain, thereby threatening Bragg's left flank; Major General George H. Thomas's Army of the Cumberland menaced the enemy's center; and Sherman, after crossing the Tennessee River in boats and over a rapidly laid pontoon bridge, moved against the Confederate right flank at the northern end of Missionary Ridge (in what Grant intended to be the main Union attack). On coming into sight of the Rebel positions at 3:30 P.M. he discovered that the terrain over which he would have to advance to reach them was more difficult than Grant and he had thought. Instead of assaulting, he had his troops dig in. As a result Thomas remained motionless, his orders being not to attack until Sherman did.

Did Sherman blunder, as some critics subsequently charged, by "going to ground" instead of pushing forward? Probably he did. When he crossed the Tennessee the Confederates had only a thin screen of pickets covering their extreme right on Missionary Ridge. Bragg did not order his reserve, Major General Patrick Cleburne's division, to that point until 2:00 P.M.; not until late in the afternoon did two of Cleburne's brigades face Sherman; and not until after midnight did Cleburne (who had expected Bragg to withdraw from Missionary Ridge because of the loss of Lookout Mountain) begin fortifying the position. It is reasonable to believe that a strong, determined attack by Sherman once he got most of his approximately 25,000 troops on the east side of the Tennessee would have enabled him to seize the northern end of Missionary Ridge, which was held for its entire length by only 26,000 Confederate infantry, and outflank Bragg. By failing to assault, Sherman showed himself to be overly concerned by what might be on "the other side of the hill."

Grant ordered Sherman to attack at dawn on November 25. He did not do so, however, until midmorning. Later he claimed that he had expected Bragg to attack him at daylight. If so, he was guilty either of timidity or wishful thinking—or both. In any event his troops gained nothing and lost heavily. They were up against some of the toughest fighters in the Confederate army doggedly defending an almost impregnable position. The only thing that prevented Sherman's casualty list from being longer was that the nature of the ground made it impossible for him to deploy his entire force, with the result that he used only six out of sixteen available brigades. Also he ignored a suggestion from one of his division commanders to outflank the enemy position by sending some of the surplus brigades across Chickamauga Creek, which emptied into the Tennessee near the northern end of Missionary Ridge and over which his engineers had also thrown a pontoon bridge. But then Grant had instructed him to assault Bragg's right, not circle around it.

At 2:00 P.M. Grant, realizing that his planned strategy was not working and hoping to draw the Confederates away from Sherman's front, ordered Thomas to seize the first line of enemy trenches at the foot of the center of Missionary Ridge. Thomas's troops did so. Then, on their own spontaneous impulse, they charged onward. The poorly positioned, thinly spread, and already half-demoralized defenders fled in utter panic. Thus Grant won another great victory, but not the way he intended, and with Sherman, to whom he had assigned the star part, playing only a supporting role.

Immediately after the battle Grant sent Sherman and the Army of the Tennessee to relieve Major General Ambrose Burnside's forces at Knoxville, where, reportedly, they were besieged by a superior Confederate army and in danger of starving. Sherman's approach drove away the Confederates and he reached Knoxville—only to discover that Burnside had been in little danger and possessed ample food. Since his own men had suffered severely from cold, hunger, and fatigue in marching to Knoxville, understandably Sherman was disgusted.

In January he returned to Mississippi. Early the following month he set out for Vicksburg with 20,000 infantry. He again occupied what was left of Jackson, then pushed on to Meridian, where he spent five days destroying factories, military supplies, and railroad tracks. Then he marched back to Vicksburg, leaving in his wake, as he put it, "a swath of desolation fifty miles broad" and followed by "about ten miles of negroes."

The professed objective of the Meridian Expedition was to make it impossible for the Confederates to assemble sufficient force near the Mississippi to endanger Northern shipping on the river. Since the Confederates in this region soon had all they could handle attempting to turn back various Federal incursions, however, the Meridian Expedition in fact served no significant strategic purpose. But it did confirm for Sherman that a large, fast-moving army could support itself deep inside enemy territory. Also it marked a further application of his belief that it was necessary to strike at the Southern economy and people if the war was to be won.

In March Grant became commander of the entire Union army with the rank of lieutenant general. In announcing his promotion to Sherman, he expressed thanks to Sherman and McPherson "as *the men* to whom, above all others, I feel indebted for whatever I have had of success." Sherman promptly replied, declaring that on the contrary it was he who was obligated to Grant: ". . . when you have completed your best preparations you go into battle without hesitation . . . no doubts, no reserve; and I tell you that it was this that made me act with confidence." Sherman then went on to urge Grant, who had gone to Washington, not to remain there and be ruined by intriguing politicians. Instead he should return to the West: "Here lies the seat of the coming empire; and from the West, when our task is done, we will make short work of Charleston and Richmond. . . ."

Grant, however, chose to establish his headquarters in the East, both to exercise with maximum efficiency his new responsibilities and to personally supervise operations in Virginia. Accordingly he named Sherman to succeed him as commander in the West. Ever since, admirers of Thomas have maintained that he deserved that post. They point out that he had never failed but had always succeeded, that he had saved the day at Chickamauga and won the day at Chattanooga. In contrast Sherman had panicked in Kentucky, broken down in Missouri; and been surprised at Shiloh, as well as bloodily repulsed at Chickasaw Bluffs, Vicksburg, and Missionary Ridge.

Grant's association with Thomas, however, had been brief and formal, and for reasons that are somewhat obscure he disliked and distrusted him. On the other hand, Grant and Sherman were the closest of friends, bound together by shared troubles, shared triumphs, and reciprocal gratitude.

Grant's choice of Sherman was not only inevitable but probably for the best. Even if it be accepted that Thomas possessed greater military talent than Sherman, he would not have received from Grant the confidence and freedom of action that Sherman enjoyed and would have been hamstrung in the conduct of operations—as in the case of Nashville in December 1864 when Grant, totally without cause, nearly removed Thomas on the eve of the most complete battlefield victory of the war.

Sherman, who had failed miserably as an independent commander in 1861, received the second most important and responsible military assignment in the Federal service. He accepted it calmly. Behind him now were three years of war, two of them under the leadership and tutelage of Grant. He had learned much about his profession but above all had acquired confidence in himself. Shortly before becoming head of the Western armies he had declared that he had "done a full share in the real achievements of this war." He did not doubt that he would go on to even greater achievements. The upcoming campaigns of 1864, he wrote Ellen, would be decisive. "All that has gone before is mere skirmishing. The war now begins, and with heavy well-disciplined masses the issue must be settled in hard-fought battles. I think we can whip them in Alabama and it may be Georgia. . . ."

Sherman, the loyal subordinate, now was ready to become Sherman the conqueror.

CONQUEROR

On March 20, 1864, Lieutenant General U. S. Grant and Major General William T. Sherman met in a room at the Burnet House Hotel in Cincinnati to formulate the strategy by which they hoped to win the war. The plan that emerged was quite obvious and quite sound: While Grant hammered at General Robert E. Lee in Virginia, Sherman was to move into Georgia against the Confederacy's other main army, that of General Joseph E. Johnston. He was "to break it up, and to get into the interior of the enemy's country" as far as he could go, "inflicting all the damage" possible on the South's war resources. Both Grant and Sherman were to attack simultaneously and not cease attacking in order to prevent the Confederates from shifting troops from one front to the other.

To accomplish this task Sherman collected 110,000 men in the Chattanooga region of Tennessee, divided into Major General George H. Thomas's 60,000-man Army of the Cumberland, the 25,000 men of Major General James B. McPherson's Army of the Tennessee (soon increased to

34,000 by the addition of another corps), and Major General John M. Schofield's 15,000 troops called the Army of the Ohio. Nearly all of these troops and their officers were tough veterans thoroughly experienced in the latest techniques of combat. Their discipline off the battlefield, however, was poor and in the months ahead it would grow worse. The artillery numbered 254 pieces and was well served. On the other hand, the cavalry, made up of 12,000 troopers organized into four divisions, was by Sherman's own admission inferior in quality to the enemy's. All in all, despite the deficiency in discipline and the weakness of the cavalry (for which he had little use in any case) Sherman rightly believed that he had "one of the best armies in the world."

His chief concern was the single railroad line connecting Chattanooga with Nashville and Louisville. It provided his forces with the bulk of their supplies. Should it falter in its operations or be cut by the Confederates the consequences could be disastrous. So prior to launching his offensive, he did everything possible to ensure its efficient functioning and protect it against enemy cavalry raids. At the same time he made well-conceived arrangements to rebuild the railroad, which ran through northern Georgia to Atlanta, so that the Confederates would be unable to bring his army to a standstill by destroying it as they retreated. Thanks to this forethought and preparation, he was never seriously hampered by a shortage of food, forage, or material during the ensuing campaign. It was the greatest logistic achievement of the war, one that made possible the Union victory in Georgia and far surpassed anything that any European army of the time was capable of doing.

On May 5, two days after Grant advanced against Lee, Sherman began his offensive. Johnston waited for him at Dalton, Georgia, with approximately 55,000 men; the vast majority were battle-hardened veterans. He hoped, apparently even expected, Sherman to attack him head-on and, accordingly, constructed formidable fortifications. But Sherman had no intention of being so obliging. Instead, he sent Thomas and Schofield to demonstrate against Johnston's front while McPherson circled westward to his rear. He instructed McPherson to proceed through Snake Creek Gap (which Johnston had left unguarded because of his assumption that the Federals would strike directly at Dalton), tear up the railroad in the Resaca area, and then retire back into Snake Creek Gap. Johnston, his supply line broken, would then have to retreat, pursued by Thomas and Schofield; McPherson would assail his flank as he passed through Resaca. If all went as planned, Johnston's army would be smashed, and not only Georgia but also the Carolinas would be open to conquest.

But all did not go as planned. McPherson successfully penetrated Snake Creek Gap on May 9 but then encountered difficult terrain and unexpected resistance of unknown strength. Instead of pushing forward in full strength, he merely skirmished, and only a handful of his troops reached the railroad and did no damage. At nightfall, fearing that Johnston might send a strong force to pounce on him from the north, he fell back to Snake Creek Gap. From there he reported his failure to cut the railroad to Sherman, adding that he could have done so had he possessed a division of good cavalry.

When Sherman learned that McPherson had passed through Snake Creek Gap he exclaimed, "I've got Joe Johnston dead!" But on receiving McPherson's report that the railroad had not been broken, he expressed anger and disappointment. Later he stated in his 1875 *Memoirs* that McPherson "could have placed his whole force astride the railroad above Resaca" and enabled the Union army to trap and destroy Johnston. "McPherson," he continued, "seems to have been a little timid. Still, he was justified by his orders."

Sherman's criticism of McPherson is correct except for the last phrase. It should read "victimized by his orders." For Sherman did not tell McPherson to place "his whole force astride the railroad." He was merely to cut it, then fall back. Consequently McPherson conceived and conducted his operation as a raid rather than a move to block Johnston's line of retreat. To have done otherwise would have been for him to have shown great boldness and enterprise—far more, for example, than Sherman personally displayed at the Battle of Chattanooga, where his excess caution and rigid adherence to orders cost the Federals a chance to inflict an even worse defeat on the Confederates.

It was Thomas who suggested the Snake Creek maneuver to Sherman and had proposed making it with his Army of the Cumberland, indicating that he thought in terms of cutting Johnston's line of retreat as well as his line of supply. Sherman, however, preferred to use McPherson's smaller army and a lesser objective. By so doing he set the stage for the failure of the movement and consequently deserves, along with McPherson, to be criticized for being "a little timid."

Upon receiving McPherson's message that the railroad had not been broken, Sherman sent three corps through Snake Creek Gap, leaving only one corps and some cavalry on Johnston's front. Assuming that Johnston would make "no detachments" from his Dalton line, he did not hurry this movement. Consequently, when he emerged from the gap on the morning of May 13, he faced most of the Confederate army, now bolstered by reinforcements from Mississippi/Alabama to 65,000, strongly entrenched around Resaca.

With the collapse of the Snake Creek Gap plan, Sherman wasted a splendid opportunity to realize the primary military assignment Grant had given him—"break up Johnston's army." Actually, though, he wished to do this only if it could be done at minimal risk. Thus in his private letters and sometimes in official correspondence, he spoke only of taking Atlanta, and that by maneuver, not battle. He found this goal and the means of achieving it personally congenial.

During the next month Sherman and Johnston performed a sort of military waltz across the mountains and valleys of northern Georgia. Always both armies entrenched on coming into contact; rarely did either make a major attack; they skirmished almost constantly. Sooner or later Sherman, realizing that he could not break through the enemy's front, would take advantage of his superior numbers and his possession of the strategic initiative and slide one of his armies—McPherson's—around Johnston's left toward the railroad in his rear. Invariably Johnston would anticipate the move and retreat to the threatened point, where he would be found waiting and ready.

By mid-June the Confederates had been maneuvered back almost to Marietta, less than twenty miles from Atlanta. But now they seemed determined to stay put. Anchoring their line on Kennesaw Mountain, a height that dominated the entire countryside, they fended off Sherman's attempts to get around them until his forces were stretched so thin that he feared to spread them farther. He preferred to fight on the defensive and took the offensive as a rule only when he assumed, almost always in error, that the enemy was retreating and so could be struck in the open. This approach to war also harmonized with a belief that the essential purpose of the campaign in Georgia was to prevent Johnston from reinforcing Lee, thereby enabling Grant to do what he took for granted—win the war in Virginia.

Fearing a stalemate that would enable Johnston to reinforce Lee against Grant, who also was bogged down, Sherman decided to do what he previously had declared he would not do—make a large-scale frontal attack in an attempt to break through the enemy center. On June 27 large portions of four Union divisions assaulted the fortifications stretching southward from Kennesaw Mountain. None of their officers and men believed that the attack could succeed. They were right. The Confederates, who had been hoping for just such a chance, mowed them down in heaps. Unable to advance and afraid to retreat, the survivors frantically dug in. When the fighting finally ended, 2,500 of some of the North's best soldiers lay dead or wounded. Two days later Sherman wrote his wife, "I begin to regard the death and mangling of a couple of thousand men as a small affair, a kind of morning dash. . . ."

Soon after the Kennesaw debacle Schofield and McPherson again began curling around the Confederate left flank; apparently such a maneuver was feasible after all. Johnston promptly withdrew to an already prepared stronghold on the north bank of the Chattahoochee River—the last natural barrier before Atlanta only five miles away. This move surprised Sherman, who expected the Confederates to make a stand on the south side of the river, but it did not baffle him. On July 8 he got Schofield's army across the Chattahoochee east of Johnston's position and forced him to fall back to the outskirts of Atlanta.

This was too much for Confederate president Jefferson Davis. Convinced that Johnston had no intention of trying to hold Atlanta, on July 17 he replaced him with General John Bell Hood, who promised to make a fight for the city.

Hood kept his promise. On July 20 he struck Thomas at Peachtree Creek north of Atlanta. He rocked "The Rock of Chickamauga" but finally was driven back with heavy losses. Assuming that the Confederates had shot their bolt and now would evacuate Atlanta, Sherman then ordered his forces to sweep forward and occupy the city.

This time he was careless. On July 22, with two-thirds of his army, Hood pounced on the Army of the Tennessee east of Atlanta. The Confederates surprised both Sherman and McPherson, killed the latter, and savagely attacked in front, flank, and rear. Only luck and stalwart fighting saved the Army of the Tennessee from disaster. Sherman helped repulse the enemy assault by forming scores of cannons into a "monster battery" that cut bloody furrows through the Rebel ranks. He refused, however, to call on Thomas and Schofield for reinforcements, explaining afterward in his

Memoirs that "if any assistance were rendered by either of the other armies, the Army of the Tennessee would be jealous."

Both of Hood's grand sorties were defeated but they stopped the Federal drive on Atlanta from the north and east. Sherman responded by swinging the Army of the Tennessee, now under Howard, around to the west side of Atlanta, his object to cut the Macon Railroad, the last line connecting the city with the rest of the South, thereby compelling Hood to evacuate or starve. Again the Confederates counterattacked, this time at Ezra Church on July 28. Although the Army of the Tennessee slaughtered their assailants, it was unable to reach the railroad. At the same time Sherman sent three cavalry divisions to tear up the tracks. Two were destroyed and the commander of one was captured in a foredoomed attempt to liberate the Union prisoners at Andersonville. Cavalry, Sherman concluded disgustedly, "could not, or would not, make a sufficient lodgement on the railroad" to break it; so, early in August he tried once more with his infantry, only to be blocked at Utoy Creek southwest of Atlanta.

Northerners began to fear, Southerners began to hope, that Sherman was as bogged down at Atlanta as Grant was at Richmond. Both Sherman and his men, however, remained supremely confident of capturing Atlanta—it was merely a question of time. Meanwhile, after three months of almost constant marching and fighting, they needed an opportunity to get their second wind physically and psychologically. Therefore during the balance of August Sherman resorted to siege war, pounding Atlanta with large cannons. This bombardment made life miserable for the civilian population but did inconsequential military damage. The only positive function it served was to give the Northern troops and people that feeling that at least something was being done against the defiant enemy inside the city.

By the end of August Sherman was ready to make another effort to slice Hood's railroad lifeline. He correctly perceived that previous attempts had failed because Hood had been able to anticipate them, they had been made too close to Atlanta, and they had been backed by inadequate strength. This time he avoided all of these mistakes. First, he pulled his army out of the trenches around Atlanta, causing Hood to hope that the cavalry raid he had launched earlier against Sherman's supply line had succeeded and that the Federals were retreating back toward Chattanooga. Next, after posting one corps to guard the rail bridge across the Chattahoochee, Sherman slowly marched the bulk of his army toward the Macon Railroad. He halted frequently, taking time to rip up the tracks of the railroad between Atlanta and Montgomery, one that served no essential purpose. As a result Hood had time to ascertain Sherman's design and attempt to frustrate it. On August 31 he attacked Howard's Army of the Tennessee with two of his three corps, but was repulsed at Jonesboro, a small town on the Macon Railroad. The next day Sherman counterattacked; although he was only able to dent the enemy line, he forced the Confederates to withdraw from Jonesboro during the night.

Hood now had no choice except to evacuate Atlanta, which he did on the night of September 1. The next day the Union corps that had been left at the Chattahoochee occupied the city. Sherman telegraphed Washington: "So Atlanta is ours and fairly won."

The strategy by which Sherman expelled Hood was well conceived but ill-executed. He took far too long to reach the Macon Railroad; he employed only a fraction of his available force in the September 1 battle at Jonesboro, thereby allowing the Confederates to escape; and he made no attempt to cut off and crush Hood's widely scattered forces while they retreated southward from Atlanta. Instead he followed the Confederates to Lovejoy Station, halted, skirmished a few days, and then withdrew—leaving Hood's army battered but capable of fighting, as fight it would, another day.

The capture of Atlanta was one of the decisive events of the Civil War. It strongly shook the South's ability and will to continue fighting, it revived the flagging determination of the North, and it assured—perhaps even made possible—Lincoln's reelection, which earlier had seemed doubtful even to Lincoln. It was Sherman's greatest military achievement, one for which he received and deserved most of the credit, and it fulfilled his forecast, made in 1861, that the first leaders in the war would fail and be cast aside, but that a "second or third set will rise, and amongst them I may be . . ."

Sherman spent the rest of September resting his army in Atlanta. In order to turn the city into a "pure Gibralter" he forced most of the civilians to leave it. The Confederates protested this act of "studied and ingenious cruelty." Sherman answered with one of the epigrammatic half-truths typical of him: "War is cruelty, and you cannot refine it. . . ."

Early in October the indefatigable Hood swung into northern Georgia with the purpose of drawing Sherman out of Atlanta by threatening his supply line, then drawing him out of Georgia by invading Tennessee. Leaving a corps to hold Atlanta, Sherman with the bulk of his army pursued

Hood all the way to Dalton, then westward across the Alabama line, but was unable to catch him. By the middle of the month he found himself in a strategic dilemma, the consequence of his failure to destroy the Johnston-Hood forces. On the one hand, it obviously was futile to chase Hood who, as Sherman put it, "can turn and twist like a fox." On the other hand, should he move into Tennessee to defend it against Hood this would make the capture of Atlanta seem a barren victory and have a depressing effect on Northern morale on the eve of the presidential election.

Sherman's solution, which he proposed to Grant, was to leave Hood to Thomas, whom he had sent to take command in Tennessee, and return to Atlanta from where he would march to Savannah and "make Georgia howl." This plan was motivated by Sherman's penchant for raiding and his desire to terrorize the Southern people into submission. Nevertheless it was his best alternative under the circumstances. Not only did it rescue him from the military impasse created by Hood's northern movement but it also—and this was the advantage he emphasized—made it possible, once he secured a new base of operations at Savannah, to carry the war into the Carolinas and threaten Lee's rear in Virginia.

Reluctantly Grant agreed to Sherman's proposal. On November 2, after obtaining assurances that Thomas would have ample strength to defeat a Confederate invasion of Tennessee, he gave Sherman permission to make the march. Two weeks later, Sherman with 62,000 of his best troops set out from the burning city of Atlanta.

He instructed his men to "forage liberally on the country." This they did—and looted and destroyed. In front of them there were only a few brigades of cavalry and the old men and young boys of the Georgia militia. Behind them they left a trail of devastation sixty miles wide. Accompanying them were hordes of blacks rejoicing in their liberation from slavery. Their presence annoyed Sherman, who considered the Emancipation Proclamation a mistake. Many of his soldiers felt the same way. Once they deliberately left hundreds of freed slaves stranded on the other side of a river.

In mid-December Sherman's legions reached the outskirts of Savannah. Possibly, had he moved in the right way and with sufficient speed, he might have bagged the city's 10,000-man garrison. But he was more concerned with establishing contact with the Northern navy than with the garrison commander's resolve not to be trapped. So the Confederates, after a brief show of resistance, had no difficulty getting away. On December 21 the

Union troops entered the city and Sherman telegraphed Lincoln: "I beg to present to you as a Christmas gift the city of Savannah."

The North acclaimed Sherman. He now surpassed Grant in popularity, who seemed to be going nowhere in Virginia while Sherman romped through Georgia. Afterward the public regarded "The March to the Sea" as his greatest accomplishment. No doubt it was highly dramatic. No doubt too it was a glorious adventure for the soldiers who made it. But what were its actual results?

It destroyed, according to Sherman's own estimate, $100,000,000 of property, but he admitted, only $20,000,000 of that amount "inured to our advantage," the remainder was "simple waste and destruction." It left thousands of civilians hungry but had little or no impact on the supply situation of Lee's and Hood's armies. Also, the miles of tracks that Sherman's soldiers tore up did not seriously handicap Confederate military operations; not until his forces reached Branchville, South Carolina, in February was the South's east-west rail system totally cut. And although the march had a depressing effect on many Southerners, especially Georgians, it also infuriated many of them and so strengthened, rather than weakened, their will to fight on. There is also no hard evidence that the march, or its eventual continuation into the Carolinas, was the main cause of the high desertion rate from Lee's army during the 1864–65 winter, as some historians have asserted. The most important and common motives were hunger, privation, and the increasingly obvious hopelessness of the Confederate cause.

The March to the Sea probably did not shorten the war. On the contrary, by making it with an unnecessarily large force of 62,000 (40,000 would have been more than ample) Sherman risked prolonging the war—even giving the Confederacy a new lease on life. Despite the fact that Hood was moving northward and was 300 miles from Atlanta by mid-November, Sherman predicted that he would follow him to Savannah. Subsequently he left Thomas with fewer than 60,000 widely scattered and mostly inexperienced troops to oppose Hood's more than 50,000 veterans. To be sure, Thomas himself expressed confidence that he could handle Hood and of course he did so, destroying his army at Nashville on December 15–16. Only a chain of bad mistakes and ill luck, however, prevented Hood from defeating or cutting through the Union forces in Tennessee before Thomas united them. Had this happened—and it came very close—the March to the Sea would stand as a classic example of military folly.

Early in December, when he learned that Sherman was nearing Savannah, Grant proposed that Sherman not even bother to seize that city but instead load most of his army on ships to be transported to Virginia, where it would join the Union forces around Richmond to overwhelm Lee. Without hesitation Sherman agreed to do this, observing that he could reach Virginia much sooner by sea than by land. The destruction of Hood's army at Nashville, however, caused Grant to change his mind about bringing Sherman to the Richmond front at once. Instead he in effect left it up to Sherman's preference. Sherman promptly chose to march northward through the Carolinas—which is what he had hoped to do all along. By so doing, he wrote Grant, "we can punish South Carolina as she deserves." Also, he asserted that by smashing Lee's supply system and making his ultimate defeat inevitable, such a campaign would be "as much a direct attack upon Lee's army as though we were operating within the sound of his artillery." Finally he stated: "I attach more importance to these deep incisions into the enemy's country, because this war differs from European wars in this particular: we are not only fighting hostile armies, but a hostile people, and must make old and young, rich and poor, feel the hard hand of war. . . ."

At the end of January 1865 Sherman crossed into South Carolina. His troops devastated the countryside with literal vengeance, for like most Northerners, they considered South Carolina the birthplace of the rebellion. The most famous episode of their march through the state, the "Burning of Columbia" on the night of February 17, occurred primarily, however, because Southern cavalry, before evacuating the town, set fire to cotton bales piled in the main street. Of course, had not the enemy unwittingly spared him the bother, Sherman would have burned at least the government buildings and military installations of Columbia anyway—in fact he announced his intention to do so back in December.

In South Carolina, as during the March to the Sea, Sherman encountered no opposition worthy of the name. But after entering North Carolina he found himself confronted by a significant enemy force under his old adversary Johnston. Near Bentonville on March 19 Johnston, manifesting uncharacteristic and unexpected aggressiveness, ambushed Sherman's left wing. Only errors by Johnston and his key subordinates saved it from a severe mauling. Then, two days later, an equally uncharacteristic lack of caution by Johnston gave Sherman an excellent chance to cut his line of communications. Sherman, however, was so intent on reaching Goldsboro, where reinforcements—brought to North Carolina by sea—were awaiting him, that he allowed Johnston to escape.

Sherman's army, now 85,000 strong, halted at Goldsboro to rest and refit. While it did, Sherman, at a conference with Grant in Virginia, proposed joining his forces with the 120,000 Union troops already outside of Richmond to overwhelm Lee's 55,000 scarecrows. Grant, however, did not want the long-frustrated Army of the Potomac (and perhaps himself) to have to share with Sherman's Westerners the honor of defeating Lee. He instructed Sherman to move against Johnston in order to prevent or at least delay a linkup between him and Lee. Sherman promised to start his operation on April 10.

But he was not needed. At the beginning of April Grant forced Lee out of Petersburg and Richmond and on April 9 accepted his surrender at Appomattox. Johnston, seeing no point in persisting in a lost war, came to terms with Sherman on April 26 at a farmhouse near Raleigh. Sherman, who in 1862 had vowed to "make war terrible" for the South and who had done so, now sought to make peace as easy as could be. In the process he trespassed onto political matters. Andrew Johnson, now president, had no choice except to repudiate Sherman's pact. Sherman, half-expecting this, was not offended. But he was incensed by the way Secretary of War Edwin M. Stanton and Major General Henry W. Halleck, who now was chief of staff of the army, handled the affair: They implied that he was betraying the Union and seeking to make himself military dictator. In retaliation he snubbed Stanton at the grand review of his army in Washington and broke with Halleck, the man who had given him his chance to rise to the top by picking him up after he fell in Missouri in 1861.

So, on this sour note, Sherman's Civil War career ended. In the years that followed he engaged in warfare and peace negotiations with the Indians of the Western Plains; he rejected an offer from President Johnson, who had hoped to exploit his popularity for political purposes, to appoint him secretary of war; he became Grant's successor as commanding general of the army, a post he held from 1869 to 1883; he rejected the possible Republican nomination for president in 1884 when he announced: "If nominated, I will not accept. If elected, I will not serve." Yet it was all anticlimactic. Although he lived until 1891, what he did between 1861 and 1865 determined his place in history and his status as a military leader. But how should he be rated?

Sherman was too cautious when conducting a battle. As a consequence he tended to hold back both in the deployment and employment of his forces. This in turn either cost him defeats, as at Missionary Ridge, or else lost him the full fruits of victory, as at Jonesboro. To a degree this cautiousness in combat reflected his personality—he simply lacked the "killer instinct." But it was mainly the result of his awareness that as commander of the stronger army he was bound to win so long as he avoided unnecessary risks and major mistakes. Even Napoleon's daring declined as the number of his troops rose.

Sherman tended to assume that the enemy would act or react in a certain way and therefore overlooked other possibilities. This is why he overestimated the danger from the Confederates in Kentucky and Missouri, underestimated it at Shiloh, moved with insufficient force and speed at Snake Creek Gap, walked blithely into a near-disastrous trap at Atlanta, and discounted Hood's tenacity and ingenuity. He was being facetious, yet he revealed something of his character as a general when he complained in October 1864 that Hood "is eccentric and I cannot guess his movements as I could those of Johnston, who was a sensible man and only did sensible things."

Sherman was guilty of making the same dubious assumption that many other war leaders before and since have made: That the enemy could be terrorized into submission by devastating his farms and towns. Rarely is this the case, certainly it was not true of the South in the Civil War. Although the havoc wreaked by Sherman's hordes contributed to Confederate defeat, this contribution was so indirect and ambiguous that it did not justify militarily, much less morally, the human misery that accompanied and followed it. This is particularly true of what Sherman himself considered to be his greatest accomplishment—the march through the Carolinas. Had his army proceeded, as at first planned, from Savannah to Richmond by sea, the war almost certainly would have been ended at least a month, probably two months, sooner. But Grant is more to blame for this not occurring than is Sherman.

But Sherman had no superior, perhaps no equal, among Civil War commanders when it came to supplying and operating large armies over vast distances. His campaign through Georgia and the Carolinas was a masterpiece of logistical planning and execution. By the same token, anyone studying his military correspondence will be impressed, even awed, by the virtuosity in dealing with multitudes of administrative details, for he was his own operations, personnel, and intelligence officer. The highly able British general of World Wars I and II, Archibald Wavell, wrote at the end of his career: "The more I see of war, the more I realize how it all depends on administration and transportation. . . ." Judged by this criterion, Sherman stands high as a commander.

Although nervous in deportment and emotional in temperament, in emergencies Sherman was calm and quick-thinking, as he revealed at Shiloh and above all on July 22, 1864, at Atlanta. He was able to do what every good commander does—react effectively to the unexpected and potentially disastrous. Equally important, he possessed that hardness of mind and spirit that is essential to a successful general. He could order men into battle without qualm: "The very object of war is to produce results by death and slaughter," he wrote his wife after Shiloh.

After taking command in the West in 1864 Sherman dominated, by the force of his intellect and personality, the generals who served under him. The sole exception was Thomas, with whom his relationship was both unique and complex. He also secured the confidence and even the admiration of the rank and file, who on seeing him ride by would say, "There goes the old man. All's right." As a result the veteran—but heterogeneous—forces that assembled around Chattanooga in the spring of 1864 became a fighting machine matched in effectiveness only by Lee's army at its peak.

To a list of Sherman's merits his biographer and admirer, the British military historian Liddell Hart, has added the highest of all—genius. According to Hart, Sherman deserves this designation because he cleverly employed the "indirect approach" both in tactics and strategy; he constantly placed his opponents on the "horns of the dilemma" by marching in widely dispersed columns, preventing—as in Georgia and the Carolinas—a concentration of force against him; he ushered in the age of modern warfare by making the enemy's home front as important an objective as his battlefront and he carried out *blitzkrieg* penetrations deep into his rear.

What Liddell Hart claims has the ring of truth, but maybe Sherman was not so much a military genius as he was a man who could attack a knotty problem with a practical solution. As an old quartermaster he knew the needs of a large body of troops; how else could his army have moved rapidly and still have lived off the land without fanning out? Also, giving up the chase after Hood to head for Savannah, and efforts at flanking the formidable Rebel defenses thrown up in his army's path make someone like "Uncle Billy" seem to be a person possessed of common sense rather than superior military intellect. His men's long and often unopposed hikes through the South destroyed no enemy army, the object of a *blitzkrieg,* and would hardly seem to place him in the military *avant-garde.* And the tactic of allowing troops to bully and rob noncombatants is no more modern than Attila or Genghis Khan.

There is a major reason why one hesitates to place Sherman among the Great Captains. Apart from his brief and unhappy experience in Kentucky in 1861, he did not hold a top command until the last year of the war. By then the Confederacy was half-defeated, its troops declining in numbers and quality, many of its best generals dead or crippled, its morale shaken, and its economy staggering. Consequently, in the Atlanta Campaign Sherman faced an enemy army decidedly inferior to his own and commanded first by Johnston, who rarely attacked when he could find an excuse to retreat, and next by Hood, who rarely retreated when he could find an excuse to attack. And during the march through Georgia and the Carolinas he was unopposed and never in serious danger. In short, his military skill and character remained untested in the sense of having to cope with an opponent of comparable strength and talent.

But there can be no reasonable doubt that Sherman was an exceptional man who developed into a capable, although flawed, commander. During the final year of the war he accomplished much—perhaps prevented the North from losing the war by losing its will to win the war. Yet he could, hence *should,* have achieved much more—by striking the Confederate army in George a crushing, at least crippling, blow. For this reason, while he definitely belongs among the top Union generals, where he should be ranked is debatable.

EPILOGUE

Why The North Won And The South Lost

The epilogue appeared in an article with the same title, published in Civil War Times Illustrated, *May 2000. I consider the only controversial aspect of it to be the unorthodox—some will think it worse than that—ranking of the top Union commanders. I hope someday to provide a much fuller rationale for this ranking in a book dealing not only with Sherman as a general but also with George H. Thomas and William S. Rosecrans, not to mention sundry others.*

ONE OF THE FEW THINGS—PERHAPS THE *ONLY* THING—THAT CIVIL WAR historians agree on is that the North won and the South lost. Why this was so, however, is a different matter. On that question, disagreement is the rule and agreement rare.

It has ever been thus and always will be. Hardly had the guns ceased firing in 1865 than some Southerners began attributing their defeat to a lack of sufficient will and determination. Subsequent historians—most, if not all of them natives of Dixie—have reasserted this thesis in books such as *Why the South Lost,* by Richard E. Beringer, Herman Hattaway, Archer Jones, and William N. Still, Jr. Others—again, most, if not all, of them Southern-born—have blamed the loss of the Lost Cause on what they consider the wrongheaded policies and stubbornness of Jefferson Davis, the mistakes of certain Confederate commanders, or simply ill fortune, such as the mortal wounding of Albert Sidney Johnston at Shiloh, General Robert E. Lee's "Lost Dispatch" during the Antietam Campaign, and the accidental shooting of Stonewall Jackson by his own troops as he was leading them to victory at Chancellorsville. If only Stonewall had been with Lee at Gettysburg . . .

There are, of course, many other proffered answers to the question of why the South lost. These reasons range from the literally sublime—it was God's will—to the inane, such as the contention that Lee's victories induced the South to devote too many of its limited resources to the war in the East rather than the West, where the war's outcome was actually decided (as if failure, not success, should have been reinforced). But the most common reason for the Union's victory given by historians from both the North and South has been the North's immense superiority in manpower, manufacturing, material, and money. These advantages enabled the North to raise at least 2,000,000 well-equipped Yankees, while the South could muster at most 750,000 ragged and ill-fed Rebels.

Indeed, the North's tangible advantages at the beginning of the war were so enormous that some historians maintain that Union victory was inevitable; the campaigns and battles were merely the unfolding of a story with a foregone conclusion. Charles Beard, for example, in his *Rise of American Civilization* (unfortunately the most influential history of this nation ever written), declared that the South was "fighting the census returns," and so devoted only two paragraphs of his 1,661-page work to the Civil War's military operations. Beard dismissed the fighting as a "fleeting incident" best left to writers who have "mastered the art of depicting tragedy and romance." Shelby Foote, whose three-volume *The Civil War: A Narrative* is the finest depiction of the conflict's tragedy and romance, stated in Ken Burns's 1990 PBS series, *The Civil War,* that "the North fought that war with one hand behind its back." Had it been necessary to achieve victory, Foote argued, "the North simply would have brought that other arm out from behind its back. I don't think the South ever had a chance to win that war."

The North's superior numbers and strength clearly played important roles in winning the war. Without them, or had they been substantially less, victory would have come with great difficulty, or perhaps not at all. But did the Union's potential and raw strength guarantee victory, dooming the South to defeat from the very start? The answer, contrary to Beard, Foote, and other historians who share their opinion, is no. Passing over the annals of warfare, which contain numerous examples of smaller, weaker contestants besting bigger and stronger foes, let it simply be stated that the South could have won. In fact, as James McPherson has pointed out, the South had victory nearly within its grasp on three occasions during the Civil War:

1. In the early autumn of 1862, when Lee, after driving Major General George B. McClellan back from Richmond and winning the Second Battle of Bull Run, invaded Maryland at the same time General Braxton Bragg swept through Tennessee and into Kentucky. These offensives caused the British government to consider recognizing the

Confederacy, an act which almost certainly would have led to British (and French) intervention on the side of the South.

2. During the first half of 1863, when the North's lingering gloominess over the bloody Union defeat at Fredericksburg the previous December and the continuing stalemate in Tennessee and Mississippi turned to alarm as Lee advanced into Pennsylvania. Only Lee's defeat at Gettysburg and the simultaneous capture of Vicksburg, Mississippi, by Grant—neither of which were "inevitable"—revived Northern resolve and staved off another movement toward recognition of the Confederate government by the British.
3. The late summer of 1864, when Grant's failure to take Richmond and Major General William T. Sherman's apparent inability to capture Atlanta caused so many war-weary Northerners to despair of victory that President Abraham Lincoln concluded he stood no chance of being reelected. His Democratic successor, he assumed, would repudiate the Emancipation Proclamation and suspend the war effort. The accuracy of Lincoln's assessment is open to debate, but there is no denying that Sherman's capture of Atlanta in September and Major General Phillip Sheridan's victories in the Shenandoah Valley in October restored the North's will to fight on toward victory.

Three times the South stood on the threshold of victory because of intangibles—the nonmaterial factors that affect the outcomes of all conflicts. These factors included the quality of the armies' leadership, morale, willpower, and sheer luck. Of these, quality of leadership was by far the most important. Sufficient superiority in the ability of Confederate commanders would have more than compensated for the South's numerical and material inferiority. To quote a nineteenth-century French general, "An army of sheep commanded by a lion will defeat an army of lions commanded by a sheep."

The South could have realized such superiority in two ways, one positive, the other negative. The positive way would have been for its top generals to have been so outstanding that their Northern counterparts, even if highly competent, still would have lost more battles than they won, especially the decisive ones. The Confederates had one such general in Robert E. Lee. Thanks mainly to him, they did have those three opportunities to win the war and their independence, despite the heavy odds against them. Unfortunately for the Confederacy, though, it had only one Lee. It needed at least two. The South produced a number of able division, corps, and cavalry commanders, but only two of them rose to the level of genius: Jackson and Lieutenant General Nathan Bedford Forrest. Because Jackson died before he had the chance to lead an army, it is impossible to determine whether he could have done so successfully. As for Forrest, it is doubtful that he would have shone as brilliantly on battlefields where he could not personally supervise and inspire his troops. The most that can be said for Confederate generals who did command major armies—Joseph and Albert Sidney Johnston, P. G. T. Beauregard, Bragg, and John Bell Hood—is that they could possibly have won offensive battles against armies of equal or lesser size. This they never did, except in the case of Bragg at Chickamauga, Tennessee, in September 1863, and even then the general owed his near-Pyrrhic victory to a fluke (an erroneous movement of Union troops that opened a huge gap in the Federal line).

The negative way in which the South could have attained a decisive edge in military leadership was if all the Federal commanders had been so inept that even competent mediocrity on the part of Confederate generals would have constituted superiority. This, obviously, did not happen. The Union developed some top generals who were, or became, highly capable—in some instances more than that, and in two cases deserving of the label "great." Ranked on the basis of their contributions to Union victory and their skill in planning and conducting military operations, these generals were as follows:

1. Ulysses S. Grant. He broke open the Confederacy's Western front at Forts Henry and Donelson, held what had been gained in battle at Shiloh, captured Vicksburg in a masterful campaign of maneuver—a major turning point of the war—and opened the way into Georgia with his victory at Chattanooga. Placed in command of all Union armies in 1864, he chose to take on Lee himself, and by refusing to accept defeat in their ensuing year-long duel, he ultimately forced Lee's surrender, effectively bringing about Northern victory in the war. To be sure, he sometimes blundered and sometimes owed his success more to luck than skill; yet he always sought not merely to defeat, but to destroy the enemy. In this he succeeded, capturing three large armies, the final one being Lee's.
2. George H. Thomas. A Southerner, he contributed more to Union victory than any Northern-born general except Grant, and would have contributed much more had Grant given him the opportunity

and Sherman heeded his advice during the Atlanta Campaign. As it was, he gained the first significant Federal success in the West at Mill Springs, Kentucky, in January 1862; anchored the Union stand in the Battle of Stone's River, Tennessee; prevented the Union defeat at Chickamauga from becoming a disaster; directed the most successful frontal assault of the war at Missionary Ridge, Tennessee; and at Nashville became the sole commander of the war to completely destroy an opposing army on the battlefield, rendering General John Bell Hood's Confederate Army of Tennessee unfit for further service. This unprecedented accomplishment made the collapse of the Confederacy a mere question of time. Thomas never committed a serious mistake and, like Grant, always sought to annihilate the enemy.

3. William S. Rosecrans. It was his plan that gained the Union its first strategic victory of the war at Rich Mountain, Virginia, in July 1861, securing West Virginia (which entered the Union in June 1863), and with it the vital Baltimore and Ohio Railroad, for the North. After foiling a Confederate attempt to regain western Tennessee and defeating Bragg at Stone's River, Rosecrans carried out a brilliant campaign of maneuver that led to the Federal occupation of Chattanooga. At Chickamauga, he would have retained what he had gained if not for a petty-minded subordinate who put personal resentment ahead of military duty and so enabled the Confederates to win when they should have lost. Rosecrans opened the way for ultimate Federal victory in the heartland of the South. He had some unfortunate personal traits, but his greatest defect was a lack of good fortune, an attribute that Napoleon once deemed more important in a general than ability.
4. William T. Sherman. During the first three years of the war, his contribution to the Union cause was at best minor, at worst negative. Not until the Atlanta Campaign in 1864, which he directed because of his friendship with Grant, did he achieve a success that made a decisive impact on the course of the war. Even then he accomplished only the minimum necessary—the capture of Atlanta—while squandering numerous opportunities to wreck the Confederate army opposing him and bring the war to a quicker end. He was simply incapable of committing his full force to combat. He never won an offensive battle during his career, since he preferred to conduct raids directed against the enemy's communications and civilian population.

This preference led to his most famous exploit, the 1864 March to the Sea and through the Carolinas, but while spectacular, strategically it merely kicked the corpse of the Confederacy. An unusual and fascinating man, Sherman was one of the most overrated generals of the Civil War. Nevertheless, he was able to marshal the superior manpower and firepower at his disposal and capture strategically important Atlanta in time to bolster sagging Northern spirits before the 1864 presidential election.

5. Philip Sheridan. His major contributions to Union victory occurred in Virginia's Shenandoah Valley during the fall of 1864, when he demolished Lieutenant General Jubal Early's army, and at Five Forks, Virginia, where his seizure of a vital road junction on April 1, 1865, compelled Lee to evacuate Richmond and begin the flight that ended with his surrender at Appomattox. Sheridan was a dashing, hard-hitting combat leader, but all of his successes came against heavily outnumbered foes. He faced Early's small army of 12,000 with 40,000 Federals, while his 53,000-man force overwhelmed the 10,000 Confederates at Five Forks. What would have been truly remarkable is if these engagements had ended in failure. Still, his generalship was sufficiently competent to contribute to Union victory.

In sum, the North produced enough commanders with enough ability to make effective use of the Union's superior manpower and material strength and thus win the war. If the Union's top generals had all been bunglers like Ambrose Burnside, or, as in the case of McClellan, highly intelligent but so fearful of losing that they were incapable of winning, then there would have been no "inevitable" Northern victory. Instead, finding itself unable to subdue the Rebel states and faced with possible British and French intervention on the side of the South, the North would have abandoned its struggle to restore the Union and accepted Confederate independence and the continued existence of slavery.

Index